Broadcasting Realities

*Real-life Issues and Insights
For Broadcast Journalists,
Aspiring Journalists,
and Broadcasters*

By Ken Lindner

Bonus Books, Inc., Chicago

02 01 00 99 98   5   4   3   2   1
Library of Congress Catalog Card Number:
International Standard Book Number: 1-56625-114-1

Cover design by Ken Toyama
Interior design by Jill Voges

Bonus Books, Inc.
160 East Illinois Street
Chicago, Illinois 60611

Printed in the
United States of America

Cover photographs courtesy of KTLA, Los Angeles.

Dedications

This book is dedicated to:

My parents, Betty and Jack Lindner. My "West Coast parents," Shelley and Bill Berman. Jack Hartley, Joe and Lanie Havens, Richard Scheer, Babette Perry, and Susan Levin: Your love and belief in me have always been my anchor and my strength.

Charles Masterson, Lee Stevens, and Ron Tindiglia: In loving memory of three beautiful humane beings who were bright lights for me and for everyone whom they touched.

Ben Cammarata, whose vision, leadership, and kindness are unparalleled.

Don Browne, whose character, wisdom, and humaneness inspire me to make this world a better place.

Phil Liebowitz and Art Fuhrer who were always there to teach and explain.

Keena Marie Bouie, without whom this book would be just a dream.

Cyndi Sarnoff, who inspired me to write.

Rob Jordan, Karen Wang, Tim Skeehan, and the rest of my wonderful associates at KLA.

Amanda Tilk, for being so understanding and supportive as I wrote this book.

All of my friends in broadcast journalism who have made my representation experience so exciting, challenging, and fun.

And most of all . . .
My clients, who have believed in me and trusted me with their precious careers:
>   To all of you, a heartfelt Thank You.
>   I hope that this book makes you proud.

Contents

The Broadcast Journalist's Conflict   *xi*

About the Author   *xiii*

Foreword   *xvii*

Thoughts for the Journey   *xix*

A Glossary   *xxi*

A Debate Regarding the Quality Level of TV News and
Reality Based Programming   *1*

I. Two Core Broadcasting Conflicts

The Conflict of: It Smells But It Sells   *5*

The Conflict Between Our Needs And Our Wants   *11*

II. Some Real-life Broadcasting Issues, Conflicts, and

   Problems

   Change   *25*

   Subjectivity   31

   Affirmative Action Versus Racial Discrimination   *37*

   The Realities of Being an On-Air Female   *49*

   A Call to All News and Program Executives   *55*

   Superman   *57*

   Why Supermen Evolve into Poor Anchors and Hosts   *59*

   On-Air Males   *61*

   The Right Of Assignability Versus Controlling

      Your Destiny   *65*

   A Conversation Between A General Manager and

      A Representative Regarding a Station's Right of

      Assignability   *71*

   Learning To Live With Hitting Singles and

      Sacrifice Bunts   *75*

   Murders, Dead Babies, and Fires   *79*

   Plateauing   *83*

   Lack of Feedback   *85*

The Pay Disparity In Broadcast Journalism　*89*

Number Three and Other Low-Rated Stations　*91*

The Pressure to Secure "The Get"　*95*

III. Solutions to Real-life Broadcasting Issues, Conflicts, and

Problems

Being Wise　*111*

The Sprint Versus The Marathon　*113*

Crunch Time　*119*

Getting It Right — From the Start　*121*

The Three "D's" of Constructive Decision-Making:

Desire, Discipline, and Delayed Gratification　*127*

Constructive Decision-Making　*138*

Constructive Decision-Making and Solutions　*139*

The Enhancing Niche　*149*

The Enhancing Niche — Highlighting Your Strengths　*153*

Understanding What Different Venues Do and

Don't Offer　*159*

The Importance of Choosing A Position For The

Right Reason　*167*

Don't Leave Your Job Until You've Secured An Enhancing

Position To Go To   *173*

At The Beginning — Less Is Often More   *175*

Understanding the Pressures That News Managers

Are Under   *179*

The Compromise In Broadcast Journalism and the Value

of Emotional Intelligence   *183*

IV. The Psychology of Securing Effective Representation and

Advantageous Contracts

Leverage   *197*

Contract Renegotiation Time   *203*

Representation   *205*

The Psychology of Contracts   *219*

V. The Psychology of Breaking into Broadcasting and

Developing Your Career

The Psychology of Breaking Into Broadcasting   *241*

Building a Foundation Step-By-Step   *251*

Attaining "Understanding" and "Ownership" of

Your Work   *255*

VI. The Ideal Fate of Broadcast Journalism

The Ideal: To Secure Higher Ratings and Also Produce a

High-Quality Newscast or Reality-Based Program   *261*

VII. Closing Thoughts

The State of Broadcast Journalism (poem)   *283*

The State of Broadcast Journalism   *285*

Don't Lose Sight of "The Gift"   *289*

A Broadcaster's Mission Statement: To Aim

Toward Attaining "The Ideal"   *291*

Bibliography   *293*

Index   *299*

The Broadcast Journalist's Conflict

I became a reporter for the satisfaction and glory
Of changing the world through a well-researched story.
To make a positive difference was my desire,
To enlighten society, seize the bar, raise it higher.

But now I often feel terribly low,
'Cause I'm given assignments that I know
Are sell-outs and therefore don't call for my best,
And I feel like I'm failing the character test.

I once had dreams, but now nothing is plainer,
I'm no longer a journalist, I'm an info-tainer.
Entertaining and titillating have become the norm;
We don't seek the truth and we rarely inform.
'Cause at the end of the day, we're way too scared
That our viewers don't care and they're attention-impaired.
So we sell sex and violence, and provocative teases;
We'll air almost anything, as long as it pleases.
Hooking the viewer has become paramount,
'Cause if ratings are low, nothing else counts.

But, if I continue to settle, instead of striving,
Morally defaulting, in lieu of thriving,
I will continue to commit the horrendous crime
Of wasting my career, my potential, my time.

God, as I look back, I had a noble quest.
But reporting degradation and death have left me depressed.
So what I need to do is clear to me;
It's to begin to have fun, and to anchor "E.T."

— K.L.

About the Author

Ken Lindner owns and is the Chief Executive Officer of one of the world's most successful and well-respected broadcast journalist representation companies.

Nationally, Ken Lindner & Associates, Inc., represents about 400 of the most prominent television newscasters, program hosts, reporters, and producers. Through the years, Ken has worked with such individuals as Matt Lauer (NBC News), Elizabeth Vargas (ABC News), Lisa McRee (ABC News), Giselle Fernandez (NBC News, *Access Hollywood*), Julie Moran (*Entertainment Tonight*), Nancy O'Dell (*Access Hollywood*), Leeza Gibbons (*Entertainment Tonight*), Jodi Applegate (NBC News), Steve Daniels (*Dateline NBC*), Chris Myers (FOX Sports), Barry Nolan (*Hard Copy*), Terry Murphy (*Hard Copy*), Nancy Glass (*American Journal*), Tom Bergeron (*Hollywood Squares*), Hattie Kauffman (CBS News), Sharyl Attkisson (CBS News), Greg Kinnear (E! Entertainment Television and Fox), Jim Moret (CNN), Leon Harris (CNN), Beth Ruyak (NBC Sports), Linden Soles (CNN), Ann Curry (NBC News), Asha Blake (ABC News), Dawn Stensland (CBS News), Sam Champion (Good *Morning America*), Jackie Nespral (*Weekend Today*), Jennifer Valoppi (*One - On-One with John Tesh*), Paula Zahn (CBS News), Brad Goode (*Extra*), Libby Weaver (*Extra*), Rolonda Watts (*Rolonda*), Susan Campos (NBC News), Lori Stokes (MSNBC), Suzanne Malveaux (NBC News), Sabila Vargas (*Real TV*), Michael Brownlee (*Real TV*), Suzanne Sena (E! Entertainment Television), Linda Stouffer (CNN), Larry Mendte (*Access Hollywood*), Mabel Jong (ABC News), Liz Cho (ABC News), Dana Adams (*Extra*), Jon DuPre (FOX News), Dorothy Lucey (*"How'd They Do That?"*), Farland Chang (NBC News), Art Rascon (CBS News), Rita Cosby (FOX News), Suzanne Rico (*Extra*), Phil Shuman (*Extra*), Lauren Sanchez (FOX Sports), Virginia Silva (*Extra*), Jerry Penacoli

(*Hard Copy*), Amy Powell (*Access Hollywood*), Don Dahler (ABC News), Liz Claman (CNBC), Claudia Cowan (FOX News), Louis Aguirre (FOX News), Trace Gallagher (FOX News), Alisyn Camerota (FOX News), Shepard Smith (FOX News), Rob Nikoleski (MSNBC), Allison Costarene (FOX News), Mike Boettcher (NBC News), Dagny Hultgreen (E! Entertainment Television), Sandie Newton (E! Entertainment Television), Ken Taylor (*Real Life*), Dana Fleming (*The Home Show*), Kim Adams (*Real Life*), Lisa Petrillo (*Real Life*), Michael Bass (Executive Producer, *Weekend Today* and Supervising Producer, *Today*), Kathy O'Hearn (Executive Producer, *ABC Weekend Evening News* and *Weekend Good Morning America*), Steve Lange (Executive Producer, *Extra*), David Friend (Executive Producer of Morning Programming, CNBC), etc. Ken also represents many of the most talented and well-respected local anchors and reporters in cities throughout the United States. In almost all of these instances, Ken found these individuals at the beginning of their illustrious careers or when they were ready to make professional changes. Ken and Babette Perry, President of his Reality-Based Programming Division, worked with these broadcasters to, as Ken puts it, "Choreograph their career paths."

Ken graduated magna cum laude from Harvard University in Social Anthropology.

While at Harvard, Ken was the Captain and the number one player on the varsity tennis team, captured the Princeton Invitational Indoor Intercollegiate Doubles Championship (7-6, 6-7, 7-6, over a nationally top-ranked University of Georgia team), won numerous singles and doubles tennis titles, defeated Arthur Ashe in a match that took place one year before Ashe won his Wimbledon Singles Title, and was the Men's National Open Paddle Tennis Doubles Champion.

Ken then attended Cornell Law School, so that he could further study conflict resolution and learn to think through and analyze issues in a more orderly fashion. It was then that he developed his strong interest in the First Amendment. In 1978, he was awarded his Juris Doctor degree.

Upon graduation from Cornell, he was hired as an attorney in the Business Affairs Department of the William Morris

Agency. During that time, Ken worked on hundreds of television talent and packaging contracts. Within two years, he became the Assistant to the President, and then an agent in the News Department. Thereafter, he was promoted to Vice President in charge of the West Coast News Division. In 1988, he left William Morris and founded Ken Lindner & Associates, Inc. Approximately 95 percent of his clients followed him.

The information found in this book is gleaned from Ken's years of experience, specializing in all areas of broadcasting (i.e., from his roles as both a career developer and as an attorney who has negotiated and worked on more than 3,000 broadcasting contracts, as well as from his hundreds of thousands of conversations with broadcasters, producers, news managers, program executives, general managers, station owners, network executives, syndicators, consultants, etc.).

Foreword — Advancing the Story

In the field of broadcast journalism, the goal of a reporter is to either break (uncover) a news story or to *advance* an existing one — that is, to build upon and enhance the body of work that has already been done and/or disseminated.

As the preceding chapter suggests, I view myself and my role, vis-à-vis my clients, as a *career choreographer.*™ That is, as a teammate, advisor, and friend, who helps individuals reach constructive, proactive, and informed career decisions.

During the past years of client *career choreography,*™ I have learned that there are a number of factors that lead some individuals to rise above the pack and maximize their potentials, while others somehow never do. One of these factors is the quality of information that individuals have at hand when they are making their large and small career decisions. Other factors are how people perceive individuals and events, and how they think when reaching their decisions.

In the broadcasting area, there are a number of books focusing on the history of news and television, as well as on various personal broadcasting stories and memoirs. *Broadcasting Realities* is different. It is intended to fill a void, by discussing, and in some cases suggesting, solutions to the often conflicting, confounding, and complex issues, problems, and realities that confront on-air individuals and news and program executives, day to day, in the worlds of news and reality-based programming. It is my hope and goal that by better understanding these issues, problems, and realities, broadcasters and journalists will be better able to reach informed, constructive, and enhancing decisions.

During the chapters that follow, I will identify a number of issues facing individuals in broadcasting. My accounts and perspectives are not meant to be critical of anyone or any company. They reflect how individuals and companies have reacted to and dealt with some of the very tough questions that confront them each day. These accounts are meant to be informational to broadcast journalists, as well as to managers, producers, and other off-air individuals.

It is also my hope, that individuals in management, who are in a position to effect positive change in broadcasting, will gain a different and fuller perspective of things after reading this book, and that they will indeed implement appropriate change. So in this sense, *Broadcasting Realities* is also meant to be provocative.

Above all, I want this book to be important, because the function that broadcast journalism is supposed to serve, is of the utmost importance to our society. And this responsibility must somehow remain a priority, in spite of the ever-constant pressure on owners, executives, and managers to increase viewership and profitability.

In the film *Dead Poets Society,* prep school teacher John Keating, portrayed by Robin Williams, shares the following thought about life with his students:

"The powerful play goes on and you may contribute a verse. What will that verse be?"[A]

I hope that what you read here makes a positive difference as to how you write some of the verses of your broadcasting career. If it does, I will have effectively advanced the story.

Thoughts for the Journey

This book is divided into seven sections. Section I contains conflicts and issues that television station, network and program owners and managers face daily; Section II identifies conflicts and issues that broadcast journalists experience and have to resolve, respectively, on a regular basis; Sections III and IV are devoted to giving solutions and insights as to how broadcast journalists can constructively resolve many of these conflicts and problems, as well as how they can effectively choreograph their careers; Section V discusses how to break into broadcasting and lay the foundation for a rewarding career; Section VI presents a proposal to station, network, and program owners and managers, as to how to secure higher ratings, while at the same time, produce a high quality newscast or reality-based program; and Section VII delivers some closing thoughts.

Please note that in order to protect the identity of various individuals, I have changed the sex of the person, the market, or some other element of many of the upcoming stories. However, the basic relevant points of information remain intact.

Although some of the ensuing material may be familiar, please resist the urge to gloss over it. Many of us have, at one time or another, been to and through places where, for one reason or another, we've not seen all there was to see, nor learned all there was to learn.

Perhaps, it may not be until the second or third time around that we are ready and able to more fully appreciate a place for its previously overlooked real virtues.

Additionally, sometimes seeing familiar things from another vantage point, or in another context, can be and often is, quite illuminating. This concept was acted out in *Dead Poets Society*, when John Keating asked all of his students to join him by standing atop their desks. A moment or two later, he observed, "The view is much different up here."[A]

Keating's observation is an incredibly insightful one. So many new perspectives, possibilities, and alternatives can be seen when you leave the ground and view things from the broader, grander perspective of the big picture. Big picture thinking is an essential component of successful decision-making and will be discussed later.

Let's begin with a brief glossary.

A Glossary

Talent
Throughout this book, I use the terms newscaster, broadcast journalist, and talent interchangeably. During my career in broadcasting, I have occasionally heard the term talent, used as a somewhat pejorative reference to on-air individuals. This is not how the term talent is used in this book. It is just one of the number of ways that I refer to individuals who perform on-air services for news broadcasts and reality-based programs.

Reality-based Programming
I refer to the term reality-based programming as television shows — i.e., talk, magazine, etc. — that supply information. Examples of this type of programming include *Entertainment Tonight, Extra, The Oprah Winfrey Show, Inside Edition, The Jerry Springer Show,* etc.

Tabloid
Merriam Webster's Collegiate Dictionary defines the term, tabloid, as: *of, relating to, or characteristic of tabloids; esp: featuring stories of violence, crime, or scandal presented in a sensational manner.* I use this term in the same manner throughout this book.

Syndicated Programming
Syndicated programs are programs that are essentially sold or distributed, station by station, in each market. Therefore, a syndicated program can appear on an ABC affiliate in one market, and an NBC, CBS, FOX, Warner Brothers, etc., affiliate in another.

Sweeps

Sweeps or ratings periods are specific times during the year when viewer ratings and demographics for programs, stations, and networks, etc., are recorded and measured.

Scripts

Scripts are patterns of behavior which we engage in, consciously or unconsciously, in order to navigate through the often stormy and dangerous waters of life. They can be hard to deviate from because they can, and often do, become reflexive and/or compulsive. Our scripts of behavior are frequently the result of the emulation of acts that we have seen or heard about, or patterns of behavior that we have personally engaged in, which have been reinforced within us.

Carpé Diem (car-páy dee-ém)

Carpé Diem is Latin for "Seize The Day!" (i.e., make the very most of the moment at hand). The concept of Carpé Diem is infused with positive spirit and emotion.

This spirit is the foundation upon which every chapter of this book is based.

A Debate Regarding The Quality Level of TV News and Reality-Based Programming

Idealist to Station Owners:
>You put on stuff that's titillating,
>Tabloid, tawdry, and desecrating,
>Praying to God and anticipating
>That you will get a higher rating.

>All of your stories are over quicker,
>You now package your pablum and garbage slicker,
>Starving a society that is growing sicker,
>Just so your viewers won't press their clickers.

One angry Station Owner stands up:
>Sir, don't put me through the ringer
>Because I air a *Jerry Springer.*
>Besides, don't forget that this defendant
>Is protected by the First Amendment.
>So, before my character you impeach,
>Remember: *Jerry* is protected speech!

Idealist sarcastically replies:
>Yes, I'm sure the framers of the Constitution meant
>To protect the prurient and decadent
>Ideas and thoughts that your station spreads,
>Putting this trash in viewers' heads.

>I have watched your station, WLUD,
>And sir, it is a travesty.
>You air the lowest and sickest crowd.
>I'm sure you must be very proud.

Another irate Station Owner retorts:
>Excuse me, sir, don't point that finger,
>I, too, purchased *Jerry Springer*, and
>While he may well be an exploitative clown,
>His ratings are up! *Rosie*'s are down!
>So don't lay this guilt trip on my lap.
>It's the viewers who clamor for this crap.
>
>And before my character you condemn and taunt,
>I'm just airing what the viewers' want!
>So don't blame me if I air bottom feeders,
>I gotta move those people meters.
>TV's a high stakes business, played for keeps.
>(He then smiles to his fellow station owners)
>Besides, it's only sick in sweeps!

Then the Idealist self-righteously inquires:
>Do you think God rewards degradation and lust?

The Station Owner laughingly responds:
>During ratings, it's Nielsen in whom I trust!
>
>So don't tell me, sir, that I'm some disgrace:
>I'm driven by the marketplace.

(A second or two passes, and in a softer and more conciliatory tone, the same Station Owner asks):

>Besides, what other path is there to choose,
>When I must get people to watch our news?
>I gotta put food in my children's mouths,
>And I can't do that if my viewers' go south.

(Looking almost despondent, the Station Owner continues):
>I agree it's a sad picture that you've depicted,
>And the pressures I feel leave me conflicted.
>So give us the answers, whatever they are,
>To get higher ratings, while raising the bar . . .

>Silence.

— K. L.

I. Two Core Broadcasting Conflicts

The Conflict of:
It Smells But It Sells

Story One

Assume that you are a general manager of a local television station that airs a highly successful and controversial talk show. This program features colorful and/or troubled individuals spilling their guts out about their personal lives. Occasionally, these guest discussions erupt into ugly arguments and on-air fights. Because of this show's arguably lowest common denominator content, your station has received calls and letters from many quarters, requesting that you cease airing the show.

To make matters worse, some former guests on the show recently came forward and confessed that things said on the program were not true, and that events which appeared to occur spontaneously, in fact, were staged or set up.[A]

Therefore, many of the stories that were told, and much of the information that was imparted on this reality-based show — may well have had no basis in reality.

The end result: Your station's viewers may well have been duped.

All of this comes at a time when you were deciding whether to move the show from 10 A.M. to 4 P.M. weekdays, where it would lead into your early evening newscasts. The reasons for making this time switch are:

5

1) It has been proven at a number of other stations that this show is a real ratings-getter in afternoon time periods.

2) This show has proven to be an excellent early evening news lead-in for many stations.

3) There is some reason to believe that airing this program in the late afternoon will attract the hard-to-come-by male audience.

4) If the switch of time periods increases ratings for the show, as well as for the newscasts that follow, your station's profits will increase substantially.[B]

The reasons for not moving this show from 10 A.M. to 4 P.M. — or for not continuing to air this show at all — are:

1) The content of the program has little or no socially redeeming value. In fact, it often is an embarrassment.

2) There are strong allegations that the show has misled your viewers in that this "reality-based" program may have no basis in reality.

3) 4 P.M. is a time when children are at home and watching TV.

4) There will be backlash and protests from viewers and various religious and non-religious groups, if your station airs this program when children are home from school and watching.

As you ponder your decision, you read the following excerpt from an *Electronic Media* article:

A growing number of stations are slotting Mr. Springer as a lead-in to local news because of the eyeballs he delivers.

"It's only been a positive for our news," says a vice president of programming and production at a top market station, where Mr. Springer is besting Ms. Winfrey. "As a mother of two, does it bother me to air it at 4 P.M.? Yes, but I can't justify moving it when it's doing this well."[C]

Or, put another way:

What we're airing is degrading,
but what the heck . . . it gets the ratings.

— K.L.

The bottom line: The show smells but it sells. This is the conflict and the dilemma that you (and other general managers) may well have to resolve, when deciding whether to move the show to 4 P.M., keep it in its original time period, or remove it completely from your air.

What would you do?

Story Two

When there's a breaking story, news divisions strive
To get there first, and air it live!!!
However, when "going live," one can't forecast
What upsetting acts will be broadcast.
Therefore, managers must never forget
That going live is like playing...Russian Roulette.[D]

— K.L.

This time, assume you're a news director of a local station. It's April 30 in Los Angeles, and the May ratings competition has already heated up like a concrete sidewalk on a Phoenix mid-summer afternoon. At about 3 P.M., a call comes into the news-room of your station, reporting that a man has parked his pick-up truck at a highly visible intersection between two of L.A.'s busiest freeways. Question: Do you dispatch your station's heli-copter in case you want to cover this event live? You decide that the answer is yes.

A few moments later, you learn that frantic motorists called police after the man aimed his shotgun at passing cars. At one point, the man allegedly dialed 911, reached a police dispatcher, and communicated that he was "emotionally distraught." You are then told that during one of the calls to the police, this same man fired several rounds of bullets; one of them through the roof of his car.

Seconds later, you are advised that your helicopter is now in place to pick up the events — live — as they unfold. The next question is: Do you break out of your regularly-scheduled chil-dren's programming to air this news event live — knowing that children inevitably will still be watching your coverage?

With a major ratings period in full gear, you, along with your other competitors, feel compelled to jump on this story and make it your own. You believe that there's nothing else you can do, as this could be one of those defining moments when your station can take a big step towards establishing its image as your market's news leader. You know all too well that news reputations can be made — and lost — in connection with big and memorable stories. Additionally, this is a breaking news event, and your viewers will expect you to bring it to them.

You decide to go for it, and air the live coverage.

Your cameras and your viewers are now locked into watching the man in the car. For a few long moments, nothing happens. Then, suddenly, the car catches fire. In a flash, the man jumps out of the car; his hair, pants and socks on fire.

You think to yourself, "Thank God! I've got this live. The viewers will love this." But then you panic: "Oh God! Kids are watching this." You try to brush your guilt and regrets away by thinking, "It's up to parents and caregivers — not the station — to monitor their children's TV viewing!" However, in your heart-of-hearts, you know that kids shouldn't be watching this stuff. But you can't allow your news operation to be set back just because your station happened to be airing children's programming when this story broke.

Suddenly, your executive producer gets your attention as he yells, "Oh sh-t, catch this!"

Writhing in pain, with legs scorched, the man struggles to pull off his pants, socks and underwear. He begins to walk around aimlessly, naked from the waist down.

You think to yourself, "This is live at its best!" But then you take a deep breath, as you think about the kids who are watching these horrifying scenes because their parents aren't around to control what their children are being exposed to. However, the next thing you find yourself doing is calling for the photographer to go in as "tight" (close) as possible on the man's face, trying to capture his dazed and bewildered look. You then ask for a close-up of his burned legs and hands. Your general manager comes into the newsroom, pats you on the back and says that you're doing a great job. You're stoked.

The televised male then walks, with his bare buttocks facing the camera, to the low wall at the edge of the freeway. He wavers there . . .

Adrenaline begins to shoot through you. All sorts of things go through your mind. First and foremost: What if he jumps? Is this something you should air? What about the kids watching? You look up at the monitors of the other stations in town. Four stations are right there with you going live, including your major competitor, who also left children's programming to cover the story. You ask yourself, "What can I do?" You know that anything can happen, as the man is positioned on the edge of the freeway, looking as if he might jump at any second . . . and if you don't cut away . . . now . . . it will be telecast live to your viewers. Once again, you take a deep breath. You decide that you must go for it. This is life!

Suddenly, the man picks up his shotgun and goes to the side of the road. Your heart is beating faster, harder. Blood is rushing to your face. You're dripping with sweat.

The man begins to shake his burned hands. He seizes the gun again. You think, "Should we cut out? Is this what we should be showing?" Someone in the newsroom yells that one of the other stations has taken its camera off the man. What do you do? You think about whether you would want your five-year-old daughter watching this. The easy answer is: Absolutely not! Your instincts tell you that something bad is going to happen, yet you don't make a move. For the moment, you're transfixed; transformed from journalist to voyeur.

The man then braces the butt of the gun against the low freeway median wall. He bends down to it. You realize he's going to do it! You yell to your director to cut away . . . too late. The man pulls the trigger!!!

On your air, in front of your viewers, the man blasts half of his head away.

A moment later, he lies dead on the pavement, with everything inside his head pouring out.[E]

What a story! You captured it live. You think to yourself, "Oh God! Thank God!"

You cannot move. You cannot speak. Newsroom members, who feel as conflicted as you do, half-heartedly come up and congratulate you on the great news coverage.

You decide to stay live on the scene for another hour or so.

As time passes, your station's phone lines continue to be flooded with callers complaining that their children are "disturbed," "distraught," and "traumatized" by what they saw. Other callers complain that the station should have cut away earlier.

The next day's ratings indicate that viewership grew by leaps and bounds as the events unfolded. By the time the suicide occurred, the ratings were through the roof.

On the other side of the ledger, the station is taking a tremendous amount of criticism for airing the suicide — especially because a reasonable news executive should have kept in mind that children were probably still watching.

The issue: What is apparently interesting for viewers to watch, may not always be in their best interest to see . . . or in the station's best interest to air.

This is a broadcasting reality.

The question is: How and where do you draw the line?

The answer, of course, is with great care, and we'll explore this challenge in the chapters ahead.

The Conflict Between Our Needs and Our Wants

> In seeking out the news, the press [acts] as *an agent* of the people at large. It is a means by which the people receive that free flow of information and ideas *essential to intelligent self-government.*
> Pell v. Procunier, 417 U.S. 817 (1974)
> Supreme Court Justice Powell, dissenting
> (emphases added)

Broadcast journalism is important to all of us. Extremely important. The nature and quality of the information imparted to us can materially impact our opinions, our ideas and our life decisions. We rely on news programs, and the individuals who work on them, to help us to make informed decisions regarding such topics as: who is qualified to represent us; what our laws and policies should be; what is the latest information regarding new and established drugs and medical procedures; what are prudent ways to invest and maximize our income; and how to raise the quality of our lives, etc. Broadcast journalists inform and educate us. As we live in our often narrowly-circumscribed worlds, we trust that television newscasts, and in some instances, reality-based programs, will be our balanced, accurate, and objective windows to all of the many worlds that — but for TV — we would have few, if any, other ways to observe.

In the United States, we live in a democracy, run by the

people. Implicit in the effective functioning of a democracy is that the people — you and I — receive the requisite information to make enlightened and wise decisions. It is the television press that often supplies us with that enlightenment and wisdom.

While in law school, I learned about the legislative history of a law. That is, the modification and edification processes that a law goes through in the Senate and House of Representatives before it is finally passed. By studying the legislative history of a law, we can ascertain the why, the what and the how of the law. In essence, we can learn how to correctly interpret and apply the law, by understanding: why the law was originally introduced and ultimately passed; why it is drafted as it is; what the law is supposed to accomplish; and how the law is intended to be administered.

Similarly, if we can truly understand some of the initial and integral whys, hows and values of broadcast journalism, we will better understand how and why we have arrived at where we are today. Therefore, it is worth spending a moment or two reviewing a bit of broadcasting history.

In 1925, more than 10,000 radio stations were in existence in the United States.[A] As these stations competed for listeners, they were constantly switching frequencies and increasing their power. According to the highly respected broadcast journalism historian, Edward Bliss, Jr., the huge number of stations and the unrestricted competition brought chaos.[B] As a result, Congress recognized the need for more effective regulation, and passed the Federal Radio Act of 1927. The words "public convenience, interest and necessity" appear in that Act[C], which referred to the Federal Radio Commission's requirement that, as a condition of granting a license to a station, that station must "take care" to meet the all-important obligation of informing the public.

Later, Congress passed the Communications Act of 1934, and the Federal Radio Commission (the "FRC") became the Federal Communications Commission (the "FCC"). In that Act, stations were required to broadcast in "the public interest, convenience and necessity." Interestingly, the meaning of this mandate isn't found in the Act.[D] Therefore, it has been left up to the FCC, through its rulings, to distill, as well as to enforce, the letter and the spirit of this now well-known phrase.

Similarly, the judiciary continues to interpret and protect the First Amendment guarantee that Congress shall make no law (abridging) freedom of the press. Here are excerpts from four of the numerous United States Supreme Court decisions citing and reinforcing the public's strong interest in being informed.

In 1919, the revered Justice Oliver Wendell Holmes, in his oft-quoted dissenting opinion in Abrams v. United States, 250 U.S. 616, expressed the belief that:

> It is only when all ideas are disseminated and exposed in a free society, can truths be ferreted out, and these truths shall enhance our society.

In the 1972 case of Branzburg v. Hayes, Justice Douglas, in his dissenting opinion, wrote:

> Today's decision will impede the *wide-open and robust dissemination of ideas and counter thought,* which a free press both fosters and protects, and which is *essential to the success of intelligent self-government.* 408 U.S. 665 (1972)   (emphases added)

Justice Douglas, in the well-known 1974 case of Pell v. Procunier, said:

> In dealing with the free press guarantee, it is important to note that the interest it protects [is] the right of the people, the true sovereign under our constitutional scheme, to *govern in an informed manner. The public's interest in being informed . . . is thus paramount.* 417 U.S. 817 (1974)   (emphasis added)

In Houchins v. KQED, Justice Stevens, joined by Justices Brennen and Powell, maintained that,

> *The preservation of a full and free flow of information to the general public has long been recognized as a core objective of the First Amendment.* 438 U.S. 1 (1978)   (emphasis added)

It is through the efforts of a free press and its responsibility to inform that we have exposure to diverse ideas and information, are afforded the opportunity to discern valuable truths and to form intelligent opinions, and can develop a foundation of knowledge, so that we may effectively govern ourselves. Because we are informed, we are also better able to develop and to make use of our faculties and deliberative processes, which can contribute to our emotional health and humaneness, and to that of our society.

The Radio & Television News Directors Association (RTNDA) states in its constitution, that its goals are "[the] achievement of high professional standards of electronic journalism and the fostering of principals of journalistic freedom to gather and disseminate information to the public."[E] The preamble of the RTNDA's *Code of Ethics* provides that: "The responsibility of radio and television journalists is to gather and report information of *importance and interest to the public accurately, honestly and impartially.*"[F]

As members of a democracy and a complex society, whose foundations are squarely built upon the concepts of self-determinism and independence, we must know as much as we can, on a continuing basis. This requires our access to necessary information. That is, information that we *need* to know, not only information that we want to know. We rely upon and trust that the TV press will give this to us. In theory and in reality, the role and the obligations of broadcast journalism and of broadcasters to the public are of profound importance to all of us. It is this role and these obligations that the framers of the Constitution, the Supreme Court, the FCC, and the RTNDA have sought to protect and to encourage.

News Profitability and the Wants of the Viewer
Years ago, when television news was in its infancy, news divisions were non-profit making entities. Their lofty goal was to serve the public interest. They viewed their responsibility as that of a public trust. As Bliss writes, "The reputation for providing a quality news product and for providing an important public service was a medal worn [by news divisions] with pride."[G] But, when it was discovered that huge sums of money could be made in

news, in lieu of a competition for journalistic excellence and achievement, TV journalism became a competition for viewers, demographics and ratings. Thereafter, news and reality-based programs began to be treated as a business — Big Business. The original end of serving the public interest with information that people needed to know often placed a distant second to the end of giving viewers what they wanted to see — that which would entertain and titillate them — so as to attain the new and almighty end — a great bottom line.

For example, a local news manager once said to me that he has the ratings of his local newscasts broken down into three-minute segments. This way, he can compare one day's news ratings with the next, and specifically identify which particular stories resulted in viewership increasing or decreasing. With this information, he then decides which stories to continue to run in a later newscast, or the next day. For this television station and for many others, the defining data is not the importance of the story to the community that the station is serving, but which stories provide the highest ratings. The end is what counts — profitability — not the means — the content of the stories, nor how important and/or beneficial the information is to the viewers.[1]

It is a broadcasting reality that many TV newscasts and reality-based shows now give us what we want — not necessarily what we need — so that we will tune in.

Michael Gartner, former President of NBC News, writes the following about the network evening newscasts focusing upon what viewers want to see, not what they need to know:

---

1. For example, two recent articles discuss how very little relevant and important news is actually given to viewers during Los Angeles evening newscasts. Please see:

   1) Swertlow, Frank, "Broadcast News, Inc. Local Newscasts Are Sensational And Superficial For A Reason: Profits," *Los Angeles Business Journal*, 24-30 August 1998, 1,14.
   2) Osborn, Barbara Bliss, "Election Neglected On Los Angeles' Local TV, Exploring an Empty News Hole," *Extra! TV News: Empty, Compromised . . . Savable?*, July/August 1997, 14.

The [O.J.] Simpson trial chewed up more time than the next two coveted events combined — the continuing war in Bosnia and the tragic bombing in Oklahoma City. The networks have spent five times as many minutes reporting on, obsessing about, and analyzing the Simpson trial on nightly newscasts, as they have spent covering the debate over Medicare and welfare, issues that truly affect our lives.[H]

Bliss echoes Gartner's sentiments, as he writes:

To a large extent, marketing researchers, not editors, determine the content of local newscasts. Since consultants have warned against the sin of boring anyone, pictures have become increasingly important, the more graphic the better — in traffic accidents, blood on the pavement; in homicide cases, bodies being removed in bags. No one argues that automobile accidents and murders should not be covered; the question is what priority to assign them. To quote John Hart (formerly of CBS and NBC networks): *"Too many producers select stories because they may seize an audience, instead of offering coverage designed to serve the audience."*[1]

(emphasis added)

Richard M. Cohen, former Senior Producer of CBS Evening News, shares the following observations in his caustic essay, "The Corporate Takeover of News":

Television news has an important job to do and, I believe, it has become an institution that fails America everyday . . . .

I thought our job in news was just to tell Americans the hard truth — the facts. What you need to know about your world. That's what the press is supposed to do, is it not? To insert ourselves under the citizens' skin and infect them with the virus of everything they probably don't really want to deal with, but very much need to know.

. . . this is a new era of television. In television, journalism is no longer a calling. It's a big-deal job with a fat paycheck. Objectives have changed. We are audience-driven now. We're not mission-driven, propelled by our responsibility to inform. We're just here to entertain, to soothe. We're here to sell our wares.

News has utilitarian value. In a free society news is fuel. News is blood. We are a society of choices. We are citizens with a franchise. We need to know our world, which means understanding our nation and our own backyards.

. . . what is the purpose of news in America today? To enlighten and edify, perhaps? *No.* The purpose of news is to make money, to generate corporate profits.[J]

So, just like separated parents who compete with each other to be the more popular with their children, by giving them what the children appear to want — gifts or candy, and leniency — as opposed to giving them what they need — their love, their time, their thoughts, their respect, and strong consistent parameters for behavior — often, news and reality-based programs give us what we want, not what we need or what is intellectually, emotionally, and spiritually beneficial and healthy for us.

The Conflict Between What We Need and What We Want

As we discussed above, two very compelling and often divergent values enter into most broadcasters' decisions each and every day. One value is that of serving the public interest by supplying necessary information. The other is that of making as much money as possible, by airing any and all material that will draw and keep demographically desirable viewers watching programs, which, in turn, will bring in the most advertiser dollars per commercial spot.

Through the years, we have evolved into a very ends-oriented society, and we rarely examine the means by which we attain our ends. For example, programs such as *Entertainment Tonight, Access Hollywood, Extra, Lifestyles of the Rich & Famous*, etc., often focus on outward success: "Who's hot today?"; "Who just signed the biggest contract?"; "Who has the most lavish lifestyle?" However, *how* those individuals achieved those ends is rarely discussed. Do these individuals have character? Have they supported and enhanced others along the way? Did the individuals behind these success stories cheat to get where they are? Or hurt others? Pay people off? These issues often aren't researched or presented.

Why? Because it seems that we basically don't care. The end — "They won" — is all that counts. Unless, of course, we can make even more money by exposing, gossiping, and pandering. If we can, we're there! Just as our heroes reflect who we are, so does the content of our programs. Can the producers of these programs be faulted for giving the viewers what they appear to want?

During the past decade, much has been written regarding the tabloid talk and magazine shows that fill our air waves. All too often, many of these shows have done their best to out-sleaze and out-sensationalize one another, especially during the all-important ratings months. The goal: To garner as many ratings points as possible. As our society continues to become more and more desensitized, the individuals behind the tabloid shows feel that they need to give us more and more titillation and degradation to get a rise out of us and to keep us watching. (How ironic, in that the morals, the character, and the spirit of our society continue to sink so low.)

The remarks of Howard Rosenberg, the respected television writer for the *Los Angeles Times*, in his critique of the televised suicide discussed earlier in "Story Two," are equally applicable to the issues and problems raised in "Story One," regarding the allegedly staged talk show:

> Even as protests against violence on TV appear to surge, our capacity to tolerate and even *enjoy* it [the violence] seems to be growing still faster. Although many are outraged by Thursday's coverage [of the highway suicide], probably just as many found it compelling; so riveting that they couldn't turn away. If so, they are as much at fault as the stations that served it to them.
>
> So how high does the bar go from here?
>
> It was only a few years ago that a producer of a notorious Japanese game show known for subjecting contestants to extreme ridicule and humiliation, was asked in an interview, how he planned to meet the rising expectations of viewers. "Someday, we might have to kill somebody," he said without smiling.
>
> Appetites do have to be fed. And so you wonder . . . what happens next?[K]

Why, before national advertisers withdrew their advertising

dollars, did so many talk and magazine shows feature degradation and negativity, knowing that there was no redeeming social value to the viewer or to our society as a whole? Because they were and are allowed to do so under the free speech guarantee of our First Amendment. And also, because sleaze translates into large profits. Our society has become obsessed with ends, and through such rationalizations as, "It smells, but it sells," and "It's business," we *sweep* our less than noble means of end attainment under our carpets.[2] In our society, a healthy bottom line has become a great deodorant, for covering up the stench of questionable decision-making and for the ends justifying the means.

As TV stations began to realize large profits from their newscasts, Bliss writes:

> . . . the treatment of news changed. Increasingly, news was packaged to attract larger and larger audiences. Consultants advised broadcasters on giving the public what it wanted, rather than what it needed. More emphasis was placed on pictures — the visuals — and on pace. "Talking heads" were discouraged. And although many broadcasts still acted responsibly, many did not. News had become golden. It was difficult, having a profit center, not to make profit the name of the game.
> This trend distressed Ed Murrow as early as 1958, when he told a meeting of news directors, "I am frightened by the imbalance, *the constant striving to reach the largest possible audience for everything*, by the absence of a sustained study of the state of the nation." It was in this speech that he said, "Television can teach. It can illuminate. Yes, and it can even inspire. But, it can do so *only* to the extent that *humans use it to those ends.* Otherwise, it is merely wires and lights in a box." This warning is perhaps better known than anything else Murrow ever said.[L]
> (emphasis added)

---

2 This strikes me as an excellent definition of the term "sweeps," in that during sweeps (or ratings) periods, some broadcasters sweep their responsibility to inform the public, as well as sweep their consciences and their higher selves under their proverbial carpets, in order to justify (or to rationalize) airing titillating, degrading and/or tabloid material in hopes of attracting viewers and attaining higher ratings.

Bliss continues:

It was [the] clash between public interest and corporate interest — between responsibility in news programming and profits — that concerned Murrow in 1958 when he spoke to the country's news directors and expressed his abiding fear of what [that clash] would do to society. Speaking boldly, realizing his own danger, he declared:

"*Our history will be what we make of it.* And, if there are any historians about 50 to 100 years from now, and should there be preserved the kinescopes for one week of all three networks, they will find recorded in black and white, or color, evidence of decadence, escapism, and insulation from the realities of the world in which we live . . . [3] If this state of affairs continues, we may alter an advertising slogan to read: LOOK NOW, PAY LATER. For surely, we will pay for using the most powerful instrument of communication to insulate the citizenry from the hard and demanding realities which must be faced if we are to *survive.*"

"And," he added, "I mean the word survive literally."

A quarter century later, John Chancellor, addressing the same group, spoke of how news had become a *money center.* "*Our greatest challenge,*" he said, "*is the corruption of success.*"[M]

(emphases added)

The values of the public need and the public want often conflict in the real world of broadcasting. Many decisions that broadcast executives make each day, in one way or another, involve and reflect the weighing of these values.

News and reality-based programming are indeed big business. In many instances, they earn big money. Almost all decisions that are made regarding these broadcasts involve finances and the maximization of profits. The pressures on news managers, general managers, executive producers, producers, and others to secure high ratings, to keep costs down, and to thereby

---

3 This was 1958, before anyone heard of *A Current Affair* or Jerry Springer!

increase profits, are very real and very intense. This book discusses what issues and conflicts broadcasters — real-life human beings — face each day, and what on-air individuals (as well as producers, news managers, etc.) must know and be aware of, in the often non-black-and-white world of television news and reality-based programming.

As Dave Mason's song informs: "There ain't no good guys. There ain't no bad guys."[N] There are (only) individuals who have conflicting values and pressures that need to be weighed, balanced, and somehow effectively and constructively dealt with.

Regarding many of the complex issues presented herein, there are no easy answers. However, if we can clearly identify some of the problems, we have taken the first step towards finding some constructive solutions.

II. Some Real-life Broadcasting Issues, Conflicts, and Problems

Change

"The one thing that remains the same about our business (broadcasting), is that there's always change."[A]

Years ago, a very successful and highly respected news executive made the above off-handed remark to me during one of our negotiations. I have come to see how very right that general manager was. Change is inevitable . . . especially in local news. During the past ten years, I have seen scores of stations change ownership and, in some instances, change network affiliations. I have also seen how ratings of prime time and other day-part programming go up and down, and with those fluctuations have come increases and decreases in news ratings — and change.

With all of these changes, come changes in management. These new management recruits, in turn, make their own changes, as they bring with them new ideas and different perspectives as to how to garner a greater number of demographically desirable viewers. The goal is: To raise news division and overall station profitability.

Along with changes in management almost always come changes in on-air talent, off-air staff members, news philosophy, news content, news format, graphics, pacing, music, sets, etc. This can also be said to varying degrees about network and cable news operations, as well as network, syndicated, and cable reality-based programs.

A number of years ago, I had a most revealing conversation

with a news executive whom I believe has done more than anyone to revolutionize local news over the past decade. The discussion focused on his perception of the positive value of change for his stations. When I asked him why he thought that he and his stations had become so successful, he replied:

> It's because my station managers have *complete flexibility.* Other stations have hard, etched-in-stone rules and ways of doing things, that take months to change. They (other stations) also have talent contracts that guarantee that their on-camera people *must* anchor and report for *specific* shows. We, on the other hand, have designed *our* operations so that we can *change* things in a couple of hours. *We can creatively and flexibly respond to the always-changing environment.* We can change our tone, our focus and even create new music. *We can vary which shows our talent anchor and report on.* This [ability to change] makes us able to be both more responsive to the news of the day, and to the needs and desires of our viewers. Basically, when a news opportunity presents itself, unlike other stations, we can jump on it and make it our own.[B]

These words of change were from an executive in charge of highly-rated stations. On the other end of the spectrum, when a news manager at a low-rated station changed his morning anchor team, yet again, I asked him why he made the particular change that he did. He replied, "We're #3 in the market and going nowhere. I gotta change something. So I changed the anchor team (again). Hell, if it doesn't work, I'll change it again and again, until it does work."

Here are six scenarios that I have constructed which, except for some modifications, reflect real-life situations with which I have been involved or have seen. The seventh pattern is one that I expect, one day, will take place.

> 1) The owner of a #3-rated station decided that this station needed to change its news image. As a result, he hired a new general manager (GM) and news director to put together a hotter, faster-paced, more highly-produced news product. They, in turn, hired newscasters from all over the country who could sell this news product with more immediacy and color.

These newscasters uprooted themselves (and in many instances, their families); some left excellent on-air positions behind, to move to this larger market to be part of the new "program." A year later, with ratings still in the toilet, it was decided at corporate headquarters that (once again) changes needed to be made. Soon thereafter, the GM and news director of the station left and another management team was brought in. This new team was so totally at odds with their predecessor's vision of news, that they even criticized and repudiated it in the local press. Immediately thereafter, the new general manager (again) completely changed the direction and image of the news product, along with hiring an almost totally new on-air staff. Furthermore, notwithstanding the fact that many of the individuals hired by the departed management had no-cut or firm contracts, and had specific duties (what newscasts they would anchor or which reporting franchises they would be given) written into those contracts, many were not given the assignments they had been promised. Instead, they were told by the new station management that they could either accept the different and lesser positions, or they could sit home (possibly hurting their careers) and collect a pay check. When the demoted individuals complained that prior management brought them to the station with a certain vision and promise in mind, the new management responded, "That was prior management's vision. We're sorry, but we have to execute our own (vision). It's not personal, it's business."

2) Joe Smith was lured away from a station where he was anchoring a 4 P.M. Monday-Friday newscast, to another station (a Fox affiliate), where he would anchor the Monday-Friday 6 P.M. and 10 P.M. newscasts. Joe received a four-year contract which provided for twice the amount of compensation that he received at his old station. About six months after he arrived at the new station, that station went through an affiliation switch to CBS. The station's consultant advised station management that, "Considering the station's new CBS program line-up, it would be appropriate to change its on-air news approach. It [the station] should have individuals in its main anchor positions, who have established news credentials in the market, not young newcomers." As a result, Joe was demoted from the promised weeknight anchor position, to anchoring the morning and noon newscasts. The anchors who were currently

anchoring mornings and noons (who had been demoted from anchoring the evening newscasts by prior management, and who had twenty years of in-market experience between them) were promoted back to their old positions.

3) (About 1984) A GM had been at a station for five years (a lot longer than most people thought he'd last, considering his station's perennially poor ratings). No matter what approach he tried, his station remained mired in third place. People said, "The station must have been built on an ancient Indian burial ground." (A statement often made in the news business when discussing the consistent futile efforts of certain very low-rated stations to increase their ratings.) The GM felt that if his station's ratings did not show significant improvement during the upcoming May ratings period, he would finally be fired. The GM called his news director to his office and told her that he had decided to "blow up" the anchor team that was put together just fifteen months earlier, notwithstanding the fact that the team was just starting to gel. He told the news director that he wanted to hire an anchor team with a high "Q" (recognizability quotient). The general manager suggested a team such as Ollie North and Fawn Hall. Incredulous, the news director was speechless. The GM quickly added, "It'll just be for the May book (rating period). We'll figure something else for July and November." The news director, who put the soon-to-be-defunct anchor team together, was inwardly irate, but until she could find another job she had to follow his orders and ascertain the availability of Ollie and Fawn. When she arrived back in the newsroom, the news director related the story to her executive producer and said, rolling her eyes, "Thank God Hitler's not still around. His Q's probably through the roof!"

4) A group of stations was sold; management was replaced at almost all of the stations. Major on-air changes immediately took place.

5) A long-time #3 station decided to put on an afternoon newscast against the strong #1 syndicated show, *Oprah*. The general manager decided that he would hire a woman who looked like Oprah to anchor it and hopefully siphon away *Oprah* viewers. The station hired this person away from a comfortable position in her hometown, for a good deal more money (however, the cost of living in this new city was a great deal higher, also). After a few months, with no increase in the

ratings, the station decided that their experiment had not worked. They then demoted the Oprah look-alike to weekend anchoring; eventually she had to leave the station and the market (because she had been tarnished by her poor positioning and lack of success at her desperate-for-a-quick-fix station).

6) A #3 station in a large market just couldn't make any upward movement in the ratings. The general manager was worried that if he didn't do something quickly, he would get axed. (He had already fired two news directors, so there was no one else he could blame.) He needed something to increase viewership and give him more time. He decided to hire away a legendary anchor in the market, and end the anchor's career in a blaze of glory at his station. With a great deal of money, a firm contract and a lot of publicity, this anchor was hired. Within one year of coming to the station and with no ratings increase in sight, the anchor was unceremoniously told to clean out his desk and go home. He would not be anchoring anymore. The station would pay him for the next two years of his contract to "sit on the beach."[1] As this anchor had already been making very good money at his former station, he realized the mistake that he'd made by changing stations. This was not how he wanted to end his illustrious career.

7) [Three years from today] "WDED" is one of the five television stations in a Top-20-size market. Each of these stations has a full complement of newscasts. The ratings for WDED's newscasts are abysmal. The ownership decides that "DED" cannot profitably compete in the news arena, and would be better off running soap operas during the day and syndicated programs in the evening against its competitors' newscasts. Within one week, all newscasts are cancelled and the entire news staff is laid off.

These kinds of changes take place in the reality-based program arena, as well. For instance, one syndicated program hired a male to be its weeknight host, but a few days before the show was to debut, management decided that he wasn't the right guy, so

---

1 This is called exercising an employer's pay-or-play right. This concept will be discussed in the chapter entitled, "Contracts."

they paid him to sit around the office until they could contractually let him go. As a result, he never had the chance to host the show — as promised — for even one day! Then, after one year, this show, which was billed as an entertainment program, switched executive producers, became a pop culture show, and replaced its two hosts with two new ones. One year later, the show decided that it needed to become harder-edged — a sort of mini-Dateline. Its executive producer and hosts were again replaced. Three months into the fourth year of the show, it appears to have changed its tone once again and has just hired another executive producer.

All of these changes took place, mind you, even though the show was doing fairly well in the ratings.

I could write volumes about the changes that I've been involved with and those that I've seen, which have been made in pursuit of greater profitability, and thereafter cavalierly explained away as, "It's just business," like someone flicks an annoying fly from one's shoulder. However, if you are the talent who is being fired, demoted, and/or humiliated, this kind of change can be devastating — professionally, emotionally, and financially. It can indeed be a life-altering experience.

Herein lies a harsh reality. Stations, due to economic pressures, want as much flexibility as possible to make changes at any time regarding on-air and off-air individuals. Essentially, if you don't deliver viewers, or you no longer fit in, management will demote you and/or let you go in a flash. And from management's perspective, it's not personal, it's business.

Of course, from the employee's perspective, what's missing here is a long-term, human commitment from management, and a true appreciation of the fact that management seems to give so little consideration to the reality that human beings and their precious careers and dreams are being willy-nilly disposed of like last night's trash.

News Tip: Individuals who are in broadcast journalism should understand that the people they work for — for the most part — perceive broadcasting as a high stakes business. The financial rewards for everyone can indeed be great, but because change is inevitable, careers will ebb and flow, and often not go as planned.

Subjectivity

"One person's passion is another person's poison."

As you may glean from the events in the last section, broadcasting can be a very reactive business. When deciding to make changes, management often reacts to: ratings and demographic information, research studies, lead-in and lead-out programming requirements, what competitors appear to do well, and the opinions of key employees and those of program sponsors, etc. Most of all, managers react to the perceptions and mandates of their bosses, who for the most part are bottom-line driven.

Where broadcasting in many instances, may be a reactive business, it is almost always a subjective one. Here are two illustrations of how different news managers' subjective tastes can radically differ:

1) Bill was anchoring for a national cable network. One morning, he arrived at work and was told that the network had just been sold. He thereafter learned that, as a result of the sale, the upper management at the network, who had hired and had been supportive of him would be immediately replaced. A day later he received a call from a program director who had worked with him years before. This program director said that he was one of two remaining candidates in the running to be named to the position of president of the network. The caller then said to Bill, "If I get the job, Bill, I will promote you to be our lead evening anchor. You and one or two others will become the go-to people and public face of the

network. I can't believe these guys [Bill's current manage-
ment] aren't using you better. Anyway, as soon as I get in there,
we'll rip up your contract, pay you more, and make you a
prominent part of the network for years and years to come."
This was indeed one of the best calls Bill had ever received. He
called his wife to share his excitement.

However, two days later, it was announced that the *other*
candidate got the job — not Bill's supporter. Shortly thereafter, the new president of the network, through his new vice
president of news, told Bill that, unfortunately, the network
just didn't see Bill as having any future there and that his services would no longer be needed. Bill's style just wasn't their
style. They would pay Bill for the remaining six weeks of his
contract and he could go find another job.

As is almost always the case, news of the firing spread
quickly through the network. As soon as Bill entered the newsroom, some of this colleagues — not knowing what to say —
avoided him; others awkwardly tried to console him.
Emotionally blown away, Bill packed up his things and quickly
left to tell his wife and children the devastating news. As he
walked to the parking lot, he wondered how one person could
see him as the future star of the network and another could
feel that he had no future there at all.

2) Stephanie, a weekend anchor, was hired two years
ago by the news director of a Top-10 market station. During
this time, Stephanie was the main fill-in for both of the weeknight female anchors, and she received excellent marks for
this work from her management. One day, the news director
called Stephanie's agent and said that in the near future they'd
begin negotiations for a new contract for Stephanie; and that
within the next six months, she would be promoted to a
prominent weeknight anchor position.

However, before negotiations for a new contract could
begin, the general manager and the news director were
replaced and all of their plans and changes were put on hold
until new managers were hired. About two months later, the
new news director called Stepanie's agent and told him that
Stephanie did not have "the heft and weight" — "the gravity"
— to be a weeknight anchor, as they perceived Stephanie's

strengths to be her warmth, her ad-libbing, and her perkiness. As a result, they'd like her to assume the station's weekday morning anchor position.

As Stephanie's goal and expectations were to become a weeknight anchor at her station, she told her agent that "It's so very disappointing that the individuals who were going to promote me are no longer here; but, if we can't change their (new management's) decision, then it's time to find a weeknight anchor position for me someplace else. Screw them if they don't want to take advantage of the time I've spent here!"

Six weeks later, Stephanie became a weeknight anchor in a larger market.

Regarding subjectivity, I'll always remember the evening when a friend invited me to a dinner party attended by her family and their friends, all of whom were from Pittsburgh. My friend told everyone at the table that I represent newscasters and that a number of my clients are television anchors and reporters in their city. As a result, for the next hour I heard: why one person loved anchor X because he was authoritative, and two others found him pompous and un-watchable; why three people loved anchor Y, but my friend's mother found her vapid and cold; why some people loved the hip way one young anchor dressed, while two others felt that she didn't look or dress like Diane Sawyer (who, for many in the viewing public, is the prototype journalist). Everyone brought his or her own subjective tastes to the table — literally.

Beauty is in the eye of the beholder, and there is no accounting for taste. These rules apply just as much to broadcast executives and managers, and to those who advise them, as they do to anyone else. Company heads, station managers, owners, general managers, program directors, sales staffers, news directors, consultants, producers — *and even their spouses or significant others* — all have a subjective say as to who is hired (and fired) at a station, and on which newscast or programs they should appear. And who's to say that any of them has good taste, a keen eye, or true vision for what can be? How many changes do we see made in broadcasting every day? Plenty!!! Obviously, somebody thought that each person being replaced was right for the position in issue when that person was originally hired. Additionally, not only do different individuals have completely different subjective perspectives regarding a broadcasting staff, but managers themselves often change their subjective perspectives. For example, one news director, to the best of my recollection shared the following (scary) insight with me: "The *worst* anchor in the country is the one that I hired three months ago. The *best* anchor is the one that I'll hire *next* (to replace her)."[A]

Because of the psychological dynamics of subjectivity, not everyone will like or highly value a given person. Not everyone will recognize how smart they are, how talented they are, or that they are the best at what they do. It *is* impossible to please everyone. This is a crucial concept to understand and a clear reality to keep in mind. For your emotional well-being, remember it. And you need to know without doubt that the reasons for the lack of approval or the rejection that a person receives, may well have nothing at all to do with the (objective) talent or the abilities of the individual being evaluated, and everything to do with the subjective perspectives and personal experiences of the person doing the evaluating. When you become an on- (or off-) air talent, everyone who comes in contact with you becomes an evaluator. One rule of thumb is: You will not be everyone's cup of tea.

There is a simple but eloquent prayer that goes like this: "God, give me the serenity to accept the things I cannot change, the courage to change the things I can, and the wisdom to know the difference." In life, there are some times — maybe many times — when we just can't win somebody over. When they just don't get it or see it or appreciate it. No matter how much we think that they should. Not everyone got Elvis when he was popular. Not everyone got the Beatles when they were hot. Not everyone likes Katie Couric or *Friends* or *ER* or *Seinfeld.* It's a free country and people can like whomever they choose. As they say, "That's (the dynamics of subjectivity) what makes a horse race." We will be much wiser and happier if we know up front that not everyone will see our talents and abilities. So, be forewarned that no matter what you do, your emotional health, self-esteem, and feelings of self-worth, at some point, will take some knocks. Just be aware, that everyone who is successful has shared these same emotionally-jarring experiences.

Fortunately, there is also good news regarding subjectivity. Where one employer may not value you enough, you may be just the answer and the right fit for someone else's subjective taste. The key is to find an employer who will understand and appreciate you and your abilities, put you in positions that will enhance you, and intelligently and effectively promote you. I can cite an abundance of previously non-successful broadcasters, who experienced many, many bumps in the road and some very tough emotional setbacks, until they found an enhancing employer and environment. I would argue that Katie Couric and Matt Lauer — the hugely successful hosts of the *Today* show — are two such individuals.

News Tip: With all of the management changes that take place in broadcasting, it is important to remember the broadcasting reality, that taste is a subjective phenomenon. There are times when some people won't see or appreciate your value. Your goal is to work for and with those who do.

Affirmative Action Versus Racial Discrimination

An Introduction

One of the issues that broadcasters deal with day to day is that of not being offered a position — or, in fact, not even being considered for one — because they are not of a specific race.

Years ago, almost *no* minorities were in news. Ed Bliss writes:

> The headline appeared in the *New York Times* on December 3, 1972. It called attention to a study conducted by the Office of Communications of the United Church of Christ. According to the study, half of the commercial television stations in the country did not employ as anchor, reporter or producer, let alone as manager, any black man or woman, American Indian, Oriental or Hispanic. News was being reported largely from the perspective of white males.
>
> Discrimination was not limited to television. A survey made by the *Columbia Journalism Review* and B'nai B'rith in 1968, found that of all employees in the news media, broadcast and print, blacks constituted only 4.2%. If the sign in some of journalism's show windows said, "Minorities Wanted," it also said, "Not Too Many, Not Too Fast."[A]

At many TV stations and, in a number of instances, at the networks, the situation has changed. Now, many managers strive to hire individuals who represent the racial composition of their

37

viewership. This has come about for the following reasons:

1) For the past 27 years, the Federal Communications Commission has had stringent Equal Employment Opportunity (EEO) regulations in place. These regulations require that TV and radio stations establish and maintain programs aimed at recruiting and hiring minorities.[B]

2) Various coalitions and interest groups have often effectively put pressure on stations to hire members of their particular race; if the stations don't, I am told, the coalition will sometimes complain and lodge protests with the FCC, with the hope that license renewal pressures will force the station to hire more of their own.

3a) By having more individuals on their air who reflect the racial composition of their viewership, stations hope to attract viewers of those races to watch their broadcasts.

3b) By reflecting the ethnic diversity of the community that a station serves, its management believes that the station will be more successful. As one well respected vice president of news said, "My belief is that if you're not a reflection of your community, you're in trouble . . . You're not going to have any viewers. They're going to say, They (the on-air staff) just don't seem to be like us. They don't reflect our views, so we're gone.[C]

3c) By striving to attain diversity of background and opinion in its newsroom, management believes that its news operation and product will be more broad-based, more balanced, and therefore more effective.

4) The individuals doing the hiring — along with deriving the hoped-for financial benefits of having one's news product ethnically reflect its viewership — believe that having ethnic diversity on the air is the right thing to do.

A number of complex issues involved in station, network, and independent producer minority hiring practices affect all broadcasters. Here are some of them.

Minorities - Their History
Professor Man Keung Ho writes that when one is a member of almost any minority group that person shares a unique social and cultural heritage that, most times, is passed on from

generation to generation. That heritage encompasses a member's sense of belonging to that group, and that group's unique way of valuing, feeling, acting and perceiving the world.[D]

One common history that most ethnic minorities share is that they, in a number of instances, have been discriminated against, held back, and treated as inferior by mainstream society.[E] Ho writes that the term minority can mean an "out-group" whose worth, culture, values and lifestyles are depreciated, devalued and stereotyped. Minority often is synonymous with blocked access to politically and economically powerful in-groups and the full benefits of the American way of life. Ho says that the prevalent American (majority culture) way of life, generally, standardizes individuals and is intolerant of cultural and racial differences.[F]

Affirmative Action

Affirmative action is a concept and practice designed to give minorities an equal chance to succeed, or, to put it another way, it is a means by which the playing field can be leveled. From my experience, there are two main ways to practice affirmative action. One is to treat everyone equally in all hiring processes and then let the most qualified person win. The second is to compensate, or overcompensate, for a minority's background and historical past mistreatment, by either favoring a specific minority or by completely excluding candidates of other races from the competition.

The first practice, ideally, would allow the best candidate, whatever his or her race is, to secure the position. The second practice guarantees that a member of a specific race will get the job. For some, this second practice smacks of reverse discrimination, and may have some detrimental side effects, both for the minority and for those who never had a chance to be considered because of their race. As I discuss later in this section, this practice could well have negative repercussions for employers as well.

Nobel Peace Prize Winner Dr. Martin Luther King Jr. was a proponent of an affirmative means to compensate the African-American for society's past injustices and defaults. He wrote:

> Among the many vital jobs to be done, the nation must

not only radically readjust its attitude toward the Negro in the compelling present, but must incorporate in its planning some *compensatory consideration* for the handicaps he has inherited from the past. *It is impossible to create a formula for the future which does not take into account that our society has been doing something special against the Negro for hundreds of years. How then can he be absorbed into the mainstream of American life if we do not do something special for him now, in order to balance the equation and equip him to compete on a just and equal basis?*

Whenever this issue of *compensatory* or preferential treatment for the Negro is raised, some of our friends recoil in horror. The Negro should be granted equality, they agree; but he should ask nothing more. On the surface, this appears reasonable, but it is not realistic. For it is obvious that if a man is entered at the starting line in a race three hundred years after another man, the first would have to perform some impossible feat in order to catch up with his fellow runner.

Several years ago, Prime Minister Nehru was telling me how his nation is handling the difficult problem of the untouchables, a problem not unrelated to the American Negro dilemma. The Prime Minister admitted that many Indians still harbor a prejudice against these long-oppressed people, but that it has become unpopular to exhibit this prejudice in any form. In part, this change in climate was created through the moral leadership of the late Mahatma Gandhi, who set an example for the nation by adopting an untouchable as his daughter. In part, it is the result of the Indian Constitution, which specifies that discrimination against the untouchables is a crime, punishable by imprisonment.

The Indian government spends millions of rupees annually developing housing and job opportunities in villages heavily inhabited by untouchables. Moreover, the Prime Minister said, if two applicants compete for entrance into a college or university, one of the applicants being an untouchable and the other of high caste, the school is required to accept the untouchable.

Professor Lawrence Reddick, who was with me during the interview asked: "But isn't that discrimination?"

"Well, it may be, " the Prime Minister answered. "But this is our way of atoning for the centuries of injustices we have inflicted upon these people."

America must seek its own ways of atoning for the injustices she has inflicted upon her Negro citizens. I do not suggest atonement for atonement's sake or because there is a need for self-punishment. I suggest atonement as the moral and practical way to bring the Negro's standards up to a realistic level."⁶   (emphases added)

Due to pressures exerted by various coalitions and special interest groups, broadcasting executives *often* engage in overcompensation, or so-called reverse discrimination, by seeking to hire a person of a specific race for a particular position, while completely excluding individuals of other races from consideration. For example, here are four illustrations of this dynamic at work.

Story #1: A number of years ago, I had a white reporter client whom just about everyone at her station respected and liked. Toward the expiration of her contract, she received numerous offers to anchor and report in various places. At one point, the then-current African-American weekend anchor, received an attractive job offer at another station which she accepted. Thereafter, my client began to fill in as the weekend anchor. From everyone's perspective, she did an excellent job. Her management — who desperately wanted to have her stay at the station long-term — told me so. Even her co-anchor went to his news director and recommended that they put my client into the vacated spot.

When I asked her management why they didn't give her the weekend anchor position, so that everyone would be happy, the news director replied, "Kenny, you know I must fill that job with a black. The black coalition will be picketing and down my throat within five minutes, if I put your (white) client in there!"

I then replied, "You know that you're forcing my client to leave your station and her hometown to take a weeknight anchor job in another city. However, if you promote her (to weekend anchor), you'll be able to groom her as your next weeknight anchor. It's the perfect plan." His response: "Yes, in an ideal world it would be perfect, but not in the real world. I gotta hire a black."

My client thereafter left her station — and her hometown — to become a successful weeknight anchor in another market. Ultimately, the station that my client left hired an

African-American from a smaller market to replace her and be the weekend anchor. About two years later, that African-American anchor left the station for a job in another city.

Story #2: A weekend Latino anchor was lured away from his station ("Station A") to another one ("Station B") in the same market, to become its 4, 5, and 10 P.M. weeknight anchor. The current 4, 5, and 10 P.M. weeknight anchor at Station B was African-American. Station B management decided to relieve the African-American anchor of his weeknight position after many years of service, because of poor research.

When the hire of the Latino individual was announced, a prominent black interest group vehemently protested the move and asserted so much pressure on Station B's management, that Station "B" reneged on part of its promise and contractual obligation to the Latino anchor; Station B retained the African-American as their weeknight 10:00 P.M. anchor — until he was ready to leave.

From my perspective, this re-thinking (or retreating) by Station B occurred as a result of the fact that the market in which Station B is situated has a significantly larger African-American population than Latino, and the interest groups for African-Americans are far more active, protective and influential than those for Latinos. In essence, it was to Station B's benefit to satisfy an employee of one race over an employee of a different race, because, one employee's race and special interest group was more important to a station's viewership and license renewal prospects than those of another.

Story #3: The Latino coalition is very strong in a major market, and Latinos make up nearly half of its population. As a result of intense Latino coalition pressure stations in this market are under intense scrutiny and pressure to hire many Latinos for their news programs — and they have. Interestingly, there are many Asian-Americans living in this market, but for many years there have been far, far fewer of them on the air than Latinos. In fact, one major station in that market, for more than a year, didn't have one Asian-American on the air. It appears that because there was no Asian-American interest group pressure put on any of the stations, hiring Asian-Americans was not a priority.

Allegedly, a few years ago, the Hispanic Coalition was

exerting tremendous pressure on one major station in this market in particular to hire more on-air Latinos. So much so, that the general manager's position was in serious jeopardy. Allegedly, one of the results of this pressure, was that two very well-respected and experienced white reporters' contracts were not renewed, and two far less experienced, smaller-market Latino reporters were hired in their places. This was accepted without incident or notable attention from any parties.

Story #4: An 11 P.M. weeknight anchor position became available at a large-market station. A day or so after the opening became public, the general manager and news director of the station called the agent for Tom, the white 5 P.M. weeknight anchor. They said that it was "very likely" that Tom would be assigned to anchor the 11 P.M. newscast, once they "went through some formalities."

However, after a series of heated meetings with prominent members of the Black Coalition, who urged that Michael, the station's African-American weekend anchor, be promoted to anchor the 11 P.M. newscast, the general manager and news director changed their plans and gave the 11 P.M. newscast to Michael.

Within a year or so, Michael attained so much acceptance and success that he was promoted to anchor a second evening newscast.

The Issues

It is a fact of broadcasting life that there will be some positions that broadcasters won't get, because they won't even be in consideration for them. Putting this reality in the most constructive way possible: Employers want to be ethnically sensitive to and reflective of their viewership. Put another way, employers can't afford to put their license renewal in jeopardy or to alienate significant portions of their viewership by not being ethnically diverse.

This fact of life has both good and bad points.

Ideally, most individuals would like to feel that they have an equal opportunity to secure any and every position for which they are qualified. However, the past practices of stations have shown that, until outside pressures had been exerted, only whites, for the most part, were hired for on-air positions. As I mentioned in Story #3, Asian-Americans were under-represented (and, in one case, were not represented at all on air at one station) in a major market, because there was no outside pressure being put upon the stations to make an Asian-American on-air hire. So, the question becomes: If employers can't be ethnically responsible on their own, what are the most effective ways to protect minorities from many executives' predispositions to hire whites? Coalition and FCC pressure exerted on station owners and executives, to practice affirmative action or minority compensation, has been the predominant means over the past ten years to accomplish this.

For many, this kind of affirmative action — of excluding some races — in order to hire others — can also be seen as reverse discrimination and pernicious. However, if Dr. Martin Luther King, Jr., were alive, he might well say that this kind of hiring practice is necessary to compensate minorities for past and current defaults in hiring practices, at least until the minorities are equipped to compete on an equal basis. And, that without some affirmative help now, the minority may never compete on equal footing.

Another issue is the ramifications of some managers' perceptions and fears that once you have someone of a particular race in a position, it's almost impossible to fire[1] or demote them; and if a minority does vacate a position for one reason or another, that person must be replaced by someone of the same race — or ironically, the station will almost surely be subject to protests,

---

1 An illustration of this fear came up recently when I was proposing that an African-American reporter be offered a *very specialized* correspondent position. Everyone concerned, agreed that my African-American client — like other of my non-African-American clients — didn't have the specific (scientific) knowledge ideally needed for this position. In the past, I had successfully overcome this obstacle by proposing that the employer in issue sign my (white) clients to a contract, which contained an employer's right-of-termination clause, after one year, if my client wasn't doing well as a result of his or her lack of expertise and comfort with the subject matter. However, in this last instance, the individual doing the hiring for this company declined to hire my (African-American) client. He said, "Kenny, normally I might try your proposal, but with a black (candidate), if (after a year) I fire him because it doesn't go well, I subject us to all sorts of (racially-based) problems. It's just not worth it."

pressures, and allegations of discriminatory practices.

I have found that, depending upon the market and the minority in issue, stations, in many instances, *do* feel compelled to replace one minority with a like minority, mainly as a result of coalition pressure, and occasionally, fear of viewer withdrawal. Not only does this practice preclude individuals of other races from being considered for these positions, but it certainly ties managers' hands with regard to how to most effectively configure and construct its talent line-up. However, there is one other question that should at least be explored: If stations feel that, once they put an individual of a particular race in a particular position, they are "forever" locked into a person of that race for that position, will this have a chilling effect upon putting a minority in that position to begin with?

Another issue is how one's newsroom colleagues feel about the situation of a minority getting or keeping a job, based solely or largely upon the criterion of race. For example, in Story #1, I discuss the situation of a very talented and popular white female anchor who had to leave her station, because the only anchor position that was open had to be filled by an African-American. Everybody at the station knew this. How did this impact upon how others perceived, treated and valued the African-American anchor who ultimately got the job? And, how did the well-known fact that this African-American anchor was offered the job — in lieu of the white female — solely or largely because of her race impact and effect the African-American anchor's own self-esteem, confidence, and growth?

These are real questions that often have no clear answers. To further cloud these issues, in April 1998, a three-judge panel of the U.S. Court of Appeals in Washington found the Federal Communication Commission's EEO rules unconstitutional, and overturned the FCC requirements that stations actively recruit minorities.[H] As this book is going to print, the U.S. Court of Appeals for the D.C. Circuit rejected the FCC's request for a new hearing on the agency's minority recruitment rules. Currently, FCC Chairman, Bill Kennard, is said to be considering whether to appeal this ruling to the Supreme Court.[I]

In defense of its regulations, the FCC cites substantial

increases in women and minority "participation" in broadcasting since its EEO rules took effect. "In 1971, women constituted 23.1% of full-time broadcast employees and minorities 9.1%. Last year, women constituted 40.8% of broadcast employees and minorities 19.9%.[I]

In an *RTNDA Communicator* article, Bob Papper and Michael Gerhard found that while almost all white news directors with whom they spoke expected no change in minority hiring practices should the FCC guidelines disappear, every minority news director whom they interviewed felt just the opposite.[J]

For example, Barbara Hamn, executive director of news and information programming at WTKR in Norfolk, Virginia, says (apparently assuming that most news station owners and executives are white), "I just think that most people are more comfortable with their own . . . and that's what they're going to go back to."[K] Hamn continues, "If nobody's holding your feet to the fire, you're not going to go out of your way to find minority candidates. You hear people complaining of how difficult it is to find minority candidates for producer and director positions . . . and (if FCC guidelines no longer exist) it's going to be easier to just wipe your hands and not worry about it. And that's frightening."[L]

WWOR news director Will Wright echoes Hamn's views when he says, "I don't think we should need a law that tells us who should get served in a restaurant. But it turns out that (we) do."[M]

When discussing some manager's statements that hiring practices won't change should there no longer be any EEO rules in effect, Phil Alvidrez, executive news director at KTVK in Phoenix, says:

> . . . I just don't believe that history gives us any promises or confidences that that's going to happen. And if anything, I see a swing back in a lot of people's attitudes toward race, and that's discouraging.
>
> The pendulum's swung (again), and that's sad because it takes a lifetime to reverse this kind of thing. There's been a tremendous amount of progress in the almost 25 years (since the EEO rules have been in effect and stations have proactively hired minorities), and I would hate to see us go back to the days when that wasn't the case. I remember working in news-

rooms where there were very few minorities and there were no women. That's not a place I want to be."[N]

I agree with Hamn's, Wright's, and Alvidrez's perspectives and concerns. Personally, I believe that managers often tend to hire people like themselves. Therefore, if most station and network owners and executive managers are white, they will hire whites. This is one of the overriding reasons why, up until a couple of decades ago, newscasts were "lily white." However, with profitability being the predominant value today, I also believe that networks and stations will often hire and air anyone who will win for them, regardless of who and what they are. So if diversity attracts and keeps viewers, newscasts may well be and remain diverse. Because profits rule.

News Tip: For a number of reasons, it is often important for networks, stations, and producers to engage in exclusionary hiring practices in order to have ethnic diversity on the air. The goal is a desirable one; the means is a debatable one.

The Issue Of Affirmative Action In Connection With Who Is Given A Particular On-Air Position And How That Decision Is Reached

When this book was near completion, the case of *Janet S. Peckinpaugh v. Post-Newsweek Stations Connecticut, et.al.* was tried and decided. Below, I have reprinted a paper that I wrote regarding the *Peckinpaugh* case, as I believe that it identifies and discusses some very important concerns and realities for broadcasting employers. (Please note that I have been Ms. Peckinpaugh's agent for over fourteen years. I was deposed twice before the trial and testified at trial.)

The Dilemma That The *Janet S. Peckinpaugh* Case Poses For Broadcasting Employers Who Seek Ethnic Diversity On-Air

For the past sixteen years, I have been a proactive representative of, and *career choreographer*™ for, some of this country's finest broadcast journalists — many of whom are "minorities." Along with many other individuals involved in broadcasting, I fervently believe that newscasts and reality-based programs must be ethically diverse, both on the air and off. However, in light of the recent federal court decision in *Janet S. Peckinpaugh v. Post Newsweek Stations Connecticut, et.al.,* I am concerned that constantly beleaguered and well-meaning news and reality-based program executives, who strive to attain ethnic diversity on-air through certain exclusionary hiring practices, may well be unknowingly violating anti-discrimination laws and thereby subjecting their companies to potentially major damage awards.

As a talent representative, I am called upon almost daily by news and programming executives who say that they have an opening, or a potential opening to fill, *but that they MUST hire an individual of a specific race to fill it.* Often, these executives say that they want to reflect the ethnic make-up of the community that their newscasts and programs serve. They may also share the belief that cultural diversity in the newsroom and on the air best serves their station, the content balance of their newscasts and programs, and their viewers.

These are all worthy goals. The issue is: How to legally attain them. I submit this paper to encourage vigorous discussion on this subject.

Below is a scenario that I have constructed which illustrates a *potentially* dangerous on-air decision-making practice:

> In a top market, where there was a very large Hispanic population, but also a substantial Asian population, a station had a 5 P.M. weeknight anchor position open. During conversations with various agents, the news director of that station confided that he needed to find an Hispanic anchor to fill the opening.
>
> After four or five months of being unable to find the "right" Hispanic individual for the position, station management eventually conducted focus-group testing to assist in finding the best (Hispanic) candidate. This test sample was comprised *solely* of Hispanic broadcast journalists.
>
> During this time, there was an Asian weekend anchor at the station who was very highly regarded. When that Asian anchor's representative called the station's news director to suggest that his client be given the 5 P.M. position, the news director replied that at another time, in another setting, the Asian anchor would be an *excellent* choice for the job; however, in this instance, he *must* hire an Hispanic individual to fill the spot. This was the case notwithstanding the fact that there was already an Hispanic individual anchoring the weekday morning newscasts.
>
> When the representative then asked that the station include his Asian client in the focus-group testing, in order to determine the community response, the station management declined. They said that they must fill the position with an Hispanic individual, as they wanted to ensure that their station's on-air personnel reflected the ethnic composition of their viewing community. Therefore, regardless of the fact that there was a significant Asian population in the station's market, and that there was no Asian weeknight anchor at the station, the Asian anchor was not included in the focus group testing.
>
> One month after the research was completed, an Hispanic individual was given the position.

Recently, in the case of *Janet S. Peckinpaugh v. Post-Newsweek Stations Connecticut, Inc. et.al.*, a federal court jury found, among other things, that the Post-Newsweek company was guilty of gender discrimination. In that case the management of WFSB in Hartford, Connecticut, hired anchor Al Terzi from its competitor, WTNH, in New Haven. When Mr. Terzi was hired, the plaintiff in the case, Janet Peckinpaugh, who had been a ratings winner at both WTNH and WFSB, was anchoring the 5 P.M. and 6 P.M. weeknight newscasts, and was one of the females being considered as a co-anchor with Mr. Terzi. The station conducted viewer research, having all three of its weeknight female anchors take turns sitting next to Mr. Terzi, in order to determine who would be the best choice to anchor the 5 P.M. and 6 P.M. newscasts with him. After receiving the research results, Ms. Peckinpaugh was removed from anchoring the 5 P.M. and 6 P.M. newscasts. These newscasts were then anchored by Mr. Terzi and another female anchor. Ms. Peckinpaugh was reassigned to anchor the Monday through Friday noon and 5:30 P.M. newscasts with another female anchor; however, she was eventually taken off the noon and 5:30 P.M. newscasts so that WFSB could have a (traditional) male/female anchor pairing on those newscasts as well. Thereafter, Ms. Peckinpaugh was offered a lesser contract to anchor WFSB's weekend newscasts with a male anchor.

The jury, in this case, found that WFSB management committed gender discrimination by taking Ms. Peckinpaugh off the noon and 5:30 P.M. newscasts after *pre-determining* that their anchor team had to be the traditional male/female pairing. In this instance, WFSB's management allegedly never considered that two females anchoring the noon and 5:30 P.M. newscasts, could be their most effective pairing.

As an extension of this theory, I would argue that the original testing of three females with only one male, Mr. Terzi, also constituted gender discrimination, because station management again allegedly *pre-determined* that the 5 P.M. and 6 P.M. news-team pairings *had* to be male/female. Since each of the females was paired *only* with Mr. Terzi, the focus-group testing precluded a finding that the best anchor team could be comprised of two women. In the Peckinpaugh case, the plaintiff was awarded both compensatory and punitive ($3 million) damages in connection with the finding of gender discrimination.

According to Mike Allen, in his *New York Times* article, "Jury Awards Anchorwoman $8.3 Million in Sex Bias Case" (January 29, 1999, A-17), "[a]fter the verdict, Mr. [Bill] Ryan, the Post-Newsweek stations president, said that the discrimination laws apply to hiring, not to pairing [of broadcast journalists]." Obviously, the *Peckinpaugh* jury found that these laws *do* extend to which particular individuals broadcasting employers put on the air and to *how* these employers reach and justify their on-air decisions. This finding can apply equally to on-air decisions based upon race.

Using the *Peckinpaugh* case as a guide, if news and program executives and their consultants *pre-determine* that an individual of a *specific race* must be hired for a particular position, and *preclude* individuals of other races from being *equally* considered for that position, they may well be found guilty of racial discrimination. The smoking gun evidence will be if stations and/or their consultants perform viewer research, and the candidates in that research are only of one specific race (or if the research is skewed in favor of individuals of a specific race).

Therefore, according to *Peckinpaugh*, broadcasting executives should not make on-air decisions or be involved with research based upon the *pre-determined,* etched-in-stone goal of having individuals of only one race as candidates to fill a particular position. The key, under *Peckinpaugh,* is to allow candidates of *all* races to have an equal opportunity to compete for any given position, and to let *neutral* research help determine who fills which on-air roles.

The dilemma in all this is: Broadcasting employers want ethnic diversity on their newscasts and programs. However, certain often-used exclusionary hiring practices which ensure diversity on-air actually place employers at risk of violating discrimination laws. On the other hand, if employers open up on-air decisions to candidates of all races, as the *Peckinpaugh* decision appears to mandate, employers run the risk of having less, or no diversity at all on the air. Therein lies the problem presented by the *Peckinpaugh* decision.

* * * * * * * * *

It is commonplace in broadcasting for news and reality-based programming executives to seek out individuals of a specific race for a particular position to reflect the viewing public as much as possible. Although the goal of having on-air diversity is an admirable and important one, in light of the *Peckinpaugh* decision, the methods by which well-intentioned employers seek to achieve this end may well need to be studied and changed.

The Realities of Being an On-Air Female

One of the main reasons why I enjoy and I feel good about working in broadcast journalism, is because it is an industry that in many instances values, respects, and promotes (on-air) women. As I will discuss, subsequently, the situation isn't perfect, but it is better than most.

The good news is that there are few professions outside of broadcasting where women can fare and be paid as well as —— or better than — men. For example, I believe that Oprah Winfrey earns more than any male broadcaster — anywhere — at any time. I would expect that with the success that Rosie O'Donnell is enjoying, she, too will earn more than 99.9 percent of all male broadcasters. Years ago, Barbara Walters was reported to be the first $1 million-a-year newscaster. Diane Sawyer deservedly has one of the most lucrative broadcasting contracts. As this book is being written, Katie Couric has entered into a new NBC/*Today* show contract. This agreement, which will reportedly pay her about $7 million per year, will certainly make her the highest paid morning show host in history.[A] Her success merits it. Additionally, Jane Pauley has just reached a new long-term agreement with NBC, which will pay her approximately $5.5 million annually.[B]

I represent a great many females who earn more than their male counterparts or their male predecessors. This is the case because the individuals who own and run networks, stations, and programs believe that they will make more money by having

49

these women on their programs than if they don't.

A number of the most successful, highly respected, and nationally-seen women are minorities. Oprah Winfrey, Connie Chung, Giselle Fernandez, Elizabeth Vargas, Ann Curry, Carole Simpson, Deborah Roberts, etc., are just a few. Additionally, many of this country's most watched and highly regarded local anchors and reporters are female minorities. These women are wonderful role models for individuals in general, and they are particularly inspirational for up-and-coming broadcasters. For example, I cannot tell you how many young Asian-American females have told me that they aspire to be like, and to attain the success of Connie Chung.

Frequently, on-air women can move up in market sizes more quickly than men. For men, with age often comes the important and sought after qualities of credibility and authority. For women, depending upon an employer's needs and how that employer perceives a woman's on-air role, qualities such as credibility and authority are also important, however other elements can often be more prominent in the equation. One is a female's appearance. Another is her ability to warm up and have chemistry with an often cold, repressed, stiff, dull and/or arrogant male co-anchor or host. Take, for example, Katie Couric's pairing with Bryant Gumbel and Connie Chung's pairing with Dan Rather. In both instances, the female's role was in large part a *chemical* one. For example, in the lighter, warmer morning show venue, the warm and effervescent[1] Katie Couric was paired with Bryant Gumbel, as a way to neutralize Bryant's edge. Sort of like a base neutralizing an acid.[2] However, this in no way is meant to be a slight to Katie Couric, who is not only a warm and energized host, but when appropriate, she is also a strong, incisive, and compelling interviewer.

---

1 In deference to Katie, I am staying away from the overused adjective, "perky."
2 By-the-by, my observation is not meant to be critical of Bryant Gumbel, who is one of broadcasting's very finest interviewers. However, his demeanor may well be better suited to an evening time period.

Generally, on-air women receive a great deal of attention — good and bad — regarding their look, hairstyle, clothes, weight, etc. Focus upon these visual characteristics comes from both men and from women.

Here's an interesting example: A number of my female clients were ruled out as contenders for network morning hosting positions because some network managers said that these women were too sexy and/or too attractive for the time period. One male executive explained that a woman at home won't watch a morning show if she feels threatened, waking up with no makeup on, "while the guy beside her is drooling" over some sexy female host. But, I consistently see articles describing how sexy and handsome Matt Lauer is. I could make a deal for Matt to host any morning show — anytime, anywhere. Different visual, visceral, and chemical criteria for women? You bet!

As stated, relatively young women can often ascend the broadcasting ranks more quickly than men. However, a problem arises in local news when a women reaches the age of 45 or thereabouts. Because of stations' desires for younger demographics, many stations are reluctant to hire a woman from another market who is over 45, because they feel that she is too old to invest in. This is not necessarily the case with men, as they begin to reach their prime in their 40s. By-the-by, if station executives question my perspective, I would love to know how many of them hire female anchors who are over 45 from outside their markets compared with those who are younger.

The uplifting news is that if women can establish themselves in their markets, they can flourish there well into their 50s and 60s. Kelly Lange in Los Angeles and the late Ann Bishop in Miami are examples.

However, as most mature women are replaced by younger ones, and as these mature women fear and find that they can't find comparable on-air positions, inside or outside their current markets, I expect a proliferation of age discrimination suits — rightly or wrongly — to be brought against broadcast employers in coming years. These will be brought despite employers' contentions that they have absolute rights to terminate a contract or not renew it "without cause" — depending upon what the contract in issue provides. As this kind of suit will be grist for many an attorney's mill, I believe that age discrimination cases — taken on a contingent fee basis — will be a prominent issue in broadcasting in years to come.[3]

On the one hand, there are many, many excellent anchoring, hosting, and reporting positions for on-air women in broadcasting; on the other hand, there are *many* more good women than men in broadcasting to compete for them. My reasons for believing that there are more good women and why women are *inherently* better broadcasters than men are:

> 1) More women than men take journalism courses and more are journalism majors.
>
> 2) Because of the many excellent, highly visible female role models in broadcast journalism, many bright, talented, and motivated women perceive an on-air career as a real way to achieve their potential;[4] as opposed to pursuing many other professions in which they are more likely to encounter and be held back by sexism. This is in sharp contrast to the plethora of advancement-friendly professions that attractive, smart, and intelligent men can choose from and excel in.
>
> 3) Women *generally* are better, more open, more expressive, and less repressed communicators than men. This is due to the way that they have been socialized in our society. As a result, women are generally more effective communicators than men. Of course, there are exceptions.
>
> 4) Years ago, with men being the primary family breadwinners, many talented males couldn't afford to start out in some tiny market, for a salary of $11,000 per year and also support a family. Single and/or married women could do this.

---

3 And if any of these cases go to trial and the plaintiff-female wins, many of the defendant-stations thereafter may look to settle them, as the monetary damages can be great, and the damage to a stations' image can be even greater.

4 For example, Oprah Winfrey says the following about Barbara Walters being an invaluable role model for her:

"If there hadn't been a Barbara, there couldn't have been a me . . . When I saw her on the *Today* show, I said, 'I want to be like that.' I would study her every morning — her position in the chair, her head movements, her hand movements, her laugh. She was the light for me . . . You can't do any better than to make someone believe in themselves. Barbara made other women believe they could do it." (*The Hollywood Reporter*, 11 September 1998, S-5.)

At the beginning of this chapter, I said that broadcasting wasn't perfect.[5] It isn't. As this book is being written, not one of the three major network evening weeknight newscasts is anchored or co-anchored by a woman. Network executives and consultants say that women don't have the authority and credibility that men do. I disagree. It just depends upon the woman and the man in issue. I could certainly make a compelling argument that there are certain female anchors who would do just as well, or better, than some males. They certainly would make great co-anchors.

One issue and potential obstacle regarding whether women will ever achieve equality with men is how male and female executives perceive women. I have heard women say that they will never attain equality as long as the top network executives are male. This may or may not be so. I know many male executives who are far from sexist. (However, in the past, I have also known some male executives who have perceived females in the stereotypical way, valuing them mainly for their looks and personalities, which is neither correct or fair.) But few women discuss the issue of how women themselves view their potentials,

---

5 One area where broadcasting is far from perfect, is how it has treated women who hold or aspire to the top broadcast management positions. In the August 13, 1998, issue of *Broadcasting & Cable*, Elizabeth A. Rathburn writes:

It has been a bad year for women in TV.

Since last September, the industry's four most prominent and arguably most powerful women — Kay Koplovitz, Geraldine Laybourne, Margaret Loesch, and Lucie Salhany — have lost their top jobs.

Whatever the reasons, the moves depleted the industry of top-level women and underscored that men are still running the show in TV. *Broadcasting & Cable's* Top 25 Media Group (April 6). No woman sits atop any of the seven broadcast networks or a major cable programming company. And there's just one woman among the Top 25 operators — Margaret Wilson of Service Electric Cable — at No. 25 (April 20).

Although Pat Fili-Kruschel thereafter was named President of ABC Television Network, her promotion is the exception and not the rule for broadcasting.

Additionally, it was reported that "The Women In Cable and Telecommunications (WICT) Foundation was shocked to learn that women in cable programming earned an average of 18.2 percent less than their male counterparts in 1997. The base salary in cable programming for men in 1997 was $72,808; for women, it was $59,531." (Rathburn, Elizabeth A., "Study Finds Cable Pay Inequity," *Broadcasting & Cable*, 15 July 1998, 57.)

and whether they themselves are truly supportive and enhancing of each other.

I cannot begin to count the number of times that women have been taken aback and disappointed by how unsupportive and undermining women are of other successful women. Some attribute this behavior to the fact that males are used to playing team sports and helping their teammates and "buddies" out. As one friend said, "That's where the boys club mentality comes in." Girls are taught to focus on individual activities, such as being a ballerina, an ice skater, or a pageant queen. There's no teamwork between them and they don't learn to support each other.

No matter what the cause, it is arguable that not only do we need more female executives at the networks — and in other high profile news and programming positions — but we also need women in those positions who will be equally supportive of other women.

One more opinion: Executives and managers of stations and programs that have two male anchors, have women in subservient roles, don't appear to value women equally, and don't seem to value them for all of the contributions that they are capable of making if allowed, you are sending damaging signals to your viewers and perpetuating an undersireable stereotype. Ideally, it should be your goal to set an example for the community that you serve. Many of your viewers are women. Respect them.

News Tip: Broadcast journalism is one of the few businesses in which women can fare as well as, and in many instances better than, men. To my mind, women are inherently more effective communicators than men; and because there are so many talented women in broadcasting, there is very stiff competition for the top positions.

If you are a maturing female broadcaster, it is wise to find a market or position that you like, and do your best to establish your importance and success in it. This will serve you well as you approach your 50s and 60s.

A Call To All
News Program Executives

I hope that you will wholeheartedly agree
That women must be treated *equally*
And that their core identity
Isn't just measured by their *chemistry*.

It's great that they can warm up guys;
That they've got great smiles and sparkling eyes.
But just like your most talented fellas,
They're compelling interviewers and great story-tellers.

Remember, your broadcasts must reflect your community,
Therefore, there should be *no* immunity
From pursuing the *appropriate* goal
Of positioning women in an equal role.

One aspect about broadcasting that's quite appealing
Is that there's *almost* no *on-air* glass ceiling.
And I assume that *one day* the networks will gather
That it's smarter to *co*-anchor their "Dan Rather."

But until then, it's *crucial* for execs
That along with handing out lucrative checks
That women be given *substantive* opportunities to fulfill
All of their potentials by using all of their skills.
'Cause with your support — the *right* women can
Improve your news product — just like the *right* man.

— K.L.

Superman
(The Socialization And Pressures Of Being a *Teenage Boy* In Our Society)

A Superman is always strong,
Fighting evil all day long.
Never feeling any pain,
Always saving Lois Lane.

While others may not have a clue,
He *always* knows just what to do.
He jumps tall buildings at a whim,
Everyone looks up to him.

Invariably he gets it right,
He obviously is Super-bright.
Always doing *more* than expected,
Not a *single* problem is ever detected.

(But in truth, this would-be "Superman:")
Fights to hold back *every* tear,
Represses every hurt and fear.
And would *never* express how confused he feels,
Not this heroic "Man Of Steel."

As *others' expectations* can be such a load,
At any point, he may well implode.
He's one step away from his ungluing,
'Cause he doesn't know what the hell he's doing . . .
Except trying to be what *everyone else* expects,
And *not* someone whom they'll all reject.

He seeks perfection for appearance sake,
This adolescent Super-fake.
But he's not sure how much he can take,
Before his heart and soul just break.

And every night while he's in bed,
The very same thought runs through his head . . .

>"I hope one day that I'll be free,
>To feel good enough . . . to just be me.
>And that they'll *encourage* me to pursue
>The things that I truly want to do.
>And they'll accept me for who I *am.*
>So I *won't* have to be a Superman."

— K.L.

Why Supermen Evolve Into Poor Anchors and Hosts

As these Supermen have gotten older,
The façades they've created have grown colder.
As they anchor with their stoic faces,
Rarely are there any traces
Of any passion or intimacy,
At least not as far as *this* eye can see.
'Cause years ago "being yourself" was forbidden,
Now it's repressed and for all time hidden.

That's the way men have been socialized,
So we *really shouldn't* be surprised
As to why there are so many anchor guys
Who are repressed, uptight, and homogenized.

It's why recruiters do whatever they can
To find an *engaging* anchor man.
Who not only is a man of steel,
But who's not afraid to just be real.

— K.L.

On-Air Males

In their book, *Failing at Fairness*, Myra and David Sadker study boys from grade school through grad school. They found that boys, in our society, are taught to be strong and independent: they are told to act like a man.[A] As a result, boys often feel that they must always appear strong and never show vulnerability. They must hide and repress their feelings. They must never express their doubts, their hurts, their sadness, their disappointments, their confusion, their conflicts — lest others think them weak.[B] (Do we see big-time intimacy problems developing here?) Boys must be in control and always self-contained. They must solve problems by and within themselves. Dr. John Gray, in his book, *Men Are From Mars, Women Are From Venus*, echoed some of the same observations, as he talked of males needing to resolve their problems on their own (i.e., as they go into their so-called emotional "caves").[C]

In the broadcasting industry, the most difficult on-air talents to find are warm, open, and genuine male news anchors and program hosts. On the other hand, stiff, defense-laden, egotistical males — who are afraid to be real and to share themselves with the audience or their co-anchors and hosts — are a dime a dozen. If you remember the character of "Ted Baxter" from *The Mary Tyler Moore Show*, his unwitting disciples exist, and can be found, in one form or another, anchoring newscasts all over the United States.

For many on-air males, their impenetrable façade is in part the result of how they have been socialized to act. It is also attributable to how some repressed, upper-crust network male executives, years ago, wanted their anchors to appear: strong, homogenized, self-contained, desensitized (which can be mistaken for "objective") — father-figures of sorts, who, like many real fathers, are cold, authoritarian, and lacking in any real intimacy. Through the years, aspiring male broadcasters have imitated these network anchors' demeanors — to their detriment.

However, the good news for males is that, if you are intelligent, attractive, a good writer, enjoy and are effective at telling a story, have a good, strong voice and are warm and comfortable being and sharing who you are on air, you may well be able to write your own ticket in broadcasting. If you are a minority male with these qualities, triple that. (And call me!)

By-the-by, on the subject of minority male anchors, broadcasting has seen many African-American males ascend the ranks, but where are all of the qualified Latino and Asian-American male anchors?

Another male anchor issue: Many male anchors, as they develop, emulate Tom Brokaw, Peter Jennings, and/or Dan Rather, all of whom solo anchor. The problem: Messrs. Brokaw, Jennings, and Rather — all broadcasting superstars — run their own shows and do not have co-anchors, weathercasters, or sportscasters to interact with. They do not have to share the stage, breaking stories, interviews, ad-libs, etc., with anyone else on set. However, this is not the case for almost all male anchors of local news broadcasts or syndicated shows. Notwithstanding the fact that males in these instances do have other talent on the set with them, all too often, these anchors perceive their role to be that of a solo anchor in a co-anchor setting. This is inappropriate and chemistry-destructive behavior. Furthermore, when there's a breaking story, many male anchors feel compelled to take over, to the exclusion of their co-anchors; as Peter, Tom or Dan would do as solo anchors.

Here's the point. Great male anchors, while strong, also work hard to develop a warm and engaging chemistry between all of the set members of their newscasts or programs. They accomplish this by making everybody on the set appear to be an integral element of the product — thereby making the sum of everyone's contribution much bigger than any of the parts.

Remember, the overall watch-ability and the ultimate success of the newscast or program that you anchor will be the measure of your success.

News Tip: Male anchors and hosts who are both strong and real are hard to come by. The key is to take ownership of your material and to be comfortable enough in your own skin so that you can be yourself and real. If you are a male and an effective, attractive, and engaging communicator, and you have a thorough understanding of news/current events and history, numerous opportunities for growth await you in broadcast journalism.

The Right of Assignability Versus Controlling Your Destiny

Let me share four stories that discuss the pervasive conflict between a broadcasting employer's desire to assign the employee to any and all assignments of the employer's choosing, and the employee's need to be assigned to specific positions and to work for specific kinds of programs, that he or she perceives are enhancing.

1) Recently, I was negotiating a contract with a general manager, "Bill," whom I have known for as long as I've been in broadcasting. He is very successful and very bright. During the time that I've known him, we have done many deals together; however, the other day we were unable to reach an agreement, because we found ourselves at opposite ends of the philosophical spectrum regarding his conviction, that as long as his station pays an employee the contractually-agreed-upon compensation, his management has the unrestricted right to assign and to re-assign the employee to any anchor position that it chooses — regardless of whether or not the employee consents to it.

My negotiation with Bill, was in connection with my client, "Alan," who has been a Monday-Friday, 5 P.M. and 11 P.M. anchor at Bill's station — "Station Z" — for the past ten years. About a year ago, Station Z was sold, and along with new management came a new company policy of not contractually guaranteeing on which particular shows an individual will anchor.

The problem for Alan is that, in all of his prior Station Z contracts, it was clearly written that he would only anchor the Monday-Friday, 5 P.M. and 11 P.M. newscasts, or else he could terminate the agreement at any time. And, with new and unfamiliar management having just arrived at Station Z, Alan didn't want to sign a new contract that would allow that station to assign him, for example, to anchor the mornings and noon, or the noon and 5 P.M., without his okay. He felt that he had established a following and a stature in his market, having anchored the 5 P.M. and 11 P.M. newscasts for years, and he didn't want to allow Station Z's management to tarnish his career by demoting him.

What Alan wanted was to control his own destiny. He said to me: "If [new] management decides during the contract, to take me off of any newscasts [the 5 P.M. or 11 P.M. newscasts], that's their choice; but I don't want them to assign me to newscasts which I feel will be damaging to my career. I must have the right to refuse the reassignment. [If they take me off the 5 P.M. and/or 11 P.M. newscasts,] I want to be paid for up to six months, while I look for another position; and [then] have the right to terminate the agreement, when I find it."

The general manager, Bill, felt that as long as his station pays Alan the agreed-upon salary (as the main anchor), and didn't lower it (as a result of changing Alan's duties), Alan shouldn't care which newscasts he's anchoring. As Bill said, "I just don't get it; he's [Alan is] getting paid the same, even if he anchors morning and noon. What a deal!"

I then suggested that the general manager consider the following: "Bill, I've known you for about 15 years. I remember you as a news director in Baton Rouge. Through the years, you've paid your news director dues, and then your general manager dues. What if your company came to you and told you that they were going to demote you to news director of Station Z, but they'll still pay you your agreed-upon contractual salary. How would you feel about the demotion, and the perceived and real damage that the demotion could do to your career?"

Bill, thinking for a moment, responded, "If they paid me the same amount of money, maybe I wouldn't mind."

"Baloney, Bill! You know you'd mind, and I, your wife and your kids would mind for you. If you want to continue to grow in this business, you need to develop and to hone your skills as a general manager in a big market. The demotion would preclude you from doing that. And, you know as well as I do, that once your general manager's contract with Station Z expires, they'll cut your salary to be more in line with what news directors make. Right?"

"Look, Kenny," he said, "I need to do what's best for my television station; and if what's best for Station Z is putting Alan on different newscasts, then I need to have the right to do it."

"Bill, I know what you need, but my client also needs the right to refuse your reassignment, as well as the right to terminate the contract, when he's found a suitable new position."

2) "Marc" joins cable network X, as a feature reporter for a once-a-week program. When he joined network X, his verbal job description was that he would do one long-form piece each week on the entertainment industry. However, after three weeks, the program is cancelled, and the network news manager (who is very happy with Marc's work) reassigns him to do a daily report for one of the network's five-days-per-week programs.

Marc is very unhappy about his new assignment, as his reason for leaving local news was to get away from day-of-air reporting. Now he's doing it again. When Marc goes to his news manager and requests the right to get out of his contract, the manager refuses by saying, "We're still paying you, and you're still doing entertainment reporting. Sorry, but we have the right of assignability."

3) Rita, who is a successful reality-based program executive producer (and has an excellent track record producing syndicated shows), signs an agreement to develop and to executive produce a new talk/magazine show. Upon interviewing for the position, Rita was told that this show would be a cross between *60 Minutes* and *Oprah*. However, after three months of low ratings, the head of the company tells Rita that her show must

become more racy (e.g., more tabloid), in order to boost ratings.

Rita strongly resists the new direction of the show. She is soon told by upper management that she can leave the show (and terminate her contract) but, if she does, she will have to give up about ninety weeks of guaranteed salary. That manager said, "You (Rita) have an agreement with us, that says you're the executive producer of our program; but there's nothing in the agreement — nor has there ever been anything in any other executive producer's agreement with our company — that says that we can't change the tone of the show and assign the executive producer of that show to execute our vision. So, if you want to quit, it will be you who will be breaking the agreement. We'll let you leave, but you must leave now, and we'll stop paying you now! And we don't want you working for another syndicated program for, let's say, one year from today. It's your decision. Stay and executive produce our show, or leave and find another position — but not in syndication."

4) Russ is a hard-news, investigative reporter at a local station in a Top-20 market. He interviews for a reporter position with a syndicated magazine show. At the interview, the executive producer describes the program as an early evening *Dateline*, and says that it will be a news show, and not entertainment-oriented or tabloid.

Weeks later, because of sagging ratings, upper management tells the executive producer to make the show more sexy and more blood and guts. In essence: Air anything that will get the viewers to tune in.

Upon being assigned to do stories that he finds embarrassing, Russ asks to terminate his contract. The executive producer confides that he, too, is often embarrassed by the kinds of stories that his show is now doing. However, he also advises Russ that "management" will not let any of the reporters out of their contracts, as they (management) can assign them to do whatever kinds of pieces that they want. That's it!

The common element in all of these stories is that broadcasting employers believe — and they often provide in their contracts — that they have the right to assign you to any position that they choose, and they can require you to work on any program that they choose — regardless of the program's content and its approach.

Conversely, talent, producers, writers, etc., want the right to control their destinies. Or, put another way, they want the right to accept and to stay in positions that enhance them and their careers. They also want the right to refuse to be assigned to positions, or to programs, which will diminish or damage their careers and their self-esteem.

I believe that when a prospective employer and a prospective employee agree on what specific position an employee will assume, these individuals have, in fact, had a meeting of the minds as to that component of their agreement. If the employee is then assigned to a different position without his or her prior consent, there is no longer a meeting of the minds as to that material element of the employment agreement. Therefore, the employee should be able to terminate the agreement anytime thereafter.

News Tip:

For employers: Money buys everything — or at least (total) assignability.

For employees: Careers are precious; and money does *not* buy everything.

Those are the perspectives. There's the conflict.

They are broadcasting realities.

A Conversation Between A General Manager and A Representative Regarding A Station's Right of Assignability

GM: So let me try to understand
        The contract clause that you demand:
        That if your client's not anchoring the early and late[1]
        He wants the right to terminate.

        But you know, it must be *our* decision
        To decide what is his *best* position.

Rep: And *that's* okay, but I believe
        That if you reassign him he should leave.

GM: But I *can't* see why your client should care,
        As long as *the same* amount of money is there.
        As we won't take *one penny* away,
        Whether he anchors weekends, *or* weekdays.

Rep: I *cannot* agree with your *specious* claim
        That all positions are *the same.*
        Demoting him *may be great* for your station.
        But he's *not* going through *that humiliation.*

---

1. evening newscasts

GM: (Somewhat heatedly replies):
Kenny, we have *years* invested in your client,
Why are you being *so defiant?!*

(He takes a moment to pause, then, tongue-in-cheek, he continues:)

Besides, I don't see why you're making this fuss.
We're just doing what's good for *us*!!

Rep: (With the tension being somewhat cut, the rep replies
in a warmer tone:)

Look, I *know* no position's guaranteed,
And that there are times when you need
To make an anchor line-up change;
And, *of course*, I do not find *that* strange . . .
But, remember, you've *worked hard* to become the GM,
And at your station you are the *creme de la creme.*

So think for a moment, with *real* empathy;
How *ugly* being *demoted* to news director would be.
I believe if you're honest, there's no doubt; that
if you were *demoted you'd* want *out!*

GM: If I didn't take a financial hit,
I'd *take* the job. I *wouldn't* quit.

Rep: Well *that's* hard to believe, you must admit,
And with all due respect, you're full of it.

(They both laugh. Then the representative becomes serious,
once again.)

Rep: So if you think you must rearrange
my client's position; and you *make that change*;
Then my client's career I'll have to save;
Remember: He may be your anchor, but *isn't* your *slave.*

My client wants to *stay* anchoring your early and late,
So just give him a clause which unequivocally states
That if you reassign him, he can determine his fate.

GM: (Wanting to bring this conversation to a close:)

Well this has been truly *more* than fantastic;
Engaging you in these cerebral gymnastics.
But I'm *still* not sure that I can agree
That we'll give up our *flexibility*.

Rep: Because you're *such* an insightful man
I *know* that you'll find a way that you can.

GM: The right of assignment. I *can't* live without it.
But I'll call you tomorrow, after I think about it.

— K.L.

Learning to Live With Hitting Singles and Sacrifice Bunts

As we discussed, in the early days of television news, the goal was to serve the public by supplying necessary information. At that time, due to the state of news gathering equipment, it took a great deal longer to put stories together and to get them on the air. Additionally, the slower news-gathering process was coupled with the fact that before news became a profit center for stations there were fewer newscasts for which to report. This state of affairs meant that reporters could take a longer time to research and craft their stories — and in many instances, they were able to derive more satisfaction from their work, while viewers received valuable information. This certainly was the case when stations and networks did more documentaries and long-form news specials.

However, at least five things have changed since those times:

1) News has become a profit center.

2) Innovations in news-gathering equipment now allow reporters to gather and present news much more rapidly.

3) For the most part, stations have many more newscasts than they did years ago.

4) Reporters have to report for more newscasts than they did before. So they do more stories and/or have to re-package or regurgitate the same ones, sometimes many times each day.

5) The MTV, give-it-to-me-as-fast, as-sexy, and-as-easy-as-

possible-influence makes news divisions get in and out of stories quickly, so as not to lose the perceived attention-impaired viewer.

In most cases, local newscasters no longer have the opportunity to research, write, and report very many meaningful, valuable and satisfying pieces. I cannot begin to count the number of phone calls that I have received from clients who say that all their station cares about is finding a warm body to throw on the air, just to fill a time slot; and then sending that same person out, to do either another story, or to do a re-hash of the first vacuous or gratuitous one over again. Or, they bemoan that their stations "go live," just to "show live" — even if there's no real reason to do so. And even when someone does get a meaningful story, unless the station feels that the story will increase ratings, one either has too little time to research it, or too little air time, in which to do little more than just gloss over it.

I will never forget a conversation that took place with one of my clients years ago. She truly cared about the content of news and about the responsibility that she, as a reporter, believed that she had to the public. She fervently wanted to research, investigate, probe, and enlighten. She had read everything about the history of broadcasting and the lofty ideals of broadcasting's most revered journalists. Month after month, I could hear a waning of her enthusiasm and see a dimming of her radiant bright light. Then one day she called to say that she was profoundly sad — even depressed — because she wasn't making a positive difference — by doing meaningful, well-thought out stories. Instead of her news management saying, "Let's be great!", or even "Let's get it right!", it was more like (to quote the late Marvin Gaye), "Let's get it on!" — on for the noon, on for the four, on for the five and the six, and then repackage it for the eleven.

She finished by saying that she never has the resources, the time, or the encouragement to hit the home run. Instead, she was stuck — due to her station's tight news budget and a news philosophy that catered to the lowest common denominator — with having to live with hitting singles and sacrifice bunts — with the sacrifice involving her values, her ideals, and her self-esteem.

I thereafter explained that if we proactively and creatively choreographed things a bit differently, she could indeed hit some triples, home runs, and maybe even a grand slam or two. (This choreography will be discussed later in this book.)

However, it was painful to agree with my client that sacrifice bunts and singles are often the sum and substance of local news.

News Tip: Having little or no preparation time, research assistance, or air time, etc., to do stories that mean little and aren't enlightening or rewarding is very often a reality in local news. However, the existence and depth of the problem depends upon each local station's news philosophy. Feeling empty and that you're anything but a good journalist, after reporting on frivolous and gratuitous stories is often commonplace.

Murders, Dead Babies, and Fires

The other day, a client called to say that she estimated that she had covered more than 3,000 depressing, bad news stories, and that she couldn't take it anymore. She was ready for *Entertainment Tonight* and *Access Hollywood*. My client wanted to tell stories that were uplifting and fun. She was tired of bad and ugly news. She feared that she had become desensitized, and that she was becoming less human. She wanted to smile on air for a change.

I hear this complaint regularly. However, the problem is that, through the years, a number of news executives have, in essence, admitted that, "When I go to sleep at night, you can be sure that I don't pray for world peace." This is a broadcasting reality, because world peace and other good news often don't attract viewers on a sustained basis. Conversely, bad news and scandals — war, bloodshed, the bizarre, gossip, popular figures falling, etc. — do attract and keep viewers. Witness the proliferation and apparent success, over the years, of tabloid TV shows, magazines, and newspapers. Additionally, witness the ratings boosts that CNN experienced during Desert Storm and the O.J. Simpson (criminal) trial, as well as those enjoyed by MSNBC, CNN and Fox Cable News during their President Clinton/Monica Lewinsky coverage.

I remember asking a general manager years ago why good news and programs devoted to uplifting stories didn't get ratings.

He replied that he and his company had done some research, and that they had thereafter scrapped a "good news" program, because, for the most part, people believe that their lives are so screwed up and compromised, that they get a lift out of seeing other people's lives being equally as bad, or worse than their own. It's sort of the misery loves company theory. Therefore, people like to watch bad news, crime, and the bizarre.[1]

Whatever the rationale, the truth in many cases is if it's negative, if it bleeds or if it titillates, it leads, it's promoted, and it's teased.

Interestingly, news magazine shows such as *Hard Copy, Inside Edition,* and the late *A Current Affair,* etc., whose content was once known as hard-core tabloid, have tried to become less sensational. This is in reaction to strong advertiser disapproval, which has been expressed by the threat and the actual withdrawal of advertising dollars. In a very public illustration of this reality, *A Current Affair,* as a last-ditch effort to save itself from cancellation, advertised that, "We're taking the trash out!" However, this campaign, which featured a garbage truck being driven off a cliff, didn't save the show from cancellation. Similarly, *Hard Copy,* in the fall of 1998, announced that it will no longer be tabloid. On the other hand, it has frequently been observed that certain prime time news magazine shows have — in many instances — become more sensational. As a result, the famous clear line between news and tabloid programming is now blurred.[2]

---

1 I'll never forget being in a newsroom, known for focusing on tabloid news, the day its city's new baseball team played its very first game. About three hours before the first pitch was thrown, the news manager half-kiddingly confided, "This should be interesting as to how (well) we cover this story. We're not used to doing good news! I don't know if we can do it!"

2 In a controversial *Playboy* magazine interview, Geraldo Rivera says the following about the "line" between news and tabloid programming:

"Let me suggest that the difference between a program like *Dateline NBC,* for example, and one of the tabloid shows — say, *Hard Copy* or *Inside Edition* — is, in degree, not in substance. The network would have you believe that it does a far superior and more honorable job. That's a canard. The topics on *Dateline NBC* and those other network shows are exactly the same ones everyone else is doing. Diana is dead. JonBenet Ramsey. (*Playboy,* October 1998, 53.)

Additionally, this line keeps moving, depending upon which kinds of stories news and program managers believe will attract the largest viewership, but won't alienate advertisers.

It is important to make the point that bad, sad, depressing, or negative news, can, of course, be worthy of reporting, as it oftentimes informs, teaches and can give viewers an insight into, and understanding of, important and relevant events and slices of life. However, when bad and negative news that is entirely devoid of pertinence for the public is aired just for the sake of hooking viewers, this is a different story.

One way or another, a steady diet of negative news pervades many news operations, and it not only can be depressing for the viewers who watch it, but it can be equally — or even more — depressing for those who come in contact with it and report on it everyday.

This broadcasting reality is one of the main reasons why a number of broadcast journalists whom I know, want to leave local news and their tabloid reality-based shows.

News Tip: Covering murders, dead babies, fires, and other bad and depressing news, on a regular and prolonged basis, is a broadcasting reality, and can have a strong negative emotional effect upon reporters, anchors, producers, and other news operation staff members.

Plateauing

Employers hire on-air individuals with the idea that they will bring the talent in, get them up to speed and then recoup their investment in them for years thereafter. That's one reason why talent contracts in large markets are often three-to-five years long.

Talent, on the other hand, often accept positions because they seek new experiences in a larger market or in a different setting; because they have new skills to learn; and/or because they see a particular move as a means toward achieving some further goals.

The problem with this reality is that talent often learn what they want to learn, or experience what they want to experience, and then they want to quickly move on to the next position, job, market, or program. But what frequently stands in the way of talent leaving for a new and more challenging position are the two or three years left on their current contract.

I cannot begin to count the many calls that I have received from broadcasters who have expressed their unhappiness, boredom, and/or frustration because they are no longer learning and growing in their current positions. They feel as if they're plateauing.

There is an inherent conflict here: Talent feels that they've stopped growing, so they must go on to the next position or job. Employers don't believe that they exist as graduate schools for talent. On the contrary, they are there to take advantage — for a number of years — of the established skills and market familiarity that their on-air staff members develop over time.

Plateauing is a prevalent feeling and frustration for young broadcasters who want to keep growing, keep having new journalistic experiences, and keep getting better and higher-profile jobs. They want things to progress on *their* timetable. However, plateauing is also a problem for individuals who have, over the years, truly stopped growing and are bored to tears, because they have — thousands of times — been there and done that. For example, it has always been my gut feeling that there has been a high incidence of alcoholism (in between early- and late-evening newscasts) amongst established male anchors, because, for the most part, they now just show up at 5 or 6 P.M. and at 11 P.M. and read copy. They have nothing to do with the creative process, and have had few, if any, new and exciting challenges in years. They derive little or no satisfaction from their jobs, and have very little real interest in them. In essence, they've become brain-dead and desensitized by, year after year, having to read stories about murders, crime, and mayhem. But the paycheck and the hours that they actually work are great. So they won't — or can't — leave their jobs.

One solution to the conflict and feeling of plateauing may well be for young bucks and established veterans to initiate, create, and enterprise their own stories, specials, series, franchises, and other vehicles, as a way to keep growing, remain interested, and be and feel part of the process. Or else, plateauing and the frustration derived therefrom will remain a major problem.

News Tip: It is important to understand that broadcasting careers almost never rise with a straight ascension. Often, career advancement will ebb and flow. The key to not feeling as if your career is plateauing is to proactively and constructively initiate opportunites, and to find and create venues in which to grow and learn.

Lack of Feedback

"Life is difficult,"[A] is the opening sentence of M. Scott Peck's bestseller, *A Road Less Travelled*. The life of a local newscaster is not only difficult, it can be totally absorbing, especially during the first half of one's career. There are no set hours; often, no set days off. Before you can put down roots in a city, you're off to take a position in another market. It is often the case that broadcasters, until they can strike a balance between their professional and personal lives, and/or put some roots down and become truly involved in a community, throw themselves totally into and are thoroughly absorbed by their careers. While singular focus is arguably an effective way to maximize one's potential for success, there is also one great danger: one's self-esteem and self-image may well become defined solely by one's success in the workplace, and they can rise and fall dramatically with one's day-to-day triumphs and defeats there. Furthermore, the nature and quality — or lack thereof — of the feedback that a broadcaster receives at the job can also significantly affect her or his sense of self-worth.

In almost all cases, broadcasters do not receive any quality feedback regarding their work from their managers. And when they do receive feedback, it's often negative.

Some observations:

First and foremost, most news managers, producers, etc., are hired because executives believe that these individuals can create a commercial and profitable product, or improve it. These managers often are hired because they have good technical and/or creative news and/or programming skills. However, news directors and executive producers are almost never hired because of their abilities to effectively manage people. Therefore:

      1) Don't be surprised if your news manager isn't adept at, or focused upon, making you feel good about your work, your talents and your future.[1]

      2) With the ever-increasing pressure on news managers to initiate and respond to change, in order to effectively compete (and survive) in this new ultra-competitive news and reality-based programming environment, they don't have the time to give very much, if any, in-depth feedback to talent.

      3) News managers, like talent, are human beings. Human beings who, like all of us, may have been raised or influenced by individuals who did not give them unconditional or positive support while they were growing up; and they have learned from and are emulating their role models. There are also a number of news managers who embrace the philosophy that you should rule through insecurity, intimidation, and negative reinforcement. That way, talent won't become cocky, complacent and/or lazy anchor/reporter monsters — especially come contract time.

      4) Some managers may have bosses who don't know how to manage people either, and treat the news managers with no respect. The managers, in turn, displace their anger and bad feelings onto the talent.

      5) Some managers aren't comfortable articulating their thoughts and feelings about a talent's work, or they have a hard time dealing with difficult issues or conflicts, so they take the path of least resistance — they avoid them.

      Regardless of the reason(s), most broadcast journalists in the news and reality-based programming areas do not receive any tangible, constructive, or quality feed-

---

1 A later chapter, "Understanding News Management," may help explain why news managers may not feel great about their work or themselves, either.

back from their managers. This obviously is a problem if you want to effectively meet and/or exceed your management's' expectations, and if you want to improve and to grow.

News Tip: It is rare that you will voluntarily receive any regular, high quality feedback from your employer. Therefore, you must proactively seek out this information from your exceedingly busy news managers and producers. It is also important to cultivate worthy outside sources of feedback.

The Pay Disparity In Broadcast Journalism

Years ago, for many broadcast journalists, gathering and reporting news was a calling, and the fruits that were reaped, for the most part, were the satisfaction of researching, writing, crafting, and telling an informative and compelling story that was of benefit to the viewer. Today, high quality news reporting still may be a calling and a passion for many broadcast journalists, but, as we know, it can also be a very lucrative profession.

It is hard for some to understand and to reconcile how networks and syndicated programs can pay some anchors and hosts millions and millions of dollars a year in salaries, when others are told that they must accept 3 percent and 5 percent raises on their comparatively meager salary. For example, an on-air reporter recently complained to me: "How can my (NBC) network station say that it can't pay me more than a 4 percent raise on my $80,000 salary, when the same company just gave Katie Couric a new contract at $7 million a year? I think she got more than a four million dollar raise! My station's making a fortune, even if they lose *Seinfeld* and the NFL. I deserve more. I work just as hard as the anchors. They're [station management is] not being fair."

As one of the wisest individuals whom I've ever met has (in essence) said to me: "[Great] talent is finite. There are very few Michael Jordans who can sell tickets and bring people into the tent. These are the Matt Lauers, the Oprah Winfreys, the Katie Courics."[A]

As this individual and I have discussed, whether it is through insightful career choreography™, serendipity, or a combination of both, these individuals and other megastars of broadcasting have been fortunate to find a positive environment in which to work and an enhancing venue on which to appear, which encourages what makes them special and compelling to shine through and to attract viewers.

Additionally, as we will discuss later, effective marketing and good timing often play material roles in how much one earns. For example, Katie Couric's new contract is, in great part, attributable to two realities. One is that she has been and continues to be perceived by her management as essential to the rise and extraordinary success of the *Today* show. The second is that she could well have received between $8 million and $10 million a year from other employers who were waiting to hire her for hosting positions on prime time network or daytime syndicated programs.

Never before has there been such disparity as to what different people earn per year in broadcasting. This disparity can exist between individuals who appear on national versus local newscasts and shows, or between those working in the same shop. The key factor is which individual has the acknowledged talent, the quantifiable ability to attract viewers, good timing, and the perceived leverage to secure other (more) lucrative offers. That person will, in most instances, earn the top dollar.

Number Three and Other Low-Rated Stations

As heretofore observed, low-rated stations tend to be reactive. If something positive doesn't happen fairly quickly after a change, or a set of changes is made, different changes are soon initiated. In essence, the philosophy of this type of station is: "We'll keep trying and experimenting, as we have nothing to lose (by changing) until we get it right."

The problem is that managers at low-rated stations often truly believe that they have little to lose by consistently making on-air changes. (They hope that if they keep throwing different things against the wall, something — anything! — will stick.) However, newscasters who base their lives and careers upon keeping the positions that they have accepted at these stations, have a great deal to lose when management makes changes that involve them. Here are two examples.

Story One: A #3-rated station was looking for two female weeknight anchors. (During the past few years, the station had gone through four weeknight female anchors.) This station was looking for one female to anchor three evening newscasts, including the main early- and late-evening newscasts, and another female to anchor one early evening newscast and report for the 11 P.M. newscast.

Initially, the station found and hired a female to anchor the three newscasts. (This choice was made after having three separate meetings with this prospective hire, and after cutting

91

two separate audition tapes with her.) Upon the closing of the deal, the female anchor and her husband moved across the country for this wonderful opportunity. Her hiring and a description of the position for which she was hired were announced at the station and in the press. However, before this female hit the air, the station found another female anchor that the station quickly decided was better for the main anchor position than the first female. So, before the already-announced main female anchor had a chance to anchor her first newscast, her position was changed and diminished. Embarrassed and let down, she wound up anchoring only one newscast. The replacement anchored three.

Then, within months, the demoted and devalued female anchor was told that she didn't fit into the station's long-term future at all. Therefore, her services were no longer needed and she could leave. That day. The station would, "of course," pay out the remaining fifteen months of her contract.

When the devastated anchor asked why the station hadn't given her any warning of her impending demise, and why she hadn't been given one bit of feedback to help her to improve or to change her on-air work so as to better meet the station's expectations, the reply allegedly was, "It's nothing we can put our finger on. You've done everything that we've asked. We just feel that you're not part of our future, so we should cut bait here."

When station management was asked how it could bring someone across the country, immediately demote her, and then let her go before one year of the contract had passed — especially since they had seen numerous tapes of her anchoring and had her do two auditions tapes prior to hiring her — the management allegedly said, "It's business. Sometimes it (TV news) is a lousy business."

Story Two: A sportscaster who has a "shtick" was sought-out by a #3 station, because management at the station perceived a need to find someone who would stand out, in order to get new viewers. Station management felt that a vanilla (non-controversial) sportscaster wouldn't get a sufficient amount of market sampling to increase ratings.

After three months, the station received a number of

calls and letters saying enough negative things about the new sportscaster that they pulled him off the air. They said that even though the number of calls and letters wasn't that great, they couldn't afford to lose any (of the small number of) viewers that they already had. So they had no choice but to let him go.

When I called that #3 station to say that the #1 station in their market had hired an equally controversial sportscaster years ago, and that that station had also received calls and letters after they hired their guy, the response that the #3 station gave me was: "Well, that station's #1, they can afford to give someone time to grow in the market. We can't. We need ratings now!"

How many stories do I have of #3, and low-rated stations, quickly bailing out on talent and their lofty plans for them? As the late Jimmy Durante used to say: "I got a million of 'em!"

It's a broadcasting reality . . . and a problem.

News Tip: Be careful when accepting a position at a #3 and other low-rated stations. There *is* a reason why these stations always have openings. It's called a desperate need and desire to raise ratings.

The Pressure to Secure "The Get"

Versus The Values Of Truth, Accuracy, Balance, and Compassion In Reporting

We've already discussed the intense pressures put upon news divisions and reality-based programs to increase ratings and to maximize profits, as well as the frequent focus they place on achieving their ends, while minimizing or altogether ignoring the importance of the means by which their ends are achieved. The result of these pressures and this focus may well be that many broadcast journalists feel inordinate pressure to come up with a breaking story, to uncover a new angle on an already existing one, to get the material that no one else has either found or aired, or to get the interview that no one else could secure — at the risk of compromising or abandoning their accuracy, their balance, and their humaneness.

"The *get* is newsroom parlance for securing the big interview or news scoop."[A] The get can increase ratings and revenues for an employer, bring prestige to a news gathering organization, and bring the reporter(s) involved much kudos and various coveted awards, greater respect, a more prestigious position with his or her employer, higher profile assignments, and a more lucrative contract.

Connie Chung writes, "A 'get' brings viewers into the tent." As *Dateline NBC's* executive producer, Neal Shapiro, puts it, "You can't live on big 'gets' alone, but they are the bright neon sign that brings them [viewers] in."[A]

These are just some of the reasons why the get makes us wet.

The problem with this reality is that with today's constant pressure to one-up and beat the competition,[1] it becomes easy for the get to take precedence over — or at least make reporters and news gathering organizations forget for the moment — the principled and thorough means by which they must research a story, gather their facts, source their material, check them, and disclose the possible motives and biases of their sources. Additionally, because there's such enormous competition today just to get a sought-after interview or source of information, these interviewees and sources — by virtue of their positions — wield a tremendous amount of power. As a result, reporters may not be as discerning, circumspect, and/or objective as they might otherwise be with their questioning and/or reporting. Why? Because these reporters want to curry the favor of these individuals — or at least not anger them — for fear that they might lose future gets.

Recently, a highly controversial article entitled, "Pressgate," appeared in the premiere issue of *Brill's Content* magazine. In that article, Steven Brill alleged that independent counsel Kenneth Starr illegally leaked details of grand jury testimony to special "lapdog-like" reporters, who then reported Starr's information the way he wanted them to.[B] Brill claims that Starr gave certain reporters scoops, and these reporters in turn — and in return — wrote these stories with little or no adequate and/or additional researching or sourcing of the material.[C] Why?

---

1 Marvin Kalb writes in his *Prospective on Journalism,* "Competition, which was always intense in the news business, has now become a brutal, relentless pressure." One big reason for this pressure, is the 24-hour appetite for news that must be constantly fed. Kalb continues, "In the late 1970s, most Americans (more than 80%) watched the evening newscasts; now they have the same three, plus three cable news networks, ten weekly news magazine programs, three cable business news networks, two sports news networks, and three news websites furnished with video."

Because these reporters wanted the get and they implicitly understood the game: I — Kenneth Starr — get my information out to the public in a controlled and choreographed manner — and you — the reporter — keep getting scoops.

Brill writes:

> The abuses that were Watergate spawned great reporting. The Lewinsky story has reversed the process. Here, an author in quest of material teamed up with a prosecutor in quest of a crime, and most of the press became a cheering section for the combination that followed. As such, the Lewinsky saga raises the question of whether the press has abandoned its Watergate glory of being a [thorough, accurate and balanced] check on official abuse of power. For in this story the press seems to have become an *enabler* of Starr's abuse of power.
>
> An examination of the Lewinsky story's origins and a day-by-day review of the first three weeks of the media coverage that followed, suggest that as it has careened from one badly sourced scoop to another in an ever desperate need to fill its multimedia, 24-hour appetite, the press has abandoned its treasured role as a skeptical "fourth estate."[D]

In reference to Brill's article, Starr wrote a strong and detailed 19-page rebuttal in which he answers Brill's allegations of illegally leaking material.[E]

Regardless of whether Brill or Starr is correct, or whether the truth lies somewhere in the middle, Brill cites numerous instances in which top national television and print journalists and their employers reported gets to their viewers and readers, respectively, which, he alleges, were not accurate or balanced nor based upon eyewitness accounts or first hand knowledge.[F]

Although Brill, in his article, discusses many offenders, here's one illustrative excerpt of a major news gathering organization reporting a get, followed by two perspectives of that report:

> At 4:42 eastern time, Tom Brokaw and Claire Shipman of NBC break into pre-Super Bowl programming with the following bulletin:
>
> Brokaw: "There's an unconfirmed report that, at some point, someone caught the president and Ms. Lewinsky in an

intimate moment. What do you know about that?"

Shipman: "Well, sources in Ken Starr's office tell us that they are investigating that possibility but that they haven't confirmed it."

The perspectives:

"Our anchor and White House reporter come on the air and say, here's something that we don't know is true but we just thought we'd tell you anyway just for the hell of it, so we can say we reported it just in case it turns out to be true," a disgusted NBC reporter says later. "That's outrageous."

Asked three months later why he aired that kind of "bulletin," Brokaw says, "That's a good question. *I guess it was because of ABC's report.*[2] Our only rationale could be that it's out there, so let's talk about it . . . But in retrospect we shouldn't have done it."[G]

The reason I quote Brokaw is because he explains that NBC went with the bulletin — the get — as a reaction to ABC's report. NBC — normally an excellent news gathering organization — acted precipitously and incorrectly in this instance. Why? The competition made them do it.

Additionally, Brill alleges that many print journalists — as well as other experts in their fields — who might normally be more circumspect in what they report in print — seem to be much less cautious and less principled when answering questions on TV — especially on "news" talk shows (i.e., those aired on NBC, ABC, CBS, MSNBC, CNN, etc.).[3] Why? Maybe because

---

2 The "report" to which Mr. Brokaw refers, allegedly, is that of an ABC network reporter. Brill alleges that the report appeared to be erroneous; however, Brill writes that ABC used it as a predicate for other reporting and interviewing and later embellished it.[140]

3 For example, in Brill's article, *Newsweek* writer-turned-NBC News-pundit for NBC's Monica Lewinsky coverage, Howard Fineman, admits:
"Television is definitely more loosey-goosey than print . . . And I have loosened up myself, sometimes to my detriment . . . and said things that were unfair or worse. It's like you're doing your first draft with no layers of editors and no rewrites and it just goes out to millions of people."[133]

these pundits and experts get great career-enhancing exposure on TV and some may even be rewarded with a lucrative full-time position on these programs if they can supply gets and spicy and/or provocative speculation to the viewers.[4] As Brill writes, "Talk TV is the speculation game."[H] However, he warns that, "A rumor or poorly sourced or unconfirmed leak aired or printed in one national medium ricochets all over until it becomes part of the national consciousness. In short, once it's out there, it's out there."[I] With today's hunger for gets of any kind, often news gathering organizations will pick up the rumors or poorly sourced material of others and run with it.

What are the financial rewards for news gathering organizations and their reporters being ahead of the curve on sexy stories such as Monica Lewinsky?

Brill says,

> MSNBC officials would later make no bones of the fact ... that with (Keith) Olbermann's 8:00 p.m. show (*White House In Crisis*) and, indeed, with the entirety of their talk-news daytime programming, they were hell-bent on using the intern scandal to do for their entire network what the Iranian hostage crisis had done for a half-hour ABC program called *Nightline* in 1979.
>
> Indeed, MSNBC's use of the alleged intern scandal was endemic to how all 24-hour cable news networks and all talk radio had come to use such topics in the late 1990s. For these talk machines, the subject matter isn't simply a question of bumping circulation a bit for a day or a week, the way it is for traditional newspapers or magazines, or of boosting ratings for a part of a half-hour show or an hour magazine program the way it is for network television. Rather it's a matter of igniting a rocket under the entire revenue structure of the enterprise.

---

4 This was the case for Fineman. Brill writes:
Within a week, Fineman would become a regular on-air nighttime and weekend analyst for NBC, MSNBC and CNBC for an annual fee that he says is "in the ball-park" of $65,000. That's about 40% of his day-job *Newsweek* salary, for what he estimates to be 5% to 10% of the time he works for the magazine. [133,134]

Thus, while the three broadcast networks' evening news ratings increased a total of about six percent in the week beginning on this day (January 21), MSNBC's average rating for its entire 24-hour day — a day when almost all of its coverage was devoted to the intern scandal — increased by 131 percent. Which meant that its revenue from advertising (which is the only revenue that varies from week to week in cable television) would also jump 131 percent if it could sustain that increase.[J]

Many articles have recently been written discussing CNN's embarrassing retraction of Peter Arnett's report, "Operation Tailwind." This piece alleged that during the war in Vietnam in 1970, the U.S. had used nerve gas in Laos as part of a mission to kill American defectors there.

When Floyd Abrams, a First Amendment attorney, was asked by CNN to investigate the story, he found that the reporter's allegations were unsupported and that the story should not have aired. When Abrams appeared on *The Charlie Rose Show*, he said,

> " . . . I concluded that there was insufficient material for the broadcast to have gone on the air, insufficient basis to sustain the broadcast today, that the broadcast wasn't fair, that the broadcast had not taken into account sufficiently the views of the people who disagreed with the thesis of the producers . . .
>
> That, [with] everything taken together, my conclusion is that the broadcast was simply insupportable . . ."[K]

Were the direct or perceived pressures that the reporters and producers of this story felt to get CNN's new magazine show, *NewsStand* off to a rousing start the cause of this alleged lack of journalistic competence? Or, was it just the pressure to secure and to air a major get? Who knows? What's clear is that the reputation and image of one of the world's most well-respected and topnotch news gathering organizations, CNN, has suffered because of someone's or some individuals' alleged poor judgment.

Recently, it was reported that writers for both the *New*

Republic and *The Boston Globe* made up information and reported it as truth; the *Cincinnati Inquirer* ran a front-page apology to Chiquita Brands International, Inc., saying that its series of stories questioning the company's business practices were untrue and based on stolen voice mail;[L] and a jury found *Dateline NBC* guilty of "negligence, misrepresentation and emotional distress," ordering NBC to pay $525,000 in damages to a trucking company.[M]

I could end this section by writing that "The hits to broadcast journalism's credibility, just keep on comin'! It's a broadcasting reality and a big problem." And, after reading such compelling articles as "Pressgate" by Brill, and those of other informed individuals who identify and deplore what they perceive as journalism's current "reign of error," I could feel comfortable with writing that these are, in fact, deep-seated problems that exist regarding many reporters' non-adherence to sound principles of journalism.

However, in the interest of balanced reporting, I must ask this question: Are the aforementioned breaches of journalistic ethics pervasive, or are they only isolated instances?

There are individuals who argue that instances of the intentional disregard or omission of sound journalistic principles are, in the grand scheme, isolated. For example, one very wise, well-respected, and experienced individual shared his opinion that the number of instances in which excellent news gathering organizations such as NBC and CNN are in the wrong is *miniscule* when compared with the number of correct reports that they file each year. This, he says, is analogous to the airline industry and the issue of plane crashes. Although crashes do occur, their number is miniscule when compared with the number of successful plane trips.

I would also add that no news gathering institution can, is, or will ever be perfect when it is comprised of human beings — because human beings aren't perfect. And when taken in that context, organizations such as NBC, CNN, ABC, CBS, etc., have heretofore established relatively great track records for accuracy.

Taking this latter perspective into account, I end this section this way: Although I cannot quantify how prevalent intentional or unintentional breaches of sound journalistic ethics are, there is no question that they are a significant broadcasting reality and a problem to be dealt with.

The Value of Being Humane

Two other pressing concerns are: Does the value of being humane — that is, the quality of having compassion and consideration for others — play any role in the equation as to what the tone of a story or an interview should be, and whether or not a news gathering organization should air a particular story? And, if compassion does count, has the competition to air the get made us lose or forget about the role of compassion in broadcast journalism?

On this subject, the story of *USA Today* allegedly pushing Arthur Ashe to confirm or deny that he was HIV positive comes to mind.[N] In his book, *Days of Grace*, Ashe, recounts how in 1992 his boyhood friend, Doug Smith, who became a tennis writer for *USA Today*, came to Ashe's house and asked,

> "We have heard that you are HIV positive, Arthur. That you have AIDS."
> Mr. Ashe responded, "Can you prove it?"
> "No, that's the point," Mr. Smith said. "My editor wants to know if it's true. They sent me to find out. Is it true?"
> Mr. Ashe soon replied, "I want to talk to your editor, Doug."

Ashe then recounted:

> I could see that Doug was relieved at that point, happy to turn the matter over to his boss. From my office, as we sat there at home, I telephoned Gene Policinski, managing editor of sports for *USA Today*. Policinski couldn't talk right then, and Doug and I waited for him to return my call. He did so promptly enough, around 4:30. We talked for 20-30 minutes. He was fairly direct.
> "Are you HIV positive, or do you have AIDS?"
> "Could be," I replied.
> I could not lie to him. Sometimes, indirectly, I had to lie about AIDS. Now and then, I had to lie about it directly.

I also told Policinski flatly that I had no intention, at that time, of confirming or denying the story. I tried to argue with him, to make him see my position.

"Look," I said with some force, "the public has no right to know in this case."

As I saw this situation, the public's right to know really meant the newspaper's right to print. Of course, there would be people interested in, even titillated by, the news that I had AIDS; the question was, did they have a right to know? I absolutely did not think so. The law was on the side of the newspaper, but ethically its demand was wrong, as well as unnecessary.

"I am not a public figure anymore," I argued. I don't play professional tennis anymore. I officially announced my retirement in 1980. I am not running for office, so my health is no one's legitimate concern except my own. I haven't committed any crimes, so I am not fair game. And I haven't been caught in any scandals. Why do you think differently?"

"You are a public figure, " Policinski insisted. "And anytime a public figure is ill, it's news. If he has a heart attack, as you did in 1979, it's news. We have no special zone of treatment for AIDS. It's a disease, like heart disease. It is news."

Match point had come, and I had lost it . . .

I reminded him (Policinski) that I had not confirmed the story, as far as I was concerned.

Policinski was polite but firm. No, it was not his role as managing editor of a newspaper to help me plan a news conference, and he could not in good conscience withhold a story if he considered it newsworthy and if he had proof of its accuracy. However, *USA Today* had certain standards and practices which it would stick by in this story as in any other. In general, it did not print stories with elaborately vague sources — information attributed to "informed sources" and the like. And the newspaper did not approve of backing crab-like into a story, by reporting a rumor and then declaring that the person or person's had denied it. Policinski and I ended the conversation without coming to any agreement, except that I stood by my refusal to confirm the story, and he stood by his determination to continue to investigate it, as well as his right to publish it if he could find confirmation. I fully expected to see the story in next morning's edition.

* * * * * * * * *

I did not want to be hard on *USA Today,* but I had to talk about what had caused me to break my silence. The newspaper had put me in the unenviable position of having to lie if I wanted to protect our (my family's) privacy. No one should have to make that choice. I am sorry that I have to make that revelation now.

* * * * * * * * *

Was I justified in claiming that I had a right to privacy? Or was *USA Today* justified in asserting it's privilege? For the record, the newspaper had acted with some deliberation. The editors had decided at 11:00 on Tuesday evening, the day before my announcement, not to carry the story. The decision had involved not simply Policinski, but also Peter Pritchard, the editor of the paper. Once I had made my decision (to have a press conference) the newspaper enjoyed only a minor scoop of sorts. At 1:00, before my conference, it sent the story to the newspaper's international edition, which mainly reaches Europe and Asia. The story was also sent to the Gannett News Service, which supplies a chain of eight newspapers, including USA Today, as well as Cable News Network (CNN). "Tennis great Arthur Ashe has AIDS," the item began, "he will announce Wednesday afternoon at a New York press conference."

No one could doubt, however, who had forced my hand. To my surprise, and my satisfaction, this aspect of my announcement generated great controversy. More than 700 letters reached *USA Today* on the issue of my right of privacy, and about 95% vehemently opposed the newspaper's position. [For example] A man in Topeka, Kansas [wrote]: "Linking AIDS with a public figure is titillating but rarely newsworthy. There is no compelling reason in this case to reveal Ashe has AIDS."⁰

Tennis champion Chris Evert, regarding the press' course of action in "outing" Ashe, said "It's like the press has given up a *touch of humanity* (emphasis added)."ᴾ

In the above instance, *USA Today* more than adhered to

sound journalistic principles and appeared to have the law on its side. The question is: Did the value of being humane — being compassionate — regarding Ashe's desire for privacy outweigh printing the get?

Let's push the envelope a little further. I am aware of at least two totally separate instances in which individuals have reported stories about two newscasters' personal lives that had the potential to seriously damage the careers of these two individuals. In both of these instances, the reporters had no first-hand knowledge of the information on which they reported.

When questioned as to whom and what they based their reports on, and after they were advised about the serious ramifications that their reports could have for these newscasters personally and professionally, both reporters admitted that they had heard the personal gossip from people with whom they in fact had little or no familiarity. The reporters then apologized.

What is the public's right or need to know potentially harmful personal gossip about someone that in fact may well not be true, regardless whether or not the person in issue is a public figure? Is this what the framers of the Constitution sought to protect in the First Amendment?

Is it humane to go with a get that has not been solidly researched or sourced, because you can protect yourself by saying "sources say" or "rumors have it," when the damage to someone professionally and personally can be devastating?

Is it humane to report harmful personal gossip about a public figure that *is* solidly researched and sourced?

Finally, if the answer to both or either of these questions is that it is not humane, should this answer matter when you decide whether or not to air the get?

One more scenario. This is a story that was told to me about a year ago.

It was a slow news day. Then, suddenly, word of the Oklahoma City bombing cut through newsrooms like a sharp knife through butter. One newsroom member allegedly blurted out, "Oh God — but, thank God!"

In essence, what that reporter meant was, "Oh God, too

bad for the many people who lost their lives and loved ones, and
for those who will be permanently injured. BUT, thank God, we
have a HUGE story. A tragedy! Just the kind of story that makes
for great news and monster ratings. 'Breaking' national stories
are defining moments for individuals and news departments.
Stars will be born. Maybe of one of those stars will be me!"

That reporter was sent to Oklahoma later that day by her
station. Upon her arrival there, she camped out for hours at the
home of a family that had lost a loved one in the bombing. She
stayed there until she could ambush her prey. Eventually, she was
able to interview the grief-stricken mother of one of the men who
had died. Throughout the interview, she allegedly asked question
after question, trying to dredge up every bit of pain, hurt and
heartache from the victim's mother. Upon her return to the
newsroom, the reporter allegedly was thrilled to report to her
news management and colleagues that, "I not only got the interview . . . but I made her [the victim's mother] cry! Wait 'til you
see it [the videotape of the interview]. It's great!"

Unfortunately, this type of story isn't a new one for me.
Much too often, I have seen tapes or read articles in which broadcast and print reporters — in their efforts to create compelling
or titillating television or copy — have trampled upon individuals' moral rights of privacy, their emotional well-being, and sound
journalistic principles. Witness the paparazzi's alleged triggering
of the high speed chase and the car accident that ended in the
death of Princess Diana. These acts were all in search of the get,
the rating point, increased readership, the Emmy, the recognition, the piece of videotape or the story that will earn the
reporter his or her next (better) position, etc. All of these are
worthwhile ends. The problem lies in the insensitive and/or
inhumane means of their attainment.

Jerry Maguire — played by Tom Cruise — said, as he was
unceremoniously fired and kicked out of his athletic representation firm, "There's such a thing as manners . . . a way of treating
people."[2] In many ways, this chapter is all about manners — the
manner in which we conduct our professional lives, the manner
in which we respect the subject of our stories and our interviews,
and the manner in which we respect the viewers.

It is arguable that if reporters do not respect the values of truth, accuracy, balance, and compassion in their reporting and their interviewing, they will severely damage the credibility of one of our most important and necessary institutions, broadcast journalism. This would indeed be devastating to all of us.

News Tip: In today's highly competitive news environment, there exists intense pressure to secure and to air the get . . . and to be the first to do it. This pressure can conflict with or overshadow the values of truth, accuracy, balance, and compassion in reporting. This is a broadcasting reality.

III. Solutions To Real-Life Broadcasting Issues, Conflicts, and Problems:

"Career Choreography"™

Being Wise

What helps cut problems down to size?
And lets you see through a disguise?
What dictates which response applies?
It's the quality of being wise.

Being clever and being smart
Don't make you wise, but they're a start.
It's not just thinking with your heart.
Wisdom requires a higher art.

It values where you want to go and where you've been,
Delayed gratification, and discipline.
It values a conscience and thinking clear,
And *constructively* dealing with your fears.

It demands that you be a master sleuth,
In order to uncover the unvarnished truth.
It requires of you the difficult mission
Of reaching a *thoroughly informed decision*
Not to live for the moment, or decide in haste,
But to decide with vision; be *higher-value based.*

Being wise knows that if you are to flourish
Your spirit and heart you'll have to nourish.
And if at the workplace you get ahead,
It won't mean much if your soul is dead.

As you look back and see time fly,
And you feel empty and wonder why,
Seeing the erosion and the compromise,
And all the times when you weren't wise.

But the wise know that it's a brand new day,
When *you're ready* to do and say that
"Instead of settling . . . I'm going to reach for the skies,
By seeing the Big Picture . . . and being wise."

— K.L.

The Sprint Versus The Marathon

It's Not How Fast You Initially Go,
But How Much In The Long Run You Ultimately Grow

— K.L.

The Marathon

Careers should be viewed as marathons, not as sprints. That is, solid foundations should be laid and enhancing decisions should be made with the big picture and the long run of one's career in mind. And, although there are exceptions and caveats to this philosophy that I will discuss, I believe that true skills are developed, real success is measured, and wisdom is attained — over time.

The Big Picture

A few years ago, I played in the finals of the Men's National Open Paddle Tennis Doubles Championships against the number one team in the country. The score was knotted at one set each. The final set was tied at eight games each, and we were in the midst of playing a tie-breaker. During the "breaker," one of our opponents, who was the best over-all paddle tennis player in the country, mixed up his shots and his strategy a bit more. (He had the confidence, flexibility, and ability to appropriately change his strategy at the right time.) This caused us to not be as effective as we might have been otherwise. They won the tie-breaker, 7-5, and the title.

I had played as well as I could have hoped; I just needed to play some points more creatively. So, at 38 years old, after a couple of National Open Men's wins and a few second-place finishes under my belt, I decided that I needed to improve my game. I would study the national champions and see what I could learn about them and myself.

During the next tournament, I sat up in the stands and watched. It was fascinating. I saw things in the stands that I had never seen down on the court when I was playing against them. From above, I saw how one of my opponents planted himself so close to the net that, by lobbing the ball over his head, we could get his partner out of position enough, so that, as a team, they might become more vulnerable. I gleaned all sorts of new possibilities and alternatives from my perspective in the stands.

At the end of a day of viewing, a thought about some broadcasters whom I know came to mind. I realized that some of the most talented communicators, with the biggest and brightest futures, were getting much too caught up with minor day-to-day job hassles. These problems were bringing them down emotionally. I realized that somehow they weren't seeing the big picture. In the big picture, these skirmishes wouldn't have the impact of the smallest zit on an elephant's back. I often thought to myself, "God, these people have everything going for them. They just need to see the big picture of their careers, the way that I do. They would enjoy the process so much more. They could also be more selective in the battles that they did choose to fight." I realized that, because I wasn't fighting on the ground — day-to-day — as they were, but was instead viewing their careers more objectively from the stands, I had a different, fuller, broader and in many respects, better perspective than they had.

The lesson was: Far too often, while fighting our day-to-day battles on the ground, we never look beyond ourselves, or the immediate moment and/or situation at hand. I have seen and been involved in so many instances in which better perspectives and new spins and solutions could be discerned and developed, if the individuals involved would have just taken the time to look at and examine the big picture — that is, to step away from the heat and angst of the moment, and calmly, creatively, and objectively study the situation that they're immediately involved in and/or the decision that they're about to make, in the context of the long-term picture of their career.

The Marathon Versus The Sprint

It is crucial for broadcasters to look at their major decisions in the context of the big picture of their careers, and to keep the perspective of the marathon versus the sprint in mind.

For example, a client who aspired to one day be a Katie Couric, was offered a five-year contract to anchor a national entertainment show, within two years of beginning her news career. Upon receiving the offer, she was (understandably) ecstatic. When she asked my opinion, I told her that because she aspired to become a Katie Couric — that is, to successfully host a live morning news program — I felt that, although the entertainment position would move her to a national venue quite early in her career, in the long run, that job would ultimately retard her great potential to secure the most coveted news positions — the ones to which she, in her heart-of-hearts, aspired.

I explained that what anchors often do on the entertainment program that she was offered is read copy, over and over again, until it's perfect. Rarely is there live reporting, live interviewing, or going live with breaking news. These are just some of the skills that someone who wants to be a Katie Couric has to master. I believed that signing a five-year entertainment show contract so early in her career would be ill-conceived, as she would not develop the varied live skills that are prerequisites for the most coveted national news positions. As a result, in the big picture of her career, taking the entertainment position might well have been sprint-heaven for my client, but it also would have been marathon-suicide.

Another story. Years ago, a 23-year-old client of mine, who was earning about $18,000 per year as a weekend anchor in a small market, was offered a position as a general assignment reporter at a network-owned station in Philadelphia. The station offered her a five-year contract, with a first year's salary of approximately $95,000, and $5,000-to-$10,000 raises each year. My client, in sprint-ecstasy, said, "I'm so excited, where do I sign?" To her surprise and disappointment, I said, "You don't." I continued, "You told me that your goals are to anchor and to report in San Francisco, or to be a main anchor in Seattle. If you take the reporting job, I have been told that you can expect to be a fill-in anchor two-to-three times a year. You will never grow to be a top anchor with so little regular on-air anchor experience. Five years from now, when you want to go to Seattle or San Francisco as an anchor, you won't be ready. My best advice is to forego the reporting offer, and let's get an anchoring *and* reporting position at a good station in a market the size of Denver, Phoenix, Sacramento, or San Diego. Although, in all likelihood, you won't make $95,000 as a weekend or noon anchor in any of these markets, ultimately, the skills and the money will come."

With some regrets, my client agreed with my perspective. One month later, she became a weekend anchor in Phoenix. Two years later, she became the weekend anchor at a station in San Francisco, with a starting salary of more than $160,000.

In hindsight, it's easy to see that we made the correct big picture decision by turning down the Philadelphia reporting offer. My client is now an excellent anchor *and* an excellent reporter, having worked on and significantly improved both of those skills in Phoenix. As a result, she now has the tools, and has put herself in the best position, to have a long and successful marathon run in the market of her choice.

One last story: A client, with a world of potential, was in a small market and was offered a job to anchor "headlines" for a national cable network. I strongly suggested that he decline the offer, as people who anchor headlines at the network generally don't do any day-to-day (or any other form of) reporting. You go in, read, and leave.

Once again, if my client was going to win the career marathon, he needed to have a strong foundation in *both* anchoring and reporting. It was much too early in his career to choose one skill to the exclusion of the other. He's now a weeknight anchor and reporter in a top market, and the networks have been calling him.

Big picture — marathon — thinking can make all the difference in the world as to whether you fulfill your most cherished broadcasting goals — or whether you never do.

News Tip: It is of the utmost importance to examine how each of your career decisions will enhance or diminish your chances of securing the positions that you will most covet and want to secure in the long run.

Crunch Time

The other day, a news manager of a television station called me. He said that he would be giving a client of mine, Terry, a plum assignment that afternoon, which would showcase Terry's broadcasting strengths. This manager told me that Terry was one of three people who were being considered for a coveted national position, and that if my client was on his game and really showed his stuff, he, in all likelihood, would get the position. The manager finished our conversation by saying, "Kenny, I can't be any clearer than this: If Terry gets it right, his career is changed for the better from here on out. It's up to him. Starting this afternoon, it's crunch time!"

The last few minutes of a close football or basketball game are sometimes referred to as crunch time — a critical point during a sports contest, when the outcome of the game can go either way. Crunch times are those defining moments when individuals are faced with significant choices. They are our opportunities to either make wise decisions and enhance ourselves (and others), or to make poor and weak decisions, settle and sink, and be destructive to ourselves (and to others).

As someone who counsels individuals throughout each day to make the most positive and healthy career and life decisions, I have found the concepts of crunch time and defining moments to be particularly useful, effective, and visual.

I believe that not enough attention is paid to the fact that each of us faces crunch times — or moments of decision — many times each day throughout our lives. And although it is constructive and healthy to say that we must give 100 percent all of the time, there are defining moments in real-life broadcasting, which can truly change the course of a career.

These are moments when breaking news events happen — such as a bombing, the slaying of a public figure, a weather emergency, a war, etc. — where everyone is watching and everyone cares. It's your center court opportunity to show your stuff.

I can think of so many instances where proactive, constructive individuals identified an important news moment, and then seized it. They tapped into their potentials and well-laid foundations, and they thereby raised the level of their performances to great heights. And, in many instances, these performances directly led to great career advancement and further enhancing opportunities.

But making the most of a breaking or important story is just one means of seizing a defining moment. Another way is to initiate great stories, and thereby create defining moments for yourself. I can't tell you how often I hear news managers complain that reporters never enterprise stories or build sources. They just take what's assigned to them. On the other hand, I'm willing to bet that many of the most successful and well-respected reporters enterprise some or many of their best works.

News Tip: If you want to be great and do great things, develop the abilities to identify, seize, and initiate defining moments. Carpé Diem.

Getting It Right —
From the Start

Getting it right, from the start,
Can certainly play a material part
In giving you a solid crack
At starting on the faster track.

It's true that you aren't assured of winning,
Just because you've had a good beginning;
But all too often you will find
You can't catch up once you're behind.

Life is easier, I suspect,
If from the start you've earned respect.
Having the right mind-set, when you begin,
May well pay off with coveted wins.

In broadcasting first impressions count,
So starting strong is paramount!

— K.L.

The Defining Moment Of Getting It Right — From The Start

Through the years, I counselled that it's not the size of the market that you start in that counts, but how much in the long run you ultimately grow, and whether or not you fulfill your potential and you're happy. On the other hand, some of the best advice that I can share with my clients, or remind them of is: "When starting a new job, beginning a new professional relationship, etc., do your best to get it right — the first time around." We often base our opinions on our first impressions. And it frequently takes a great deal to change our minds, when and if individuals or events happen to get off to a bad or a lackluster start. In some cases, we may never change someone's first perceptions

— even if these perceptions are inaccurate.

From my childhood, and to this day, I am one of those individuals, who people, in many instances, underrate. Therefore, if and when I succeed, people are surprised. In fact, just a few months ago, I played a series of sets against the Head Pro of a well-known resort — and beat him in a number of them. Apparently, later on, a few guests walked up to the pro and commented that they couldn't understand how I could fare so well against him. They just didn't get it.[1]

The pro responded, "Kenny's deceptive! You don't get it, until you play him." The other pro, whom I'd also played some sets against, then added, "I said the same thing when I first saw him. Then I played him. He is really good. We call him, The Deceptor, 'cause his playing deceives everybody."

Being underrated is something that I've experienced many times in my life. I've learned to understand it and to deal with it. However, I have also experienced the great advantages that can be derived from getting it right and earning people's respect — from the get go. For example, it's much easier to be highly seeded (or ranked) in a big tournament: you get right into the main draw; you may not have to play a match until the second round; and you may not play another seeded (or top-ranked) player until the later rounds. This is in sharp contrast to having to play through three or four qualifying rounds just to get into the main tournament; and then if you make it, you may play a top seeded player such as Pete Sampras, in the first round. If I am going to lose, I'd rather lose to a Pete Sampras in the finals of a tournament than in the first round.

During my freshman year of high school, I signed up to try out for the varsity tennis team. I told the coach about my paddle tennis successes, and he scheduled me to play a match the following week against the returning #1 varsity player, who was also the team captain. I knew that this match would be my shot to get

---

1 Interestingly, I had been playing paddle tennis exclusively for the past two years, and those were my first sets of tennis during that entire time. The point being, I probably would have done even better had I been playing more tennis.

off on the right track. It would be a defining moment to show that I belonged on the varsity team. During the intervening days, I practiced and mentally prepared. I wound up beating my opponent, 6-1, 6-0 in about fifty minutes. For the next four years, I was automatically given the #1 spot on the varsity team, and I never again had to play a challenge match against any of my teammates. The perception — true or false — was that I was the best player on the team, and that no one was going to beat me. So, as a result of my first and only inter-team match: The case was closed: I would play #1 singles.

In college, the same thing happened. My first day at the tennis courts during my freshman year, I was introduced to the #1 player (a senior) on the varsity team. He was waiting until other team members arrived, so that he could practice with them. After a moment or two, the varsity coach suggested that the number one player and I play a quick set. As the coach had never seen me play before, I (once again) knew that this could be a big opportunity for me. I focused and played the best that I could. I won the set, 6-3. We played another. I won it, 6-2. By now, a number of varsity team members were watching, along with a now amused and excited coach. We played once more. I won, 6-4. Although, according to Ivy League rules, I had to play on the freshman tennis team, as a result of that fateful match, my situation immediately and noticeably changed. From then on, I was extended the privilege of practicing with the varsity, along with attending separate practice sessions with my freshman teammates. The keener competition that I faced at the varsity level, helped me to remain undefeated in inter-school match play my freshman year.

A few months after I began my career at the William Morris Agency, I was given the important assignment of writing all of the contracts and being the William Morris business affairs point-person for the new morning *David Letterman Show*. This program would make William Morris a fortune in commissions. Upon receiving this assignment, similar to my high school and college tennis matches discussed above, I knew that this would be a defining moment for me vis-a-vis my new employers. With this in mind, I busted my butt, spending late evening and weekend time making my very best effort, right from the start. The work paid off.

David's managers were so pleased, that one of them, Jack Rollins, sent a letter to one of the heads of William Morris, detailing how happy he and his client, David, were with my meticulousness, the amount of responsibility that I had assumed, and how well I interacted with the show staff members. All of this allowed my career to get off to a very (visible) positive start, and I was immediately accorded respect for my efforts and effectiveness.

Conversely, I didn't initially focus on my high school assignments, as I was almost totally focused on my tennis and paddle tennis. As a result, I was perceived as someone who wasn't very bright. And some individuals, such as my senior English teacher, could never get over their first impressions of me as strictly a dumb jock. Had these particular impressions been given greater weight, they could easily have influenced my headmaster to decide against writing a recommendation for me to Harvard.

In the broadcasting arena, I have a number of clients who have been fortunate enough to begin their careers in markets that are relatively large and advanced for their early stages of development. Often, this occurs when individuals begin as interns, writers or associate producers in their hometown or college markets, and they work themselves up through the ranks to on-air positions. Since these individuals didn't have to start out in the usual small market setting, where they could make their expected and accepted rookie on-air mistakes, they wind up making them in markets where others are much more seasoned and polished. Therefore, their mistakes are greatly magnified, and are tolerated a great deal less. One problem with this situation is that news management at these stations will forever — or at least for a long time thereafter — have in their minds those rookie mistakes, and these managers are often never able to objectively see and acknowledge the subsequent growth of these newscasters. This reality is reflected in the fact that these newscasters continually make lower salaries and are promoted at a slower rate. The first impressions that they make as rookies, and the perception of their being given a break in being allowed to start on air in large markets, generally stay with these managers throughout these newscasters' careers at these stations. As a result, these newscasters are often forced to leave their first station, even if they ordinarily would have been happy to stay there. They must go on to a station where management's first impression of them is a more positive one and accurately reflects their advanced stage of development.

I remember my first paid summer position at a law firm between my second and third years of law school. As I had no prior real law practice experience, there were many issues and nuances that I just didn't get. Either other (more experienced) peers of mine did get them, or they hid their befuddlement better than I did. But I knew that I had gotten off to a poor start there. It was evident to me that partners and associates treated me with less respect and with lower expectations than they did the other interns. I felt it. It began to hurt my confidence and my performance. Eventually, I didn't care enough to prove anyone wrong. Their (initial) perception became a reality. Conversely, when people expect the best from you and believe in you, these feelings and their positive energy can inspire you to perform at a higher level. Some of my tennis coaches in years past unconditionally believed in me. They never expected me to lose. Unquestionably, I played my best for them. In counselling my clients, I am acutely aware of how very important it is for them to work for people who believe in them, are excited about them, and want to enhance them. I also know that these employers will be much more likely to continue to do good things for my clients, if my clients make a good first impression. It's just a fact of life.

News Tip: In our society, first impressions count. When beginning a new professional relationship, try to get off to the best start possible.

The Three "D's" of Constructive Decision-Making: Desire, Discipline, and Delayed Gratification

Desire

It's nice to say that you "aspire"
And that the goals you choose will take you higher,
But worthy goals aren't attained without the internal fire
Of the compelling emotions of want and desire.

— K.L.

I have learned, seen, and counselled that if you aspire to achieve a goal, "You've gotta really want it," and you've got to be fully focused on attaining it. There's no question about it. If you lack either the desire or the focus, it will be too easy for you to be diverted into settling for more immediate and ultimately, less gratifying substitutes.

Desire is a powerful concept. It conjures up energized qualities such as passion, need, want, and belief. When these emotional and sexual energies are channeled towards healthy and constructive ends, they can have a HUGE positive impact upon your goal-attaining efforts. These energies can initially have a catalyzing effect upon you. Thereafter, they can help you to sustain your efforts and focus, as you face problems, crises, distractions and weak moments.

You cannot be defensive about what you want in order to hide your true feelings from yourself or from others, in case you fail or fall short. To the contrary, you must clearly identify your goals, and not be afraid to put yourself on the line in your efforts to achieve them.

In your quest to identify and attain your goals, you must not only identify your most important values, but you must also identify, feel and tap into your desire and passion for goal attainment. You will need all of the desire and focus that you can muster, when trying to incorporate the other two "Ds" of decision-making — discipline and delayed gratification — into your behavioral repertoires.

People who are successful, know what they want, and they have the drive and focus to go after it.

> Goals aren't achieved through Hocus Pocus.
> They're achieved through your tenacious focus.

Discipline

M. Scott Peck, in *The Road Less Travelled*, writes, "Discipline is the basic set of tools we require to solve life's problems. Without discipline we can solve nothing!"[A]

I agree. In almost all instances, individuals who achieve their goals know that the practice of discipline in their thinking and in their actions is an indispensable element of their formulas for success.

Much of the career counselling that I have done in order to help my clients achieve their potentials, in one way or another, involves the qualities of discipline and its soul-mate, delayed gratification.

For instance, just the other day, one of my clients, "Julianna," called me to say that her news director summoned her to his office and asked whether she would forego her long-awaited two-week vacation so that she could fill-in for the main weeknight anchor of her station.

As we often try to do, my client and I examined the appropriate values and behavioral scripts in an orderly, objective and careful manner. We each wrote them down.

Julianna's values were that she and her husband had planned and paid for their upcoming vacation months in advance, and neither one of them had taken a vacation for about a year. They both needed and wanted one. On the other hand, Julianna and I knew that the main anchor at her station would leave in the next few months, and that Julianna was the front-runner to replace her. However, there was one other female anchor at the station, "Cindy," who was also a candidate for the position, and Cindy had openly made her desire to attain the position known to management. Julianna also knew that if she took her vacation, Cindy would be assigned to fill-in for the two weeks.

We continued to list Julianna's values. If she did get the main anchor position, her annual income would certainly double, and maybe triple. She would also ascend to a very prestigious position, in a city that she wanted to make her home for the long term. All of these values were of significant importance to her.

I then recounted the following story. Years ago, a client of mine, "Rita," left for a week's vacation. On the Friday before Rita left, the news manager of her station told us that upon Rita's return she would be promoted from being a morning anchor to a weeknight evening anchor — a position for which she had worked hard for the past twelve years to attain. During Rita's vacation, the noon anchor, who had been at the station for a little over a year, filled in on the broadcast that my client was to be promoted to.

Allegedly, during that week, the station manager went to a gas station on his way home, and the attendant there said that, "All of the guys here really like the red-headed woman you have anchoring this week." The next thing that we knew, the station management changed its collective mind and Rita didn't get the promotion upon her return from vacation. The red-headed noon anchor did. This turn of events was emotionally and professionally devastating to Rita.

Julianna got the point. She then asked me: "We all know that I'm the front-runner for the job, right?" I answered, "Right." She continued, "So, I shouldn't have to worry about taking a vacation and having Cindy fill-in. The question is, do you think that she has any chance of blowing them away while I'm on vacation?" I answered that I felt that Cindy was actually pretty good, and in reality, we never know what can happen when we allow a variable that we don't have control over to enter into in an equation.[1]

---

1 This is a strategy that I believe in. The more you can control the variables in a situation, or the more often you can eliminate variables that you can't control for or accurately predict, the more likely you are to succeed in attaining your goals.

Therefore, there was a chance, however small, that letting Cindy fill-in could indeed result in an undesirable outcome for us.

I then ended by saying that, "According to my calculation, the professional equation clearly weighs out in favor of opting to be disciplined and putting off your vacation for a while — even if it's needed and it will cost some money to postpone it. I wouldn't give Cindy the opportunity to show her stuff. However, only you can calculate the personal equation of the value to you and your husband of not taking your vacation together at this particular time. The decision depends upon how much the personal values mean to you in this instance. Do they outweigh the professional?"

About ten minutes later, Julianna called me back after speaking with her husband. She'd decided that she would fill-in for the two weeks and that she and her husband would take their vacation a couple of months later. She knew that this was a defining moment for her and that she had to be disciplined, in that she had to delay the gratification of taking her vacation as originally scheduled.

Julianna clearly made the right choice (according to her value system). Three weeks later, she was promoted to the main weeknight anchor position . . . and before she left on vacation, we negotiated a wonderful new deal for her, which included two extra weeks of vacation each year.

Julianna has been extraordinarily successful at achieving and fulfilling many of her dreams, primarily because she has developed healthy and constructive scripts. She understands when discipline is required — and when and where it is appropriate, she practices it.

Most of my clients start out in small markets and move a number of times during their careers. Often, many of them work six, and occasionally seven, days a week. Some of my network correspondent clients travel more than 200 days per year. Sometimes, talent who ascend to the highest rung may be less naturally talented than others, but they may well be more disciplined (and have better scripts for success) than many others. They understand and accept that they have to give up things of value now (their hometowns, leisure time, the stability of their relationships, etc.) in order to attain — at some future date — something that they perceive is of greater value (i.e., the fulfillment of their dreams).

As a teenager, when I was competing in tennis tournaments throughout the country, there would usually be an exciting event or a party to attend each night. I often had to weigh whether I would go out and enjoy the festivities, or go to bed early and be physically and mentally at peak condition for the next day's match. (In reaching my decision, I always had to take into account the fact that I needed more rest than many others, in order for me to perform at my best.) With disciplined thinking, I almost always opted to get my rest. My value system said to me: "I have travelled throughout the country, and I have sacrificed and practiced a lot to get to this point. I now have the opportunity to win. I have put myself in the best position possible to succeed . . . don't be stupid and blow it at the end by going out to the party."

I have attained many of my goals and dreams by practicing appropriate discipline.

When I entered Harvard, I knew that I would be competing for grades with some very bright individuals. I knew that if I wanted to do well academically and play on the tennis team, I would have to be disciplined about how I allotted my time. With the help of much discipline, I graduated magna cum laude and became captain and the #1 player on the varsity tennis team. I also won national titles in two sports — tennis and paddle tennis.

At a later time, when I left the prestigious William Morris Agency and established my own company, I knew that I'd have to be twice as good and effective on my own, once I didn't have the William Morris name to back me up. For the first three years of my company's existence, I worked a minimum of six days a week. I put many pleasures on hold. In retrospect, my discipline yielded great rewards (according to my value system).

I fully understand that not everyone desires to be as focused as I am, and not everyone has my value system. However, one thing is for certain. Appropriate use of discipline in your thinking and in your behavior can be one of your greatest allies when trying to attain your goals and enhance your life.

Delayed Gratification

Keeping The Ball In Play Until The Right Openings And Opportunities Are Presented: Not Always Opting For The Quick Fix

In my experience of career counselling, I too often see people who desire to attain positive ends and grab the gold ring immediately. Today, we live in an MTV world of quick, visual bits of stimulation, a McDonald's fast-food era. We also live in an often dysfunctional society, in which many children and adults have been raised and/or surrounded with little consistency, and/or little or no love. They therefore want things and relationships now, as experience has taught them that by tomorrow these coveted things and special individuals may be gone. As a result, many people hunger for and rely upon immediate gratification — even if the gratification in the short or long-term will prove to be worthless, worth little, or unhealthy. Among other things, it is this kind of indiscriminate hunger and reliance on the quick fix that is likely to lead to poor and destructive decision-making.

I can't begin to estimate the large number of bad professional and personal choices that I've seen people make because they wanted an inappropriate quick fix or immediate closure to a situation.

Sometimes, attaining immediate gratification is possible, at no great subsequent cost. But in a great many instances, we have to patiently and proactively continue to lay a solid foundation before we can achieve our most precious goals. In these latter situations, we have to keep hanging on, winning some battles and losing some skirmishes, or vice versa — and learning from both experiences, before we can win the war. Or, put another (athletic) way: With discipline, we must "keep the ball in play" until we get the right opening or opportunity — then go for it.

I have been involved in numerous instances that have proven that there are times in life when it's best to hang in and stay sharp long enough to learn what we truly do and don't want. During this (growth) process, values, perceptions and information may change, and with these changes our goals may be modified and re-prioritized. For example, I have represented a number of individuals who initially thought that their ultimate goal was to become a network correspondent. However, after they got a taste of anchoring a newscast, or hosting a program (or saw others do it) — and they discovered the perks that go along with those particular positions — their aspirations changed. Also, as people's life situations change, reporting for a network can lose its allure when you're asked to be on the road 200 days or more each year. It can be great for a single person, but it might be much less attractive if you get married and/or have a family.

The key is that we often have a much better opportunity to identify what we truly do want, and secure it, if we have carefully and correctly laid the right foundation — and this, in many instances, takes time, discipline and the practice of delayed gratification.

There are also situations when you just have to keep going, even when there is no immediate pay-off in sight. This requires the greatest discipline! It's sort of like driving a car in a fog or through a torrential downpour. We just have to keep a careful and steady course until there's a clearing. We have to be guided by the heartfelt belief that, "If I do things right and do the right things, something good will come of it." Very frequently, this turns out to be the case.

An illustration of this constructive script occurred when my dad was retired by his former employer at the age of 69. I know that my dad, in his heart-of-hearts, felt that he still had a great deal more to give to an employer and that he wasn't at all ready to be put out to pasture. As time passed and no one rushed to offer him a job, he began to realize that he might never again work in the merchandising field. Although he never let on to anyone, I believe that he was sad, and a bit dejected and angry by the abrupt ending of his career. Nevertheless, despite the overwhelming odds against his ever again being offered a job in his field, he diligently kept himself in tip-top physical shape — just in case a position became available. In addition, he continued to maintain his contacts with his longtime friends in merchandising. Then, at age 70, he was offered a wonderful job opportunity as a market coordinator, teacher and negotiator by a major department store company. Twenty-one years later, he is still working, has travelled cross-country and abroad with his job, he has been promoted, and he has received numerous accolades and raises in salary. And, he's still going strong at 92 years old.

In this instance, disciplined thinking and preparation met opportunity, and a successful professional relationship, further self-fulfillment and an inspiring story were the fruits. Once again, if you do things right and do the right things — i.e., having faith in oneself and developing the ability to accept and wait for delayed gratification — the ultimate results may well be quite positive. Indeed, the positive results may far exceed all expectations.

Take Abraham Lincoln, for instance. Anthony Robbins, in his book, *Unlimited Power*, gives a list of how many defeats Lincoln suffered before he accomplished his lofty goal of becoming the President. Here it is:

1) Failed in business at age 21.
2) Was defeated in a legislative race at age 22.
3) Failed again in business at age 24.
4) Overcame the death of his sweetheart at age 26.
5) Had a nervous breakdown at age 27.
6) Lost a congressional race at age 34.
7) Lost a congressional race at age 36.
8) Lost a senatorial race at age 45.
9) Failed in an effort to become Vice President at age 47.
10) Lost a senatorial race at age 49.
11) Was elected President of the United States at age 52.[B]

All broadcasting careers have small and large ups and downs. Everyone — even the most talented and celebrated broadcast individuals — has suffered some setbacks, losses, and very painful public defeats. The key is to just hang in, and calmly — yet proactively — keep your ball in play, knowing that tomorrow, next week, next month, with constructive thinking, you can seize and enjoy a victory that will put the past in its proper, grander perspective.

Here's an example. Years ago, I received a call from a news manager regarding a very talented newscaster client of mine. The manager told me that in spite of my client's obvious talent, my client didn't fit in with his station's format and presentation, and that she would be demoted in about two weeks to a lesser anchor role. I immediately called my client, knowing how devastated she would be.

After the initial shock and trauma wore off, sadness (about having to pick up and move yet again), anger and fear started to set in. During the process, I assured my client that things happen for a reason despite the fact that we sometimes don't always immediately see why. And that perceived negatives can be excellent learning experiences and opportunities to seize other valuable experiences. I told her that the good news in all of this was, "That when a very talented person that I represent suffers a setback, or cannot, for some reason, accept what appears to be a great opportunity, something better almost always comes along later." I continued by telling my client that she just had to be positive, and that I had to be intelligently and creatively proactive in making that better opportunity materialize as quickly as possible. My client was indeed fortunate, because a top station which had been looking for someone just like her still hadn't found their perfect person. Within four weeks, my client was hired for this position, which, from everyone's perspective would unquestionably enhance her career. In fact, it has, to an extraordinary extent! My client's devastating experience, in retrospect, turned out to be the best thing that could have happened. It allowed me to market, and then to extricate her from, her contract.

Another problem with opting for immediate gratification, is that we don't have the opportunity to experience and enjoy the process. For example, I've seen way too many broadcasters so focused on their next move and then the next, that they take no time to enjoy the uniqueness and beauty of their current stage of development. They don't even take time to enjoy the city that they're in. It's a pity — because in all likelihood they'll never be there again.

News Tip: The issues of whether it's appropriate to delay gratification, and for how long, is a matter of wisely identifying and weighing your values. There are times when it's right to go for the gold and seize the moment. There are other times, when keeping the ball in play — until we can produce the right opening or that opening is produced for us — and then going for it will produce a healthier, a more satisfying, and a more long-lasting result.

Constructive Decision-Making

The key is to make constructive decisions
That will put you in truly enhancing positions.
So start today, before it's too late
Begin to take ownership and determine your fate.
'Cause it's truly exciting to begin to create
A fulfilling career that makes you feel great!

— K.L.

Constructive Decision-Making and Solutions

The Defensive and Destructive Script Of Overcompensation

The two most important problem-solving scripts that I learned while in law school are: When faced with a problem, first try to understand the situation; and then identify the crux of the problem — or, as we used to say, "spot the (real) issue." (For example, this is a case of negligence, or this is a case of breach of contract, etc.) By performing these steps, we are then better able to find the best course of action, resolution, or proactive, enhancing solution.

In making career decisions, one of the reasons some people make constructive decisions and thrive, and others make destructive ones and never fulfill their potentials, is that the former individuals are open to identifying and correcting their mistakes and non-strengths, whereas defensive individuals try to ignore, rationalize away, and cover up their perceived deficiencies. One of the most prevalent, self-defeating — rather than self-enhancing — behavioral patterns that I have come across is that of "overcompensation." To illustrate the dynamics of this defense mechanism, let me depict two scenarios which, for the most part, raise similar issues:

1) Allegedly, a local station morning show host, who had been a network news correspondent prior to assuming his hosting duties, had the following experience and reaction. One day, after he finished his show and was walking back to his office, he ran into a news anchor at his station, who sarcastically chided him, "So, how are those cooking segments going?"

Allegedly, the host became quite upset and defensive at hearing the remark. He perceived that the intended implication was that he had forsaken his journalistic ideals. The host's on-air performance changed immediately thereafter. From that point on, his demeanor on the (light and fun) morning show became serious and sullen, and he became confrontational with his guests.[1]

For this and other reasons, viewership for the show slipped, and he became more of a liability than an asset. Eventually, he was replaced.

2) Allegedly, a beautiful blonde female with a wonderfully warm, effervescent, and engaging presence was offered the chance to become a host on a nationally syndicated entertainment program. At the time, she was making a transition from being a fashion model and commercial actress to becoming a TV broadcaster. Because she no longer wanted to be perceived as a lightweight, and because she wanted to be taken seriously and to be viewed as intelligent, she chose to decline the extraordinary offer. Instead, she decided to find a hard news anchor position in a local market. After many months of being out of work and looking, she finally secured an anchor job in a small market. In trying to fulfill her quest to be taken seriously, she was so cold, stern, and icy on the air, that she turned off the viewers — as well as the management of her station. She lasted about nine months before she and her station had a mutual parting of the ways.

---

1 This morning show host had already established that he was a very good journalist during his network news correspondent days. Evidently, he didn't really believe it, as he allowed himself to feel put down and diminished by someone who wasn't important in the grand scheme of things.

In the scenarios outlined above, both individuals reacted by defensively overcompensating for a felt inadequacy that they harbored within. They also proceeded to go down the tubes with their destructive decisions and scripts.

If these individuals had their decisions to make over again, and they truly aspired to be constructive crunch time performers, they could step back from the situation in which they're involved, and examine their behavior from the perspective of the big picture. This could help them answer the all-important questions of:

1) Why did the morning show host feel that he needed to constantly remind everyone of what a good journalist he is, despite the fact that his behavior, in many instances, was inappropriate and job threatening?

2) What did the host, in his heart-of-hearts, truly want to accomplish with his decision?

3) What was the most self-enhancing way to correct and improve his situation? In essence, make it a win/win situation, or at least the most positive one possible?

4) Why did the female choose not to take a national position that she was incredibly well-suited for, and then in the job that she did take, perform in an inappropriate manner?

5) What did the female, in her heart-of-hearts, truly want to accomplish with her decisions?

6) What was the most self-enhancing way to take advantage of the national entertainment program host offer, so as to make it a win/win situation for her?

In the instances outlined above, the individuals needed to proactively and objectively explore what alternative scripts of behavior might have been more constructive means of achieving their heartfelt values and desires. For example, the morning host could have requested that he do some hard news reporting assignments to go along with his hosting duties. If this could have been accomplished, he could then derive the pleasure and satisfaction of being a (reporting) journalist again, and he could also show his detractors that he is a well-balanced news person, as he hosts and also reports. This situation might well have provided a means for the host to feel more comfortable with having fun and being warm on a morning show, which required a lighter and softer touch for ratings success.

Similarly, the female could have requested that she cover some harder-edged entertainment stories on her network show, such as the O.J., the Bill Cosby, and the Marv Albert trials, along with other more serious (non-fluffy) stories. Local stations that aired her program might well have welcomed the opportunity to have her do some in-depth stories of her choosing, just to have a national host on their station. Additionally, there might have been venues such as cable television, where she could have done some in-depth interviews, which would have showcased her intelligence as well as her interviewing and writing skills. The constructive behavior in this instance would have been for her to make the most of her high profile national host position, by seeking out and finding supplementary avenues to fulfill her goals, while allowing others (her own program, local stations, cable networks, etc.), to reap the benefit of having her appear on their programs. This would have been a win/win/win strategy to design and act-out.

In the above scenarios, the individuals reacted so defensively by adopting the subjective script of overcompensation, that they never gave themselves the opportunity to explore what their real strengths were, and what constructive, self-enhancing solutions could have been created to counteract any deficiencies — real or imagined.

Overcompensation is a self-defeating script of behavior that I encounter numerous times each day.

The above individuals also needed to explore, analyze, and determine, as objectively as possible, the real agendas of those who made the derogatory and/or disrespectful comments to and about them. In addition, they needed to openly explore their own reactions to the comments, in order to discern why they felt the urge to react so strongly and defensively. Only then could they begin to determine, in any balanced way, what an appropriate response to those detractors might have been — or if any response, in the big picture, would have been appropriate or necessary at all. Had these two individuals openly examined the true big picture of their detractors and their relationships with them, they might have come to see that the real issue was not about what others said or did. Rather, it was all about how these two felt about themselves and how they inappropriately attempted to cover-up their perceived flaws and insecurities.

Constructive Strategies and Solutions

I believe that the key to making the most of your broadcasting career is: When faced with a decision, don't react, but instead, calmly step back and look at the issue, problem or challenge in the richer, broader scope of the big picture of what your true values are, and the impact, if any, that your decision will have on your broadcasting career in the short and long terms.

> My rule of thumb has been:
> When I react, without thinking clearly,
> All too often, I pay dearly.
> So, no matter how intense the pressure, or how loud the noise,
> I'll step back and see things clearly, and never lose my poise.

Once you identify what your true and most cherished values and goals are, openly and objectively figure out a creative and constructive way to attain them.

Individuals who achieve cherished and sustained successes in broadcasting often identify and/or create healthy and constructive means of reaching enhancing decisions and finding win/win solutions.

As an illustration of this process, I would like to refer back to my client, Julianna, who was faced with the decision as to whether she would forego her much-awaited and extensively-planned vacation with her husband, so that she could fill-in anchor for the individual whose position she desired to secure. Let's examine her decision-making processes in more detail.

Once Julianna identified that a decision needed to be made and she clearly stated to herself what that decision was, she engaged in the following constructive thought processes to help her reach a decision which we both believe, ultimately led to her attaining the anchor position that she coveted.

    1) First, when Julianna's news director asked her to postpone her vacation, just five days before her scheduled departure, she listened, but didn't react. When she did respond, she was wise to carefully explain her predicament to him, but to also say that she wanted to be a team player, and that she would do everything possible to try to help him and the station out.

    This was truly constructive thinking and decision-making. Julianna chose her responses carefully and effectively. She made sure that her news manger was aware of all of the plans — both hers and her husband's — that had been made regarding their vacation, so in case she couldn't or wouldn't change her vacation, he might better understand why. And, if she did rearrange her trip, hopefully, he would better appreciate all that she had done.

    She consciously expressed her sentiments about wanting to be a team player, and that she would do everything she could to try and work things out, as she knew that in the past other anchors had not been team players and that the news manager had resented it. I often recommend the script of, "You catch more flies with honey than with vinegar." In this case, in spite of the fact that my client felt that a great deal of pressure was being exerted on her to postpone her vacation, she didn't act negatively. Instead, she used a warm, constructive response, that she knew her news manager would respect and respond to positively. In doing this, she seized the opportunity to bring him philosophically and emotionally closer to her.

    Finally, she told her manager that she would need some time to see what she could do about rearranging her vacation. This period of time would give her the opportunity to think things through, with the aim that she would ultimately make her very best decision under the circumstances.

    2) The next thing that Julianna did was to step away from the situation, first, by herself, and then with me. She looked at her decision in the context of the big picture of her broadcasting career, her relationship with her husband and what his wants and needs were, and the state of her overall mental and physical health. Upon viewing the big picture, she assessed that doing all that she could to secure the main

anchor position, at a top station, in a city that she desired to make her long-term home, was a top priority. And, although she was both disappointed that she couldn't take her vacation and irked that the news manager had waited until the last minute to make his request, she determined that she was not so mentally or physically tired, that her health would be at risk if she were to delay her vacation for a month or so. Additionally, after consulting with her (understanding and supportive) husband, she learned that he would be okay with postponing their time off. He loved his wife, encouraged her professionally, and knew and appreciated the great value that getting the weeknight anchor position had for her.

3) After examining the big picture, Julianna realized that this was a time to delay the gratification of taking her vacation now. She would be disciplined and sacrifice her vacation — for the time being — in hopes of getting a bigger pay-off later.

4) Julianna also objectively and correctly assessed her competition (Cindy) for the weeknight anchor position. She acknowledged that Cindy was in fact talented, and if she were given the opportunity to fill-in for the two weeks, she might well become a much more serious threat to get the weeknight job when it became available.

5) My client also took time to assess the various agendas of the individuals who were involved in her decision. Although she knew that her husband was looking forward to their vacation, and had taken pains to clear the time from his very demanding professional schedule, she also knew that he truly appreciated what was at stake for her, and that he would be supportive if the vacation was postponed. Julianna sensed that her news manager was behind her, and that if he wanted her to postpone her vacation and fill-in, he must have had a good reason.[2] She also knew that Cindy wanted nothing more than to fill-in for the two weeks and to leap-frog over Julianna and get the weeknight job.

---

2 As we later found out, the news manager knew that the weeknight anchor would be leaving the station in about a month. By having Julianna fill in for those two weeks, he wanted their new general manager (his boss) to watch Julianna in the main anchor role, in hopes that the GM would subsequently approve her as the main anchor's permanent replacement.

6) Julianna knew that she had gotten off to a good start at the station by immediately being pegged as the #2 anchor there. By temporarily foregoing her vacation and not giving Cindy the opportunity to fill-in, she would, in all likelihood, maintain that position. This could greatly increase her chances of being named the #1 female anchor if and when the position became available.

7) Julianna realized that in order to attain her dreams, from time to time, she would have to be flexible and adopt a soft hands approach. In this instance, she was disappointed and a bit angry that her plans had to be changed, but she also knew that she needed to have a positive — or at least an accepting — mind-set if she in-deed did change her plans. She didn't want any of her feelings of disappointment or anger to show on the air, because if they were evident, then rearranging her vacation to fill-in would turn out to be counterproductive. In essence, if she performed poorly, she could set herself back. We both agreed on the same script: "If you're going to do something positive (i.e., sacrifice your vacation), the intended recipients — in this case, Julianna's news management and her audience — need to enjoy it. Or else, the excellent effort that you make can mean nothing, or can even work against you."

8) Julianna recognized that winning the battle of being able to take her vacation as scheduled — because she was able to get her news manager to (somewhat reluctantly) under-stand her predicament — would be no victory at all, if she lost the war, because Cindy did such a good job of filling in that Cindy was given the weeknight position.

In this instance, Julianna examined the (relative and sometimes illusory) concept of short-term winning, by weighing her values and goals in the insightful context of the big picture.

9) Julianna continued to look at her decision through the grander perspective of the big picture, in order to see if there were any alternative ways of approaching the situation, that she hadn't yet thought of and/or explored. She asked if there was any constructive way to take her vacation as planned and still keep herself in the best position possible to later get the main anchor job? Was there a win/win solution here? We came up with one possible alternative. I would call her news manager and ask that his station consider not only committing to Julianna becoming the main weeknight anchor upon the incumbent's departure, but also negotiating a new, more

lucrative agreement reflecting this promotion, *before* Julianna's vacation. The news manager responded that, had the prior general manager still been running the station, our proposal might well have been accepted; but with a new general manager in place, he wasn't ready to make any commitments of that magnitude.

With this information in hand, Julianna and I agreed that there was no real satisfactory alternative available.

10) Julianna then applied a strategy which had produced positive results for her in the past. That script was: "Like a full-back in football, when you see a hole (an opening), run like hell for the daylight; and keep running until you score (the touchdown)." The translation is: "If you have an opportunity to proactively seize your goal, do it!" Julianna was appropriately confident about her anchoring skills. As a result, she felt strongly that if she filled-in for the two weeks, she'd significantly enhance her chances to get the weeknight position permanently.

11) After going through this extensive study of the situation, as we know, Julianna decided to postpone her vacation.

12) She then engaged in some creative decision-making. She and I decided that along with Julianna telling the news manager that she would change her plans, I would also ask the station to reimburse any expenses that she and her husband incurred in changing their reservations, along with the station committing to two specific weeks, plus some other holidays off, for Julianna later that year. The news manager happily agreed to all of our requests. I also reiterated to him that Julianna was truly a team player, and that I hoped that her team spirit would serve her well when her station managers were deciding who should become their next weeknight anchor. He said that her professionalism would serve her well.

Julianna's talents and professionalism did, in fact, serve her well. Three weeks later, she was named as the weeknight anchor of her station.

News Tip: When faced with problems and issues to solve, step back and see the situation in the enlightening context of the big picture. Then proactively and creatively design a constructive formula for achieving the best possible short-term and long-range outcomes.

The Enhancing Niche

It is of crucial importance that you know what you want to accomplish in the short and long terms, when you look for and ultimately accept a broadcasting position. The key to fulfilling your potential is to thoughtfully choose your positions with sophistication and with your most important goals and values clearly in mind.

The Enhancing Venue

Treat a man as he is and he will remain as he is.
Treat a man as he can and should be and he will become
as he can and should be.

— Goethe[A]

My take on Goethe's insight is that if you are in a non-supportive, negative, and diminishing environment, you are less likely to flourish as a performer, than when you are in a nurturing, supportive, and enhancing one. For example, as I mentioned earlier, I know that I performed far better as a tennis player for coaches who believed in me and expected the best from me. I remember my freshman coach at Harvard. During my competitive tennis career, I may have had more accomplished coaches, but I never played better than I did for him. He thought I was great and he never expected me to lose — and I never lost for him. His belief in me inspired me and lifted my performances. Because I felt safe with him and supported by him, I was never afraid to take a risk on the court and push the envelope in order to improve and grow.[1]

News and reality-based programming are *performance* mediums. In general, you will perform better when you work for individuals who will support, promote, and enhance you.

Therefore, you must do your homework and seek out companies and individuals who have a reputation for being supportive of their staff. This isn't always easy, because there is so much management change in broadcasting. One of the keys to your success in this area is to identify companies which are known for staying the course with their management and talent. Ones that don't make changes every year or so. If managers feel more supported and less vulnerable, they are apt to be more supportive of others. As a journalist, you must do your research.

The Enhancing-Skill-Developing Niche

It is also important when deciding upon a position, that you understand what a particular position will, and will not do for your skill development and career.

For example, if you want to learn to report and to anchor, make sure that you will at some point be guaranteed to do both. If you desire to work on one skill specifically, make sure that your management understands this and that your employer is on the same page with you — spiritually and contractually. For example, if you desire to do packaged or long-form reports, as well as live reporting — as a steady diet — be sure that this has been made verbally and contractually clear with your employer.

Certain stations or programs, with specific philosophies and formats, will allow you to accomplish certain goals better than others. Before accepting a position:

---

1 As this book is going to press, Lindsay Davenport just defeated Martina Hingis to win the 1998 U.S. Open Women's Singles title. In discussing her road to success, Davenport, during her post-victory CBS interview, said, "There are many who said I couldn't make it, but I stuck with the people who believed in me." Once again: Great things can happen if you surround yourself with people who enhance you.

1) Know which skills you want to develop and focus upon;

2) Know which employers and venues will allow you to develop those skills on a regular basis; and,

3) Make sure that with management changes being as prevalent as they are, that you have something in writing to protect you and your position, in case your management allies and/or your management's news philosophies change.

Here's a rule of thumb:

> If you don't get things in writing,
> There's *no question* you're inviting
> Problems and arguments some future day.
> So get *in writing* what your managers say.

News Tip: One key to correctly choreographing your broadcasting career is to know what you want to learn, to experience, and to accomplish in connection with each position that you accept.

The Enhancing Niche —
Highlighting Your Strengths

As you grow in broadcasting, it is also important to know what your strengths are, what makes you special, and what kinds of venues will allow you to truly shine (and which will not). The goal is to then find positions that showcase and amplify your strengths. For example, some individuals are more effective reporters than they are anchors. Somehow, they look and/or perform better in the field. At some point, they may want to focus on positions that strictly play to their superior reporting strengths. However, there are caveats and nuances here. Some individuals who aren't effective local anchors, because they don't ad-lib or chit chat well, may make very effective network and cable news anchors, as these venues often require solo anchoring, and little or no on-set interaction with others. Therefore, it is important to very carefully define your strengths and non-strengths, and to find which particular venues positively highlight what you do well.

Here's an example of an individual not knowing his weaknesses, and not understanding why he had been a very successful weeknight anchor at his prior station.

After a number of years of anchoring one newscast at his top-rated large market station, "Bob" entered into a deal for more money to anchor two newscasts at a competing station in his market. When I asked the news director of the station that Bob was leaving if he thought that Bob's departure would hurt his station, he told me that he sincerely believed that Bob would not be anywhere as successful "across the street" as he had been at his station. He explained that Bob was a very poor ad-libber and that his station had taken that weakness into account, by very tightly scripting and producing Bob's newscasts. Therefore, Bob almost never had the opportunity to expose his weakness. During his debut week, I happened to be in the town where Bob worked, and I watched firsthand what his former news director meant. Bob's newscasts at his new station, were loosely scripted and allowed him to ad-lib and chit chat away. I agreed with the former news director's assessment. Bob did not ad-lib well. Within one year, one of Bob's newscasts was cancelled because of very poor ratings. Since then, his salary has been cut, and he has never been as successful at his new station as he was at his old one. In this case, Bob's old station's news format amplified his strengths and minimized the impact of his weaknesses. Neither he nor his new station understood this — to his and his station's detriment.

In Bob's case, the devil who knew him was better (for him) than the devil who didn't. This is an important insight. When talent is thinking of switching or leaving a successful situation, they must take into account *why* they are successful at their current station and program, and whether the reasons for this success can be duplicated or improved upon at a potential new station or program. (Additionally, potential new employers should do their best to understand *why* someone is successful at their current venue, and then try to duplicate that environment and improve upon it.)

* * * * * * * * *

Another reality: Some individuals are better hosts than they are anchors. Some people have a great presence, comfort level and ease on camera, a sharp mind, a quick wit, and an ability to engage compellingly not only the viewer but all of those on the set with them. They somehow can make the sum bigger than the parts. In contrast to hosting, anchoring — for the most part — is a very structured and tightly scripted environment, which often doesn't allow for one's warmth, sense of humor, wit, and on-the-spot analytical skills and interviewing abilities to come to the fore on any regular basis. For example, Katie Couric, Matt Lauer, and Jodi Applegate are *great* hosts. They have a wonderful mix of talents and warmth that naturally work on morning television — which requires a softer touch. While these individuals are also very talented anchors, arguably they are more successful as hosts, because this venue allows their special qualities to shine more brightly. The other night, Matt Lauer was interviewed by Larry King. At one point in the interview, Matt was asked what other kinds of shows could he picture himself doing. His response in essence was, "Larry, I think that I am on the perfect show for me. Early in my career, when asked about what I aspire to do, I always responded, 'I'd like to host the *Today* show or be Larry King'"[H] Matt understands what makes him special. I, too, agree that the *Today* show is the perfect, enhancing venue for him and he is perfect for it.

Would Oprah Winfrey be as successful if she were just reporting or anchoring? I think not. Some of the qualities that make Oprah special are her personality, her sensitivity to issues, her interviewing skills, her intelligence, and her charisma — all assets which won't be as evident in other, more tightly scripted and produced venues. Furthermore, all of the individuals mentioned above can be taken and enjoyed in large doses, and they therefore thrive in these more loosely scripted, more human formats.

Conversely, there are extraordinary anchors who will not be as good, likable, or effective in hosting venues.

An instance of this comes to mind. Years ago, someone who was a very successful news anchor was given the opportunity to become a host of a very prominent program. When I asked the very insightful individual who had discovered and had mentored her how he thought she'd fare in her new position, he — to my surprise — (in essence) said, "I don't think she'll do well. She doesn't have the depth, soul and life experience to pull it off. She's great reading copy. But when she needs to dig down deep and find empathy, sympathy, and honesty, it won't be there." He was right. The host's stint was short-lived.

Of course, there are some individuals, such as Jane Pauley, Elizabeth Vargas, Giselle Fernandez, Lisa McRee, etc., who are excellent anchors *and* hosts, because they possess exceptional and diverse communication skills.

One of the keys to success is to know what makes you special, and to take positions that allow you to be your best.

Creating Your Own Enhancing Niche

Throughout this section, we have discussed seeking out and identifying positions which will most help you to grow and shine. Here's one other thought. Once you've accepted a position, do all that you can to make it the most enhancing one possible. Here are four suggestions:

1) If you are a reporter, do your best before each show to tell the anchor who will be tossing to you and to your story some of the interesting things about your piece. This way, he or she may be able to make an informed introduction, and when appropriate, he or she will thereafter be able to ask intelligent questions and/or engage you in an interesting dialogue.

2) If you're an anchor, as we discussed earlier in the chapter on "Males," do your best to make everyone on the set look good, and appear to be an integral part of the product. Good group chemistry can play a material role in a broadcast's success and in the enjoyment that the participants derive from their work.

3) Enterprise and initiate worthwhile stories. Be proactive.

4) Do your best to know your audience and what it is that they expect and want from their broadcast journalists.

Besides being a wonderful broadcast talent, and an extraordinary communicator, I have always believed that one of Oprah Winfrey's great strengths is her ability to identify what it is that her audience really wants, and then effectively and compellingly give it to them. There have been many times when the various talk shows have all done the same subject. One of the differences between Oprah and the others, is that she knows or senses how to touch and reach her audience. This is an incredibly valuable skill and advantage.

Regarding creating your own niche, one very inspiring story comes to mind. It is about a woman who was hired as a general assignment reporter at her station. To the best of my recollection, at some point midway through her contract there, she approached station management about anchoring and reporting sports. At first, station management denied her request, as they wanted to keep this woman's excellent *news* reports on their newscasts five days a week. Additionally, they already had sportscasters to cover all of their existing newscasts.

However, to her credit, the woman suggested that she work an extra day each week so that she could anchor sports on one of her station's new weekend morning newscasts. Her station news director agreed to let her try it.

The result: This individual became so very good at sports anchoring and reporting (while at the same time working as a full-time news reporter) that, upon the expiration of her station contract, she later became a much-praised national sports anchor/reporter in her next job.

I have tremendous respect for how this individual *created* her own enhancing niche, by working six — and sometimes seven days a week — in order to learn her craft and polish her skills.

Seeing and Seizing the Opportunity

Throughout this book I have warned against working for employers that are low-rated, because they all-too-often keep looking for the quick fix, and they don't stay the course long enough for the talent to succeed. However, there are opportunities with employers who aren't #1 or #2, that are worth taking. For example, a few years ago, both the ABC and CBS networks had a great array of news stars on their staffs — especially ABC. On the other hand, the NBC News division was in a rebuilding phase and was looking to develop their next generation of front line talent. Because ABC and CBS had so many established veterans in place, there was little room for younger journalists to grow and receive plum assignments. However, this was not the case at NBC. It is one of the reasons why Matt Lauer, Elizabeth Vargas, Brian Williams, Giselle Fernandez, Ann Curry, Jodi Applegate, David Bloom, Deborah Roberts, and others fared so well at NBC. And although not all of these individuals stayed at NBC, all of them were given the chance to grow and to accomplish things they might not have accomplished at the other networks.

In this instance, there were opportunities to seize at NBC, even though its news division, at that time, was not on top of the ratings heap.

News Tip: Your career is precious. Choreograph it with your eyes wide open. Be as honest and as objective as possible. Know your strengths and non-strengths. Understand what makes you unique and special.

There's a time to work on developing your strengths and non-strengths. There's also a (later) time in your career to take a position in which you shine — big time.

Understanding What Different Venues Do and Don't Offer

Weekend Versus Weekday Anchoring

We have all heard the term "weekend warrior," which refers to someone who gives a sport his or her all on the weekends only. Not only can this be dangerous for one's physical health, but it is also hard to maintain one's skill level, and even harder to improve it. For instance, I have always found that when I play paddle tennis or tennis on Saturday, after a five-day lay-off, I'm often stiff and I don't play as well as I do on Sunday. The reason is that by Sunday I've had one day of play under my belt, and I've found my rhythm. If I play on Monday after two days of practice, I almost always play better than I do on Sunday. If I play five days a week, I have my best chance to reach my potential.

It is this way with broadcasting. I cannot count the number of weekend anchors who have complained that they always feel out of sync when anchoring on Saturdays, after not having anchored for five days. By Sunday evening, anchors begin to find their groove, only to once again not anchor for five more days thereafter.

The point is: If you want to grow to be the best anchor possible — generally — anchoring five days a week will be more beneficial than anchoring only two days per week. It allows you to not only maintain your anchoring skills, but to enhance them.

This five-day-per-week anchor perspective, however, should not in any way diminish your reporting growth. Just report before or after you anchor. Preferably, you can report after you anchor; this way you're fresh for your anchoring and then can focus effectively on your reports.

The Morning Anchor Shift

Make sure that you work out your reporting schedule ahead of time. Most producer and assignment desk individuals come into newsrooms around 9 A.M. They don't realize that the morning anchor has been in since 4 or 5 A.M. and, as assignment desks look for the first warm body that they can send out on a story, they may collar you. As a result, you may not be done with your story until 4 or 5 P.M., or later, each day.

One way to work this out is to have an agreement that you will have two or three reporting days each week and two days when you leave right after anchoring your newscasts.[1] Try to make Friday a short day, so that you can have a reasonable amount of turnaround time on the weekend.

Long-Form Reporting, And Finding A Venue That Gives You More Opportunities To Hit The (Reporting) Home Runs

If you aspire to be a network correspondent one day, then along with perfecting your live shots you must develop your skills in writing, crafting, and packaging compelling long-form pieces. In order to do this, you should suggest sweeps pieces, and you should initiate your own stories: These are ones that will afford you the time and the resources to put together some great demo tape material.

Interestingly, a number of my clients have been given their best opportunities to do great long-form work at independent and certain Fox stations. In some instances, these stations have fewer newscasts for which to report than affiliates and other network-owned stations, so reporters have more time to research, write and craft quality pieces.

---

1 Of course, if there's breaking news, all agreements are off.

Format-Driven Vs. Personality-Centered Newscasts

During my years representing talent, I have seen the spectrum of how news executives have perceived and promoted their broadcasts. On one end of the spectrum is the format-driven broadcast, where *format* is king. WSVN in Miami and CNN *Headline News* are two such places. In these situations, management finds talent to fit the format. And, as a result of building a product this way, on-air individuals, for the most part, are perceived as interchangeable and, therefore, they will never earn great amounts of money — because management doesn't perceive talent as bringing in the viewers. Additionally, these entities promote the product, not the talent, so talent often doesn't show up as strongly in research as it otherwise might, if they were promoted.

On the other side of the spectrum, there are managers who believe that people watch programs because they like and establish a bond with the on-air talent. In these instances, talent is often promoted, often shows up more prominently in research, and often makes more money. Why? Because they're perceived as being more important to management's financial success, so they have more leverage. Of course, many managers fall somewhere in the middle of the format/talent spectrum. Additionally, stations and program philosophies change, depending upon what the competition is doing and how well they're doing it. For example, with MSNBC having so many identifiable stars on their programs from NBC (Katie Couric, Matt Lauer, Jane Pauley, Brian Williams, etc.) CNN has responded by pursuing and hiring more well-known names, and by also making the effort to differentiate their programs more clearly. In essence, their new goal is to attain appointment-viewing, as opposed to offering a string of fairly similar newscasts that one can tune into whenever they have the time.

The point being that if you work for a strictly format-driven employer, you probably won't be promoted, you will have to fit into the format, as opposed to the employer accenting your strengths, and, in all likelihood, you won't earn as much money as in other — more talent-focused — operations. But, there may well be some very compelling reasons why working for a format-driven news operation or program is the most enhancing one at a given point in your career.[2] Just weigh the pros and cons.

Health/Medical and Consumer News Reporting Franchises

If and when my clients are looking for a reporting franchise that will enhance them and their careers, I often suggest such areas as health/medical and consumer. I believe in the power of these franchises for a number of reasons.

First of all, they supply valuable information that the viewer can use to better the quality of his or her life. The act of giving this valuable information can endear the reporter to the viewer and develop positive equity between them. Because of this, and the fact that these franchises are frequently highly promotable and promoted, an effective franchise reporter's on-air research will, in all likelihood, be materially enhanced.

Additionally, health/medical and consumer reporters often do "set" pieces and have set debriefings, with the result that these reporters get a good deal more on-set air time than other reporters. This also contributes to positive research.

Furthermore, whereas management can argue that there is no real way to equate ratings success with individual reporters' contributions, not so, with good franchise reporters. Ratings jumps and positive research can definitely be tied to an effective franchise reporter's day-to-day appearances and contributions, respectively. Therefore, compelling franchise reporters should and do earn more money than other reporters.

Finally, supplying news and information that can better people's lives can also result in the reporter feeling good and positive about his or her work. This certainly can bolster and/or raise one's self-esteem and self-image.

Entertainment Reporting

Generally, if you aspire to be an investigative or hard-hitting general assignment reporter, you'd be best off not to expect to gain valuable experience in those areas by working for most syndicated and cable entertainment shows. Why? Because, for the

---

2 For example, I believe that the format-driven WSVN in Miami is an ideal station for talent to develop and to sharpen their live performance skills.

most part, it pays for these shows to be celebrity/guest/intervie-wee-friendly. This way, these sought-after individuals will want to make return visits to the show, and maybe even give that show an all-important "exclusive." However, if you criticize the guest and/or his or her work, or ask "off-limits" questions, you risk alienating the guest, as well as his or her publicist, manager, and/or agent. This is a no-no.

So you play ball — soft-ball.

You lob an enhancing question to the guest about his or her latest movie, TV series, or CD, and he or she hits it out of the park. However, there is nothing wrong with this, as all of the indi-viduals involved — the guest, the owner and the producer of the show, and the viewers — who expect nothing more and nothing less, are happy.

If You Leave News and Go Into Reality-Based Programming — Know the Risk

Notwithstanding the fact that news programs look more and more like shows such as *Hard Copy* and *Inside Edition*, beware that there will be stations and networks who will be reluctant to hire hosts of these shows to anchor their newscasts. Hiring prac-tices vary from employer to employer, depending upon how tabloid the show is perceived to be, and upon the degree of your involvement and visibility on the show.

Some Reasons Why Anchors Or Hosts Don't Succeed

Upon finishing the preceding section, a fortuitous event happened. As I was driving home (from where I had been writ-ing), I turned on the radio to hear the host of a sports show dis-cussing the All-Pro San Francisco 49ers quarterback, Steve Young. That host said that Young, during the early part of his career, had spent two horrible years at Tampa Bay before coming to the 49ers. The host then observed that, as bad as Tampa Bay's *system* and *situation* were for Young, that's how great San Francisco's team has been for him.

This reality is analogous to one so often found in broad-casting. There is no question that the most talented broadcasters can have the world's worst ratings and incredible lack of success if they are not used correctly, not promoted, have horrible lead-ins, or have management who just don't see it or get it when it comes to them. Conversely, I have seen people hit incredible strides and enjoy wonderful successes when they are put in the right places with the right people and have the right programming in front of and/or behind them. Witness Katie Couric, who allegedly was once told that she was not good enough to anchor (in a big market). It is amazing how someone can be so unsuccessful in one situation and be a superstar in another. Or vice-versa. This is a broadcasting reality.

If you are not presented by your station in your best light . . . you may not be successful.

If your station is poorly rated for any reason . . . you may not be successful.

If the lead-in programming to your newscast is poor . . . you may not be successful.

If your station doesn't promote you . . . you may not show up in the research as well as possible, and you may be perceived by your station as not being successful.

There are many, many reasons — that may be totally out of your control — as to why you may not research as well as possible; why your ratings are not as good as they might be; and why you are not deemed to be as successful as your station and/or you would have hoped. It is important to understand this.

Along the same lines, broadcasters often ask whether they can use the fact that they have good ratings at one station as a reason why a different station in another market should hire them. Generally, prospective employers will not be significantly influenced by one's past ratings success — especially if the success is achieved in another market — for the following reasons:

1) Just because one is successful in one market doesn't mean that one's success will necessarily translate to another market.

2) One's ratings success can be attributed to good lead-in programming or being at an already successful station.

3) Ratings success can be attributed to factors other than one's anchoring, hosting, or reporting presence and impact.

News Tip: It is important for all anchors, hosts, and reporters to understand that there is a confluence of factors that lead to ratings success or non-success. You may be a truly great anchor and/or reporter, but, except in extraordinary circumstances, the exceptional talent of one person cannot significantly change a station's ratings.

The Importance Of Choosing A Position For The Right Reason

Discerning What You Really Want

If you want to know what lies deep inside,
You must drop your defenses and no longer hide,
And become the most effective sleuth,
By searching your heart and discerning the truth.
Don't take a job 'cause you think it's expected,
As your emotional well-being can be negatively affected.
Don't aspire to positions just because they're in fashion.
Make your heart sing! And follow your passion.
Seize a career that will make you happy and proud,
Make the most of your life, don't play for the crowd.
'Cause in life there are few greater sins
Than ignoring the dreams you've repressed deep within.

— K.L.

Primary Versus Secondary Reasons

Throughout my career as a talent representative, I have found that individuals all too frequently make dissatisfying career decisions because they are driven by "secondary" reasons, as opposed to "primary" ones. In order to define "primary" versus "secondary" reasons, let us, for a moment, examine some reasons why some individuals whom I know or I've heard about apparently got married. For example, one of my friends confided that the only reason why she married her first spouse years ago was that it allowed her to move out of her uncomfortable home environment at the young age of 17. Three years later she was divorced. Others have shared the fact that they wound up getting married upon completion of college or graduate school because they had "always planned it that way;" because their friends were married by that time; or because that's the way their parents had done it. I remember being told, years ago, about a woman who was so intent on getting married during the month of her college graduation, that when her fiancé broke off the engagement in late April, she met another guy and quickly became engaged to him. She allegedly sent out an amendment to the original wedding invitation, substituting the current flame's name for the original one. (However, it was a bit embarrassing when she and her printer forgot to delete the original fiancé's parent's names from the revised invitation.) So, except for the new groom, everything about the ceremony remained the same. Same day. Same time. Same temple. The facile change of grooms certainly made for some spicy conversations in the pews — but not for a lasting marriage. I was told that this woman and her husband were divorced soon thereafter.

I believe that I could compellingly argue that a marriage to either of the guys (the starter or the pinch hitter) was a means toward meeting the woman's pre-determined marriage schedule — which was the real "end" of her marriage (figuratively and literally). I would label wanting to get married to somebody — just anybody — on a predetermined date or at a set time, as a *secondary reason* for the marriage. Entering into a marriage for the *primary* reasons that she truly loved and respected her partner and that she wanted to spend the rest of her life with him never entered into the picture. If your sole reasons for marriage are wanting to move out of your house, wanting to do what your parents or friends have done, and/or wanting to please your parents, then these, too, are secondary reasons.

Another example. I would argue from all that I have heard and read that one is more likely to be an effective, loving, and joyful parent for the primary reason that one truly wants to have a baby and is emotionally ready to do so. However, if your reason for having a child is to keep up with the child productivity of your friends or your parents, to please your parents, or as a way to try to solidify an already shaky or bad marriage, these are secondary reasons and arguably not the best ones to become a parent.

When one engages in behavior, for reasons other than one's true love of, or passion, excitement, etc., for the behavior or process itself, but does so because of the "secondary" by-product derived or desired (i.e., pleasing one's parents, doing what one thinks is socially acceptable, patching up one's marriage, etc.), one does so for a secondary reason.

An example of someone making a professional decision based upon a secondary reason involved a friend who took a job (against my counsel) as a field reporter in a particular city, because she had heard that the city was beautiful, and that it had lots of single men. The problem was that the new position's job description didn't include any regular or fill-in anchoring. Up to that point in her accomplished career, my friend had been a very successful news anchor and loved anchoring. From the moment that she started at the new job, she worked as a reporter about 14 hours a day, six days a week. After about three months, she called to tell me that she was miserable at work. She was feeling that she shouldn't have taken a job that she wasn't truly excited about, as a way to possibly meet Mr. Right or to enjoy a skyline. Because of her heavy schedule, she barely had any time to do either. When she did have some time, she was either too unhappy or too tired to enjoy either. She concluded that she should have taken or declined the job based solely upon the primary consideration of whether this was the *right* job for her.

Eventually, the newscaster extricated herself from her station contract, and she is now happily anchoring in another city.

She has a steady boyfriend whom she's crazy about, and I've sent her posters of skylines of beautiful cities.

Another instance of an individual making a decision based on secondary reasons occurred in college, when I became friends with someone I'll call "Scott." On three separate occasions, Scott had to skip class because he had been throwing up or hyperventilating. After the third instance, I invited him out for dinner to see if I could help. I learned that Scott, who had one of the highest grade point averages in school, had been accepted into law school. However, he dreaded going, as he had no interest in studying or practicing law. The reality was that he originally chose pre-law as his major, as a response to the intense, life-long pressure heaped on him by his mother to become a lawyer. She would accept nothing less. This unhealthy situation was compounded by the great amount of attention that he received from the undergraduate co-eds who either knew or were told (by him) that he was pre-law and at the top of his class. Scott loved the attention that he received and the exalted position that he was accorded by being one of Harvard's strongest candidates to be accepted into Harvard and Yale law schools. The big problem was that Scott pursued law for the secondary reasons of placating his mother and attracting women (who themselves, were interested in Scott for their own secondary reasons — his degree, his status, and his future earning potential.)

As a result of Scott making the decision to pursue law for secondary reasons, he hated his life and he became physically ill. With time and further conversations, Scott decided to defer his admission to law school, and eventually he declined the opportunity for all time. Instead, he pursued his passion — painting. He is happy and much healthier, both physically and emotionally. Scott has also found a mate who appears to be with him for the primary reason that she loves him, and not because she loves being with a would-be lawyer or a famous painter.

One of my heroes is my former college roommate. While in his early 30s, he quit his position as a comptroller of a major national company to become a high school teacher, and to help his very accomplished wife raise their three terrific daughters. He teaches because he loves it. He is also the world's most loving father. He and his wife are best friends. He entered into all of these relationships for primary reasons. And except for the weekends, when he spends too much time playing tennis with me, he and his wife get along wonderfully. He has been true to himself and to those around him. He appears to be at peace and happy.

Earlier, I discussed the concept of finding positions that will enhance you. This practice involves honestly knowing what your strengths and non-strengths are and trying to ascertain as correctly as possible, what positions, with which employers, will afford you the best opportunity to grow.

This chapter is devoted to honestly discerning what positions will make you happy and excited to go to work each day. My dad is now ninety-two years old and he travels all over the world as a marketing coordinator and negotiator for T.J. Maxx and Marshalls. In the past twenty-one years, he hasn't missed one day of work. Part of his longevity and success is attributable to his extraordinary genetic constitution; part to the disciplined way in which he has exercised and valued his physical well-being through the years; and a big part, according to him, to the fact that he loves his job and he's good at what he does.

In deciding what positions to accept and remain in, don't forget about the values of passion and happiness. Working for the networks, or anchoring in a large city, may not be for everyone. For example, I have plenty of clients who have at one time or another said to me that they don't like the 150-200 days of traveling that they do for their network. They long for a geographically stable, good paying local anchor or reporting job. Many also miss the daily reporting "fix" that local news provides, that you may not get at a network, when you're one of two or three correspondents in a bureau.

Just remember, it's nice to receive kudos when you get to the network or you land a big market job, but the applause dies quickly thereafter. Then you're left with your good or bad decision. You only live once and you spend a great many of your waking hours working. Don't play for the crowd or for others' validation. At the end of the day, do what makes *you* happy and what *you're* passionate about. If you do this, I am willing to bet that you'll enjoy your work a lot more, you'll be a great deal more effective at what you do, and you'll be physically and emotionally healthier.

News Tip: Everyone who aspires to achieve their life goals generally has to perform some tasks that they may not like doing. This comes with the territory. However, when and if we make significant life-goal decisions based upon secondary instead of primary reasons, we usually don't enjoy the goal attainment process much, if at all, and the ultimate pay-off is more times than not hollow. Whereas, when individuals pursue activities for true primary reasons, these individuals tend to feel congruent and in harmony with their heartfelt passions, values, and beliefs; they usually have more fulfilling and satisfying experiences; and they are much more likely to achieve good and gratifying results.

Don't Leave Your Job Until You've Secured An Enhancing Position To Go To

With all of the changes that take place in broadcasting, clients often end up at places which are no longer as desirable or as enhancing as they once were.

When someone first hires you, they're excited about you, they believe you're *the* answer — or are *an* answer — to their problems — and they look to use you as much as possible. However, when management, research, goals, or perceptions change and you're no longer coveted, loved, at the top of management's list, etc., these changes can not only profoundly affect you professionally, but they can also affect you emotionally. When you work for someone who doesn't see your talent, doesn't believe in you, or doesn't treat you well, you can lose self-esteem and confidence. It's like being in a bad or abusive relationship. You can begin to think everything is your fault and that you're not much good at anything or to anyone.

For these and other reasons, you may want to move on to new and healthier venues. One rule that I usually share with my clients is: If possible, don't leave your present position until you've got another one to go to.

I say this for a number of reasons. First of all, when you're out of work and looking, you're almost always on the defensive. People ask, "What happened?" and "Why didn't it work out?" as if the departure from your job was your fault. Additionally, financially, you can lose some or a great deal of leverage regarding your next contract, as employers often feel you now need a job. Additionally, if you've had any real discord or problems at your last station that you would rather a prospective employer not hear about, then I'd definitely stay at your current position until you've found another one. I recommend this, because a prospective employer, in all likelihood, won't consult with your current management about you, while you're still at that station; however, they will ask questions of your last employer, if you've left. My advice: Keep your friends close, and keep working for your potential enemies and detractors until you've secured your next job.

However, there are times when your self-esteem is so low, when you're so unhappy and feel so underutilized and unwanted, that you just don't want to endure any more anguish and humiliation. In this instance, it may well be professionally and emotionally healthier to leave. However, this is a last resort. But you can take comfort in the fact that, because changes do take place in broadcasting so often, prospective employers will understand that you had to leave a non-enhancing or destructive environment, and will hire you. We've all been there, and we all know what it's like to work for people who don't value you. You may not have all the leverage in the world if you leave before securing another position, but in the long run, leaving a bad situation may be the healthiest alternative.

At the Beginning —
Less is Often More

Pushing The Envelope

Years ago, as a beginning agent, I acquired the representation of a sportscaster who was very opinionated, animated, and often pushed the presentation envelope too far, too soon. The problem was, he kept getting great positions, and then losing them because he polarized and alienated a significant portion of the audience so early on in his tenure, that his #3 stations' employers felt that they had to terminate their relationship with him. Even though they liked what he did, they felt that the early negative response was so overwhelming, that it was either irreversible or that it would take way too long to reverse.

Upon acquiring this sportscaster's representation, a general manager at a top-rated station, in a large market, expressed interest in hiring my client, but on one condition: That my client ease into the market slowly, by not pushing himself on the viewers until they were more comfortable with him. My client accepted his offer, and, in time, this strategy proved to be absolutely correct.

I am a big proponent of the idea that at the beginning of your tenure at a station, let people get to feel comfortable with you before you start pushing the envelope. This situation is analogous to that of being a guest in someone's home, in that you must show sensitivity and respect as a guest until you and your host achieve a positive comfort level. Then, certain appropriate liberties can be taken by the guest.

Similarly, once you reach a positive comfort level and you develop equity and a rapport with the viewers, you then can slowly begin to push the performance envelope and stretch. Often, with the right choreography and sensitivity, the stretch and transition will be seamless and warmly accepted.

Publicity

During my career, I have seen instances where a person was preceded with such hype and publicity that they were doomed from the start, or as one network executive expressed it, the newcomer was "dead on arrival."

My suggestion is to keep the pre-arrival and early publicity to a minimum — especially, if you're just coming into a market and the individuals at whom the publicity is aimed don't know you or haven't seen you before. This is wise, because you haven't yet developed any equity with them. Here are some other reasons why early publicity should be shunned or kept to the barest minimum:

> 1) Very high or impossible expectations to fulfill the hype will be set — and the pressure upon you to meet those expectations will be great. Additionally, you will be quickly branded a failure if you don't meet those expectations.
>
> 2) It is not unusual that people in-house will resent you, if your arrival is preceded with a lot of publicity. You don't want your colleagues looking for you — or helping you — to fail. Most of them won't need any additional incentive to resent you, other than the darkness of their own insecurities.
>
> 3) I have found that many individuals do not hit their performance stride at a new position until between six and eighteen months after they have assumed it. Therefore, if you get too much press at the beginning, you will be under the microscope and expected to be at your best, at a time when it is least likely that you will deliver.

"Equity" Expanded

Earlier, I discussed how by starting out slowly and not pushing the envelope too far, you can develop a comfort level and an equity with individuals. And, as these trust levels are established, you can then more safely venture out and take some risks. Here's another example of this dynamic:

A nationally-known client wanted to do a new and different kind of talk show. This program would be a good deal more intelligent than most, and would have an unorthodox format. In speaking with one of the most successful programming individuals in TV, he said that, "The way that you (my client) accomplish what you want, is by doing a more conventional show, with more conventional topics at the beginning. Give people what they're used to and comfortable with. Then, as time goes on, subtly begin to make some changes and slip in some of the more cerebral topics that you want to do."[A] My client responded that she wanted to do some of the self-help and new age topics that Oprah had discussed on her show. My wise friend responded, "It's taken Oprah over ten years to become *Oprah*."[B] Meaning that originally Oprah did many of the same interviews that others did; and as she developed a large and loyal following, she could then experiment with and interject more and more non-conventional topics and interviews into her show. It took time and the evolution of viewer equity to do this seamlessly. On the other hand, if you begin a show way out of the box, you may well turn off so many viewers, that you may never recover from your bad start.

Said another way: When you take fewer risks at the beginning, this behavior is more likely to allow you to successfully do what you would like to later on.

Another instance where this theory applies are the components of an anchor's or a host's appearance — especially women's hairstyles. There have been times when some women have worn their hair three or four different ways during the first couple of weeks that they're on the air in a new position. When it comes to hair, clothes, makeup, etc., dress and look the part of an anchor, journalist, or host at the beginning. Let your audience become comfortable with you. And once you develop equity with them, then begin to experiment.

One last thought. When making demo tapes for prospective employers or consultants, once again, dress and look the part. That is, look like what anchors, hosts and reporters are supposed to look like. The reason is that your tape may be put into focus group testing, where a group of individuals are asked to watch your tape and say whether they find you trustworthy, credible, likable, etc. Since these respondents will in all likelihood have never seen you before, you've developed no equity with them. I believe that you'll have your best shot of securing high marks with these new viewers, by looking and acting as they expect anchors, hosts and reporters to look. In other words, immediately tap into what they've grown comfortable with.

News Tip: At the beginning of a broadcasting relationship, develop a comfort and trust level with the audience, before you experiment or push the envelope very far.

Understanding the Pressures
That News Managers Are Under

Some things in life are inevitable. Change, death, and taxes are inevitable. If you're a news director or news manager, changing jobs every two years or so also appears to be inevitable, unless you're Marty Haag, who's been at WFAA for more than twenty years.

For the most part, news managers have little or no job security. They also get much of the blame when ratings are poor, and little credit, fanfare and financial reward when a news operation is successful. If things aren't going well, and the anchors are under long-term contracts, in many instances, it is the news director who gets fired or is asked to resign to pursue "other interests." If a general manager is in trouble, before he or she gets nailed, he or she can often buy a bit more time by blowing-out the news director. It's a broadcasting reality.

Essentially, news directors are relatively easy to fire. They usually don't have contracts and they're not in a union. And unlike talent, who are on the station's air regularly and assumably have established some viewer recognition and rapport, news directors are relatively anonymous. They just disappear into the night.

I am often amazed as to the large number of duties that a news director must assume and handle effectively. For example, many news managers may well be responsible for daily news coverage, breaking news coverage, overall news philosophy, sweeps strategies, sets, music, selecting and hiring on-air and off-air talent, negotiating deals and reviewing their contracts, managing a news operation, answering to and communicating with station owners, general managers, station managers, talent and their representatives, being involved with union negotiations, and working with promotions and sales departments, etc.

When you combine these awesome responsibilities with the intense ratings pressures that are heaped on to news managers each ratings period, it is understandable why many news managers are often only able to be reactive — rather than proactive and preemptive — when running a newsroom and solving newsroom problems.

Self-help book authors have in various ways written that each of us "write" certain scripts of behavior that we act out in order to navigate through the often stormy waters of life. Some of our scripts are healthy, constructive and appropriate. Others are defensive and destructive to ourselves and to others. Some scripts of behavior may have been appropriate once, or in a specific situation, but they may no longer be appropriate in the situation that one currently faces. The problem is that we often don't have the ability, the security, the confidence and the objectivity to step away from tried and sometimes true scripts, in order to discern if they are still appropriate, effective and constructive ways of thinking and acting.

As news managers change positions, they often bring the same old scripts and ratings enhancing formulas with them from job to job — even if the markets, audiences, and operations are different. The reality is that ratings pressures to produce are immediately put on to these managers. As a result, they (correctly) feel that they have no time, leeway, or support to step back, calmly and intelligently study the new terrain, and make appropriate adjustments to their scripts and formulas. They certainly don't have time to patiently put things in place and then let them grow through the years. In broadcasting, it's quickly produce, or you'll be cut loose.

So, for example, if news managers have a script of always blowing-up a station or a production and then bringing in all of their own new people, they often won't (and can't) take the time to re-examine this script, as to whether a massive round of on-air dismissals is appropriate in the situation at hand. They'll just routinely follow their past behavior. That's all there's time for.

News Tip: There is an intense pressure to produce positive results quickly that is placed upon most general managers and program executives by their bosses. This pressure is thereafter placed onto the shoulders of news managers. It is this pressure, along with unrealistic ratings expectations, that may well be major obstacles to news managers performing at their highest levels, for their employer, for themselves, and for you.

Remember, when trying to understand your news manager's behavior, realize that he or she, in all likelihood, has less job security than you have, is overextended as a result of all of his or her managerial responsibilities, and has at least as much pressure to perform as you do.

It's not fair to him or her, or to you. However, it is a broadcasting reality.

The Compromise in Broadcast Journalism and the Value of Emotional Intelligence

Unfortunately, I am no longer surprised (but I'm still profoundly disappointed) by the large number of individuals who reach decisions which allow them to settle for too little, to opt for the easy way out, and to be destructive to themselves as well as to others. In my opinion, one of the foremost reasons why some broadcast journalists rise above the crowd and achieve their most cherished goals is that they are not only intellectually intelligent, but they are emotionally intelligent as well.

Some attributes that seem to be characteristic of emotionally intelligent individuals are the qualities of zeal and appropriate persistence, along with the ability to exercise *self-control.* Generally, these individuals know how to motivate themselves and to correctly read and understand the actions and emotions of others.[A] They are inclined to see people, things, and events in the insightful perspective of the big picture, and thereafter act constructively and appropriately with that big picture in mind.

Often, broadcast journalists — like most individuals in our society — view their daily career actions and decisions in terms of "me": How does "x" act or event affect *me?* What's best for *me?* How do I increase *my* visibility and thereby enhance *my* career?, etc. I understand the many compelling reasons for talent feeling that they always need to protect themselves and their work product, however, I am of the opinion that the more that you can work in concert with, are sensitive to, and are considerate of the needs and goals of others, the more likely it is that you will achieve your full potential.

Emotionally intelligent people know how and when it is appropriate to protect and enhance themselves. They also understand that for real success to be achieved, everyone and everything involved with their work product must shine. Witness the wonderful chemistry, the excellent production, and the insightful topicality of NBC's *Today* show. Everything works.

A requisite for success in broadcasting is emotional intelligence, especially when making and implementing your decisions, be they large or small. Here are some illustrations.

Less Than Stellar Colleagues

One issue that all broadcast journalists must understand and be ready to face is that mediocrity is a reality in broadcasting, as it is in every other field, profession, and industry. Unfortunately, it seems to be woven into the American fabric.

Much mediocre and destructive behavior can usually be traced back to how individuals were raised, their earlier (non-positive) experiences, and the destructive and counterproductive defensive scripts that they have adopted and acted out over time. Of course, there are myriad other reasons why people don't strive to give their maximum efforts in all that they do, or why their work may not be of the highest caliber.

One reason for the average or less-than-average work effort of some individuals, may be the end effect of unions. Years ago, unions were a wonderful sword that was used to carve out certain rules and regulations, so that workers were treated fairly, even-handedly, and humanely — all worthy goals then and now. However, it is arguable that some individuals[1] currently use union

---

1 But by no means all, or even many.

memberships as a shield; that is, as a means by which to get by with delivering minimum work efforts — or less — knowing that their jobs will be protected by their unions.

For example, one day a client called me, nearly apoplectic. He was on his way to cover a huge breaking story for his network-owned station in a top market, when his photographer informed him that he (the photographer) unequivocally had to stop for his union-guaranteed lunch break. The one-hour delay caused the reporter and his station irreparable damage in the ultra-competitive climate of covering this story. The reporter's comment to me was, "I know that I just arrived here from Sacramento, but our smaller market [non-union] photographers never would have pulled this. They were our teammates in beating the competition. This guy [his photographer] couldn't care less; he's just collecting his paycheck."

I am not against what unions stand for, nor do I want to imply that many union members don't come to work hard every day, but near-complete security in the hands of non-proactive, less-than-excited individuals can — and in many instances does — produce less than top-grade results.

Additionally, with the vast proliferation of news, business, sports, and reality-based channels, newscasts, and programs, the pool of available quality writers — who can write, spell, and know what Bosnia is and where it is, and why the word "alleged" must be used in certain circumstances — is all but empty. Similarly, competent and experienced producers, directors, photographers, etc., are also hard to come by. And that's assuming management is willing to pay for quality! Often, the case is just the opposite — especially for non-Monday-through-Friday evening newscasts, such as weekend evenings, weekend mornings, and noon newscasts. In many instances, management wants to hire cheap; which translates into hiring young, inexperienced individuals who have to learn — by the seat of their pants — on the job.

The bigger-than-life problem for talent is that it's your face that's on the air and it is you who are reading the material written on shows produced and/or directed by these novices — however well-intentioned they may be.

I am endlessly amazed by how many stations and production companies can pay so much money for on-air talent, for new sets, for research, etc. — and have so much riding on their on-air individuals — yet, countless times, these managers don't protect and enhance their talent.

So, quite often, talent winds up being angry with poor writing, producing, directing, lighting, editing, or shooting, and they angrily criticize the shoddy work — sometimes publicly. The writer or producer at whom the anger and criticism are leveled feels demeaned, embarrassed, and angry at being taken to task by a highly paid prima donna. And you (the talent) become labeled as "difficult," a pain in the ass to work with, or worse — especially if you're a woman.

On the one hand, you must protect your biggest assets — your on-air performance, your reputation, and your credibility. On the other hand, you can't let someone else's low standards or inexperience make you react in ways that are counterproductive for you and can diminish your reputation. For example, all too frequently, poor behind-the-scenes work can lead talent to publicly treat off-air people without respect or sensitivity. This is not only poor and non-constructive behavior, but it is not going to encourage the criticized and demeaned person to support the talent thereafter.

The goal here is to act with a lot more forethought and emotional intelligence. As suggested earlier, I believe that you catch more flies with honey than with vinegar. That is, you will probably get the best efforts out of people when you treat them with respect. Sit down with them and clearly explain what you do and don't want from them. Also, from time to time, try to compliment them on the things that they've done well and explain why you were or are pleased. Take an honest interest in their well-being and in their growth. Off-air individuals who respect and like the people with whom they work can be great and enhancing allies, and can spread the good word about you. They are often proud to be associated with a high quality talent, who is also a thoughtful and considerate human being.

Conversely, if your relationships with off-air individuals are negative and vitriolic, these individuals can unintentionally or intentionally make you look bad. Additionally, they can label you as a bad-show citizen or worse. Therefore, having a positive relationship with those you work with deserves your attention, focus, and best efforts.

However, if after trying to work things out with the staff member in issue, you are unsuccessful at improving the situation, then it is absolutely appropriate and necessary to discreetly go to your management and discuss the problem and an appropriate and enhancing solution with them.

The Squeaky Wheel

With news managers and producers as ratings-driven and as busy as they customarily are, it's no wonder that they don't have the time to be (intimately) familiar with, or to summarily remedy a bad situation in which you are involved. This reality is coupled with the fact that most individuals in our society deal in reactive, crisis management, and often never think in terms of being proactive or preemptive. Therefore, squeaky wheels often do get managers' attention, whereas, good show citizens are often overlooked, since they are not problems. In my experience, I have found that certain squeaky wheels, in many circumstances, do get the grease. Sometimes, they get (much) more grease than their talents and work merit. Thus, when there is a real problem which you can't resolve, or you have an appropriate issue to discuss, don't be reticent about approaching management. But be sure that you have all of the facts and that you're right — or, at least have a firm basis to stand on. Because, if you complain too often, and you're not correct in your facts or your perception, you will lose credibility with management and you're less likely to get what you're looking for in the future.

I also believe that, in many instances, squeaky wheels do get more and better assignments, because they keep themselves on managers' minds.

However, there is a point on the spectrum when the squeaky wheel becomes truly difficult, and then that individual can fall into the undesirable "life's too short" category.

The "Life's Too Short" Label

When a talent becomes too much of an internal problem or complains too frequently to management, he or she can run the risk of being branded with the "life's too short" label. This can occur when no matter what the positive benefits are from having a talent at the station or on a show, these benefits don't outweigh the internal poison that the talent has created.

Although being perceived as a problem by management is never a good thing, you may well not get fired because of this — if your ratings are good. However, if you are deemed expendable, then watch out! Additionally, where you may well get hurt, if you are labeled a major troublemaker or a pain in the ass, is when prospective employers hear about how poorly you are perceived by current and past employers and colleagues. And, if there are candidates for a position who, on paper, are equally as talented as you are, management may opt to not get involved with a malcontent, because "life's too short"!

* * * * * * * * * *

The key is to make emotionally intelligent decisions — that is, to have the insight and the discipline to know what is the appropriate, constructive, and enhancing behavior to engage in given the unsatisfactory situation. It is so very important to know which battles are worth fighting and how to make win/win situations of the battles that you do choose to wage.

Your career and reputation are precious . . . act accordingly, appropriately, and considerately. Doing this will pay great career and self-esteem dividends.

News Tip: There are many people that you will work with who don't strive to do their best. This can detract from your performance and from the on-air product in which you're involved. Do your best to remedy problems through constructive and enhancing means.

There is a time to be a squeaky wheel, and a time to lay back and not be a problem. Be as sensitive as possible to what is the most appropriate behavior for you to engage in given the specific situation.

Less Than Stellar Talent

Earlier, I discussed Stephen Brill's article, "Pressgate," in which he alleges that a number of well-respected reporters did a poor job of sourcing, checking the accuracy of, and balancing their President Clinton/Monica Lewinsky reports.[B] In essence, he also contends that the values and standards of these reporters and their employers should have been higher. In that same chapter, I identify various other instances, in which broadcast journalists allegedly made up stories and/or allegedly had serious ethical and technical lapses in their reporting. One thesis of that chapter is that the intense competition to secure the get and to enjoy the sweet fruits of success caused reporters (and others) to materially lower their values and standards.

Recently, there has been much discussion about the role — or lack thereof — that Pulitzer Prize winning reporter Peter Arnett played in the retracted CNN story, "Operation Tailwind." It was reported that the senior producer of CNN's *NewsStand* resigned because of this story, and that the story's two producers were fired.[C] However, Arnett received *just* a reprimand. Apparently, one reason why CNN treated him differently lies in the fact that Arnett claims that he was no more than a "script reader," who relied totally upon the reporting of the two fired producers. Interestingly, Arnett shared the byline on the *Time* magazine story about "Operation Tailwind" with one of those two fired producers.[D]

The implication of all this is that Arnett was apparently happy to take and to share the credit for this seemingly great get, but he failed to, or for one reason or another couldn't, do his correspondent homework for it. The fact that Arnett was billed as the reporter for the piece, but was in reality just a front for it — or, as they say, just a talking head — is an embarrassment to CNN and to broadcast journalism in general. However, "Operation Tailwind" is by no means an isolated instance of this kind of misleading presentation. For various reasons, such as time and logistical constraints, ratings pressures, desires to promote key talent, and talent non-interest, fronting the work of others frequently takes place in broadcast journalism. It's not done everywhere or by everyone — but it is done.

Maybe, the bigger issue is: What does all this mean? To me, it means that many broadcast journalists are willingly or reluctantly compromising their standards by fronting work on which they have not reported. It means that talent and their roles as working journalists are often manufactured and hyped, but have little or no basis in reality. It means — as I've said earlier — that reporters are often far more interested in achieving the ends that we covet — the ratings, the Emmy, the money — than they are in adhering to principled means to achieve those ends. It appears that they're frequently more excited about attaining the quick fix than they are in delaying gratification, by taking the time to do their homework accurately and thoroughly, so that they are fortified with the real goods — having all the facts and a thorough understanding of their stories.^E It means that because they don't engage in or truly value the research, writing, and reporting process, they derive little, if any, meaningful ownership of their work and very little job satisfaction. And it means that every time a reporter presents a story researched and crafted by someone else, he or she plays Russian Roulette with his or her career. Just ask Peter Arnett.

To be sure, this compromise of journalistic ethics and techniques is of great consequence and is of critical importance.

As a result of the national attention being given to broadcast journalism during this low period, there has been a great deal written by individuals who are aghast that stories such as "Operation Tailwind" can be aired and that someone such as Peter Arnett could have done absolutely no research or writing for "his" report. For me, the issue isn't whether there is or is not mediocrity and compromise in broadcast journalism today; there definitely is some, and possibly, a good amount of it. Rather, the pressing issue is how broadcast journalists can rise or remain (as the case may be) above it.

One way to keep your standards high and protect yourself is to be emotionally intelligent and meticulously disciplined regarding your career decisions. First of all, maintain a passion and zeal for — and take pride in — what you do. Ideally, you will take as much pride and ownership, and derive at least as much pleasure in researching and writing a piece, as you do in presenting it. As I wrote in the chapter discussing primary and secondary reasons, if you don't relish the process, in all likelihood the pleasure and satisfaction that you derive from your work will be minimal, at best.

Your career and reputation are precious. Whenever possible, do your own work, so that you truly know and understand what you're reporting and what you're putting your name and reputation on. There is no question that, with all of the newscasts and newsmagazine shows being produced today there are indeed time and logistical pressures, that may cause your management and/or your executive producer to opt for you to play little or no role in the development of your piece. If at all feasible, in an appropriate and constructive manner, find a way to do your own work. The good news is that after the CNN/Peter Arnett embarrassment, management and producers should be much more sensitive to your desire.

Be forewarned: Do not make Peter Arnett's mistake. The damage to your credibility, reputation, and career could be irreparable. And remember, networks and programs, in most instances, survive these debacles; you may not.

Finally, take note that current network stars such as Katie Couric, Elizabeth Vargas, Brian Williams, Scott Pelley, Giselle Fernandez, Ann Curry, Deborah Roberts, (and of course, Tom Brokaw, Dan Rather, and Peter Jennings) all have their roots in reporting. It was out in the field that they learned about, experienced, and reported on real-life issues, problems, tragedies, and celebrations. It was this experience, in part, that has given them the depth, the breadth, the scope, and the compassion to be successful in-studio interviewers and personalities.

Don't compromise your career potential by opting to front pieces and just sit behind the anchor desk. As the aforementioned individuals chose to do, become a master of your craft, by gaining your experience, your insights, and your stripes by researching, writing, and reporting in the field. It will pay great long-term dividends.

Mediocrity Today

As this book is going to print, the NBC network has just

announced that it is planning to cut (an estimated 200-300) jobs in order to save money. During the past few weeks, I have been told by various NBC station general managers and news directors that salaries, raises, and expenses — such as moving and travel — will be cut, as well.

This announcement followed those made by CBS and ABC that they, too, will be seeking to sharply cut news costs. It has been written that the CBS network's goal is to reduce its annual expenses by $180 million — with the bulk of the layoffs coming from its News Division. It is also rumored that CBS and CNN are considering merging their news divisions, which would allegedly save CBS between $100 million and $200 million.[F]

When discussing this broadcasting reality, a high-ranking network executive said that what he's seeing at his network and the network owned stations is a three-step process:

1) First, the network has gotten rid of all of its "C" players (the mediocrity);

2) Now, the network (unfortunately) must layoff a number of its valued "B" players; and

3) Thereafter, there will be "compression"; that is, the network will then squeeze more out of those who remain.

ABC News president, David Westin, reiterated this perspective in a recent article discussing his goals of paring down his news budget and boosting news division profits.

> As to headcount, Westin says he has no internal goals concerning reductions and that corporate executives have not ordered personnel cuts. But there have been departures and, he adds, "I expect there will be further departures. We have to be looking at our people all the time, and, for better or worse, grading them. We don't have room for C's. We do have room for A's. And if they're B's, it's a question of can we make them into A's or not."

It sounds harsh, and Westin says it's "not a pleasant part of management. But that's what the organization expects. We need to convey that we know what excellence is, and we'll reward excellence." If, on the other hand, you're an ABC News staffer who 'is not doing a great job,' you ought to be nervous."

The message: Being mediocre today won't cut it. In this tough economic climate, there are two etched-in-stone realities:
1) You've got to be consistently on the top of your game; and
2) You will be asked to give significantly more of yourself than you have in the past.

* * * * * * * * *

Mr. Keating in *Dead Poets Society* says the following to his students, in an effort to compel them to make the very most of themselves, by seizing each and every moment of their lives:

> Gather ye rosebuds while ye may,
> 'Cause we are food for worms, lads.
>
> Gather ye rosebuds while ye may,
> Old time is still a-flying.
>
> And this same flower that smiles today,
> Tomorrow will be dying.
>
> Make your lives extraordinary.[G]

There's something very satisfying and rewarding about doing whatever you attempt to the very best of your ability — win or lose. There are (still) many wonderful opportunities and values inherent in broadcast journalism. Make the most of your opportunities to make a true, positive difference. Don't be mediocre.

> "I'd rather aim for a star, and end up a bit short,
> Than aim for mediocrity and attain it."
>
> Betty Lindner
> (My Mom)

News Tip: Don't settle or compromise your work or your career. Personally make every report and interview with which you're associated extraordinary.

These are the constructive, the enhancing, and the intellectually and emotionally intelligent things to do.

IV. The Psychology of Securing Effective Representation and Advantageous Contacts

Leverage

Leverage exists when your employer believes
That if the deal's no good you will leave.
Leverage doesn't, in fact, have to be real
For you to get a really good deal.
But it's great when you can back up the talk,
That if you're not happy, you will walk!

— K.L.

Whenever I open an airline magazine and I see Dr. Chester Karrass' advertisement for his negotiation seminars and tapes, I am always struck by his quotation:

> "In business you don't get what you deserve,
> You get what you negotiate."[A]

When it comes to broadcasting, in almost all instances, I agree with Dr. Karrass.

Whether or not a talent can negotiate a fair, good, or great deal, almost always depends upon whether that talent has the leverage to do so. Leverage is comprised of (at least) four elements:

• How much an employer or a prospective employer wants to retain your services or to acquire them, respectively. (This is

usually the most important element.)
• What the employer perceives your marketability or your ability to walk away from the deal is.
• How much you want or need the deal.
• If you are willing to — or actually do — walk away from the employer's final offer.

Here are four illustrations of the impact that leverage had upon my negotiations.

1) A few years ago, I was negotiating a deal for a well-established "franchise" reporter in a top market. The news director with whom I was negotiating told me that his station would absolutely not pay more than a 5 percent annual increase over the reporter's $150,000 salary,[1] for a new three-year contract. When I told him that I wanted in the mid-$200,000 range as a starting point for my client, and that I thought that I could get an offer of about $250,000 at a competing station in the market, he responded by saying, "Kenny, if he can get that kind of an offer, he should take it. But we're not going to pay more than a 5 percent raise. That's it!"

Two days later, I received a three-year offer of $240,000, $250,000 and $260,000 for my client to work at a competing station. An offer that my client would have been more than happy to accept if his current employer didn't appropriately respond. With leverage and confidence in hand, I called the news director at my client's current station, to advise him that my client had decided to decline his offer of a 5 percent raise. No hard feelings. The news director (obviously shaken) nervously said that I shouldn't do anything until he called me back. Within ten minutes, I received a call from the station's general manager, who said, in as friendly a manner as possible:

"Kenny, my goal in running this station, is to have as many (on-air) employees as possible receiving 3-5 percent raises."

I replied, as cavalierly as possible, "We know that, so

---

1 The negotiation began with the news director offering a 3 percent raise.

we're not pushing you to pay any more. My client will just turn in his resig——"

"BUT," he interrupted, "there are times when we have to and need to keep someone, and we'll do what it takes. You've forced us to pay the (perceived) market price. Let's get this one over with. We'll pay your client $260,000, $275,000, and $300,000 for a three-year, no-cut (firm) deal."

Because we had leverage, my client received an average of over $100,000 per year more than what the news director told me his final offer was.

Isn't leverage great?!

2) Another client of mine was offered an anchor position by a prominent network. However, this client was already a successful and well-paid anchor in her local market, where she was happy to stay. Twice she turned down the network's generous offer. However, after the second offer was declined, she decided that she would accept the position, if the network would agree to the almost nowhere-to-be-found clause of: "If my client was unhappy for any reason, she could terminate the contract and work for someone else." Upon asking the network negotiator for the clause, he responded that he could *never* give that clause. "No how, no way." I took his reply back to my client, who was happy to forget the whole thing.

However, two weeks later, the network once again offered her the position, along with an increased compensation package. My client once again said, "No — but thank you."

The next day, the negotiator called and said (in a tone of half-resignation and half-admiration for my client being able to get the network to give in): "Okay. Your client can leave at anytime — except during a ratings period — with sixty days notice, and one caveat: She can't terminate to go to another network."

Because of the leverage derived from my client's (repeated) willingness to walk away from the network's offer, she was able to secure a truly extraordinary deal.

Leverage is beautiful!!

3) There is a middle-market station at which I have done a great deal of business through the years. Because of the

high quality of both the station and my clients' work, I have been able to take three or four of their on-air people to wonderful and prominent positions. Additionally, because of my track record, and because of how talented and marketable this station perceived a particular client of mine to be, a year-and-a-half into a three-year agreement, the general manager called me up and said, "Kenny, I know you're gonna move your client if we don't sign her now (to a new deal), so let's just double her salary and cut through the bulls—t."

I called my client, who had every intention of staying at her station for the foreseeable future — as long as she had the right contract. After hearing the offer, she told me to get whatever else I could, and then accept it. A little later, I called the general manager, appropriately improved the deal, and then closed it. My client was ecstatic.

In this instance, my perceived ability to effectively market my client and her perceived marketability gave us leverage — in spite of the fact that not one prospective employer had even been approached (so early in her contract).

I do love leverage!!

4) A client of mine, who was at a network-owned station in market "A," made her wishes known that she really would like and, in fact, needed to be transferred across the country to a station, owned by the same network, in market "B." The market "B" station was willing to find a spot for her, but they could basically "take her or leave her."

When it came to her moving expenses, they stayed firm at $2,500, to move all of her belongings cross-country. When she secured three moving estimates, the lowest one came in at $3,500. When I learned that my client would have to go out-of-pocket to move to her desired station, I called to reason with the news director of station "B" in hopes that he would authorize the payment of all of her moving expenses. Here's how the conversation went. I began (with some tongue-in-cheek sarcasm), "My client just got three moving estimates, and the lowest one is $1,000 more than your extraordinarily generous offer of $2,500. So why don't you cover her total expenses (of $3,500), we'll call it a day, and you can feel good about yourself on your deathbed?"

"Nope. $2,500. That's it."

I responded, in my most humane tone, "But Steve, three months ago, you gave me a $35,000 as a moving allowance for my other client to move from his home two hours away. Be fair!"

He replied, with what he perceived as perfect logic, "We really wanted your other client, and by giving him all that money for moving, he was able to put more in his pocket, because we couldn't pay him all that you asked for in his salary. In this client's case, she wants to move here; and so as far as we're concerned, we're happy to have her, but we'll live if we don't. The 'deathbed stuff' was a good effort, but sorry, $2,500."

Leverage sucks!

News Tip: Moral of the story: *You* want the leverage.

Contract Renegotiation Time

They coveted me when I was hired,
Made me feel like I was truly desired,
But now that my contract's almost expired,
They tell me I'm lucky that I'm not fired.

They were great in the courtship, but not in the marriage,
There were compliments early, but now they disparage.
I was once their prize, but now I'm slime,
I'm not surprised, it's renegotiation time.

All of a sudden, there is so much that I lack,
And I'm under a constant barrage of attack.
I must say I'm truly taken aback,
As up until now I've had *no* feedback.

So we'll have a lunch and a little chat,
In their effort to keep my salary flat.
I'm so tired of hearing, "We must hold the line,"
While station profits continue to climb.

Last time my news director told me to delay gratification,
That "I'd get him back," *next* renegotiation,
And I'd be in the "driver's seat" and "in my prime,"
"Just wait 'til the next negotiation time!"
But now my news director's been replaced,
And all of his promises have been erased.
And I feel that it's a bloody crime,
That I blew it *last* renegotiation time.

So, from the depth of my heart and soul I vow,
I'm gonna get *all* I can, and get it *now!*
I'll get a no-cut deal and every last dime,
And *not* feel screwed this negotiation time.

Yes, I'll even the score with my station,
'Cause this renegotiation, I'll have *representation*!

— K.L.

Representation

I am a talent representative. Therefore, in writing this chapter, I will try to be as objective as possible. However, it is important to understand that I have had a unique set of personal experiences that strongly influence my thought processes and my perspectives on this subject.

Here are some key concepts that you might want to consider when attempting to choose the most effective representative for yourself.

Understanding

It is of great import for a representative to understand the broadcasting business and its inner workings. Your representative should understand the impact of the choices with which you are presented, as well as what kinds of opportunities need to be created specifically for you. In essence, your rep should either know or have access to the information that will allow you to make informed and wise career decisions for the short and long terms. Here's an example.

The Story Of The Ice Skating Boot Vs. The Rollerblading Boot

The following is a story about a client of mine who now reports for a national show. I first met her as a result of a San Francisco news director's glowing recommendation. She was an intern-writer at his station. To this day, her intern demo tape is one of the three best tapes of its type that I have received in my fifteen years of agenting.

Besides having a great tape, this individual is very smart and has a great natural ease with the camera.

Within weeks of getting her representation, she secured an overnight position in Sacramento as a writer and overnight cut-in anchor. She was soon promoted to a full-time reporter, whereupon she signed a two-year agreement with her station. During the next year or so, I critiqued three or four of her tapes; and, although she was growing quickly, I felt that she hadn't yet hit the stride that I believed that she, in short order, would attain. So I held off sending any of her tapes out.

Then one Sunday afternoon, about sixteen months into her two-year Sacramento contract, I screened her newest tape, and I was blown away by how comfortable and compelling her storytelling had become, by the way she engaged me, and by the way she filled the screen. She was unquestionably on her way to being great.

Upon finishing her tape, I immediately called her to share my excitement. I was now ready to introduce her to the top-ten-market broadcasting world.

For the remainder of the afternoon and early evening, I re-edited her tape, so that I had a great montage of her stand-ups at the beginning, followed by her best live and packaged reports. This way, the viewer, within ten minutes, would see the wide range of my client's reporting skills.

Monday morning I called general managers and news directors in the top markets and alerted them that a tape of a potentially great talent was on its way to them. By the end of a week or so, I had heard from a number of stations in New York, Los Angeles, Chicago, as well as from one station in Miami and one station in Dallas, all wanting to fly my client in for an interview.

After doing some extensive interviewing, my client felt that one station in Los Angeles, two stations in Chicago, and one station in Miami should be left in the running. She then asked my opinion as to which station she should choose.

I believe that my thinking and advice proved to be correct, and for instructive purposes, they are repeated here.

First: Although my client was receiving interest and

offers from top stations in top markets, what station executives saw on my client's demo tape was the great potential of a smart, extraordinarily talented woman, who was half-Latina. However, as my client's advisor, I had to remain absolutely aware that my client had only been on-air for about sixteen months. And although her tape was good enough to make a deal with Blockbuster Video, she still had a great amount to learn. Therefore, I didn't want to push her too quickly and thereby jeopardize her future growth.

Second: The four stations that were interested in hiring my client were all network-owned and reputable. However, the station in Los Angeles and one of the stations in Chicago had one thing in common: I felt that both stations in the past had been great in the courtship of some young up-and-coming broadcasters, but didn't follow through with any real nurturing or support in the marriage. Therefore, a number of their younger, less experienced recruits fell by the wayside and they either never evolved into the talents that they might have been with more support, or they suffered major setbacks from which they had to eventually recover. As a result, I would rule these stations out, no matter how well-intentioned and enthusiastic these suitors were.

Third: This left the station in Miami and the other station in Chicago. Now the choice became really tough, as Miami and Chicago are great news towns. The station in Miami had a brand new General Manager, whom I consider to be one of the very brightest, most evolved, and most humane mentors that I have met in all of broadcasting. He is a true inspiration and my dear friend. My client immediately concurred with my raves about this individual, after a dinner with him and his accomplished wife. However, there were some problems regarding the Miami station. First, no news director was there, as the previous one had left and no replacement had been hired. Additionally, the station was in turmoil, and needed a complete overhaul — which would take place during the ensuing months. On the other hand, the station in Chicago, was dominant number one, with a wonderful on and off-air staff that had been there for years. Continuity and high ratings reigned at the Chicago station.

Fourth: After recounting all of this, I then gave my client my answer and my reasoning.

My recommendation to my client was that she go to the

Chicago station, notwithstanding the brilliance of my general manager friend in Miami and his more than obvious strong commitment to my client's growth.

I explained to my client, that at another time, when a news director was in place, when all of the anchors and producers were hired, and the station was more settled, Miami might be the better growth venue for her — but not now. Besides, one executive producer whom she met in Miami said that he could see my client immediately doing the big story at 11 P.M. each night in order to increase ratings. This scared me, as I felt that ratings success should not be put on the shoulders of someone who had been on the air for such a short time.

Conversely, the Chicago station had many seasoned veterans and didn't need any great new flashes to improve ratings or increase viewership. Their agreement — which they fulfilled in every way — was to bring my client along slowly, but surely.

I then asked my client to picture an ice skating boot. Generally, it is made of soft leather, with one characteristic being that, if you move the wrong way or your ankles are weak, you can turn an ankle and sustain an injury. There's very little support.

In contrast, a rollerblading boot is strong and keeps your foot firmly in place, so there is little chance of turning your ankle, even if it is weak. I then analogized the current state of the Miami station to an ice skating boot, in that there would be little support or day-to-day nurturing for her at the then-troubled station. Whereas, the Chicago station, with its rock solid internal news operation, would give my still-green client all of the support and protection that she would need as she began to compete in the highly competitive news market of Chicago.

My client agreed with my advice, and she accepted the Chicago station offer. Within months, she was excelling as a reporter, and within a year-and-a-half she began anchoring. Soon thereafter, she secured a regular anchor position there. Step, by calculated step, she grew.

The moral of the story is that when deciding on what your early moves should be don't be seduced by quick fixes. Keep the big picture of your career in mind. Make sure that you go to stations or programs that will give you the support and nurturing that is truly appropriate for your stage of development. Early flashes and subsequent crashes aren't pretty. Don't go too fast, too soon. You should have a representative that has the knowledge and the wisdom to help you to choose your moves wisely. And remember, rollerblading boots are great until your ankles and your skill level are ready for softer, more supple ice skating boots.

The Short- and Long-Range View

I believe that the best representative for a given person needs to have in mind the long-range view of that person's career as well as his or her long-term relationship with that person. For example, an agent must be willing to counsel a client to take a lesser-paying position, because it is in the best interest of the client long-term, even if the agent must forego a larger commission. Similarly, agents often get kudos for having clients who make big market or much-publicized moves. The agent must be able to put the career of the client ahead of what may bring the agent more positive publicity. If, for example, a client would be best served having an additional local market experience before accepting a network position, the agent should put the client's long-term best interests ahead of the agent's (and the client's) desire for immediate — but inappropriate — gratification and applause.

On the one hand, I could argue that already successful and well-respected firms would be less likely to (need to) compromise a client's career for their own good. However, at the end of the day, I believe it all comes down to the agent's character and whether the agent in issue has a true long-term commitment to the client.

Marketing

If you have aspirations of moving up in market size, going to a syndicated program, or working for the network, it is optimal to find a representative who has a successful track record for marketing talent in those specific areas. Additionally, with aggressive marketing, ideally, you will have numerous employers interested in you, which will enable you to have the all-important asset of leverage when you and your representative negotiate your deal.

It is obviously of the utmost importance for an agent to understand what makes you special when marketing you to others. For example, here is a story that had a great conclusion, because I knew what made my client unique.

Years ago, we took on the representation of a prospective client — not from a demo tape, as was our practice — but as a result of a commercial picture, a stellar résumé, and a wonderful in-person meeting. It was at that meeting that the extraordinary sparkle and humanity in that prospective client's eyes mirrored those qualities found in her head shot. Her very impressive background included graduating Phi Beta Kappa from a fine university, being an All American college basketball player, winning the Miss U.S.A. Junior Miss title, and possessing a thorough knowledge of basketball and other sports. She also appeared to have great character and strong values.

Two of the goals of this talented woman were to become a major network sports broadcaster and to have a prominent role on a program such as *Entertainment Tonight*.

Within a few weeks of our association, an on-air position at *Movie Time*[1] opened up. She tested for it and got it. From that position, our client got some daily on-air experience and a demo tape with which to market her.

Months later, a major sports opportunity opened up for a woman at a network. We were told that the prerequisites for the job were breakthrough talent, and prior local, cable, and/or network sports experience. Notwithstanding the requirements of a prior sports broadcasting background, we submitted our client's tape. The network's response was: "She's got the talent, but how can we hire someone with no sports broadcasting experience for this job? Thanks, but no thanks."

The orthodox route of submitting our client's tape didn't work. It was time for an *out-of-the-box* approach. I took

---

1 *Movie Time* was the forerunner of *E! Entertainment Television.*

a day or so to think things through. My associate, Babette Perry, and I knew that our client had a thorough knowledge of sports. She just needed the opportunity to show it to the appropriate individuals. Unfortunately, the person who would ultimately make the decision didn't think that a meeting with our client would be worthwhile. This was coupled with the fact that he was someone with whom we had no prior history or working relationship. But we decided to try our plan anyway.

I called the network executive and identified all of the people whom our company had brought to his and to other networks and syndicators. I did this in hopes that this would establish my credibility. Before I finished giving my full list, he acknowledged my eye for spotting breakthrough talent. I then said that we were positive that, if he were to have a one-on-one meeting with our client (who was based in Los Angeles — he was in New York), she would win him over with her sports knowledge. I would bet my credibility and my future relationship with him on it. I then offered to send him a first class, round-trip ticket to Los Angeles, if he would sit down and have a meal with her. If he didn't hire her, I'd paid for his ticket; if he did like her, I'd be reimbursed.

I could tell by his reaction that I'd gotten him to seriously acknowledge my strong belief in our client. The unorthodox nature and novelty of the approach worked. He said that "I can't accept your proposal, although I do like the effort. But, here's what we *can* do. I'm going to be in Phoenix next week. How about having your client fly down and meet me there?"

I instantly accepted the offer on behalf of our client, and once again reinforced my client's thorough sports knowledge. The next week they met. Three days later, she was offered the job.

Two factors played major roles here: One was that we *knew* our client and her abilities well, and we understood that if she met the network executive in person she'd dazzle him; and two, we needed to step back, get another perspective, and find a more unorthodox and creative approach that would shake up the unfavorable status quo. In this instance, we found it.

Representing Your Values and Goals

It is of equally great importance for your agent to understand you, your values, and your goals. It is up to you and your agent to initiate conversations regarding what your goals and values are, and how they change over time. It is important to be aware that as people grow and have different experiences, their expectations and goals may well be modified.

By understanding who you are, your representative is better equipped to correctly and effectively represent who you are to others. Clients often say that being represented, in some instances, is a passive position, because someone else is out there marketing and speaking for you. You will be a lot better off and you should feel more secure, if you know that your representative understands and is able to effectively articulate who you are and what you aspire to achieve.

Achieving The Desired Outcome

Once again, if a representative *understands* you, and what you want to achieve in the short- and long-terms, you and your agent will have a much better chance of achieving a desirable outcome.

Access and Track Record

It is of the utmost importance that the representative that you choose has access to information about openings that currently, or will in the future, exist, and about what kinds of positions can be created for you. To do this, your representative needs access to the news managers and program executives who will potentially hire you. Additionally, there are specific agents who have a reputation for having a keen eye for identifying and representing top talent. Therefore, in many instances, these representatives' (client) demo tapes will be looked at before others — which, of course, can be a distinct advantage for their clients.

There are also certain representatives who have developed long-standing positive relationships with many news directors, and network and/or program executives.[2] As a result, these representatives may be contacted to submit candidates for a position well before an opening becomes public, because a news manager or executive may quickly want to see who's out there, without conducting a more public search. Therefore, some positions can be filled without some representatives even being aware that a need existed and that a discreet search took place.

On the other hand, news directors, recruiters, and program executives will generally look at all tapes that come in, and it doesn't matter who reps you and what that person's relationship is with the prospective employer. If the talent is good and a deal can be made, you'll get hired. As it's generally the bottom line that counts, people will deal with the devil if they feel that they can hire someone who'll increase ratings. And if they won't deal with the devil, they'll get their assistant to make the deal.

The Concept of the "General Practitioner" vs. the "Specialist"

Currently, there is a proliferation of news agents in broadcasting. Why? I guess that it seems like fun; it looks easy — it appears lucrative — and you need no special training or educa-

---

2. Long-standing relationships with employers can make a great deal of difference in at least two instances. First, knowing how to negotiate with someone can pay great dividends for a client, because the representative knows how far he or she can push the envelope with a manager with whom they're familiar, as well as what attractive things are attainable for a client, and what is the best means to attain them.

Second, having a positive working relationship with management can be of great help, for example, when a client needs to be released from an employment contract. A number of times I have been able to extricate someone from his or her personal services contract (without any ugliness or bad feelings), because I have a good working relationship with a manager and/or his or her company. For example, I remember one client who had signed a five-year renewal of her network contract, and during the first year of that agreement a career-making opportunity with another employer became available to her. Partly because of how positively the network felt about my client, and partly because of my longtime positive relationship with that executive, he let her out of her contract so that she could accept the position.

A representative's long and/or positive course of dealing with a particular broadcast manager can absolutely work to a client's advantage.

tion to do it. Anyone, yes, anyone, can become an agent. I am truly amazed that broadcasters, whose profession it is to research stories and to search out the truth, so often do so little — or no — research on an agent's background, experience, track record, and his or her access to information and to prospective employers. It is incredible how many beginning and not-so-inexperienced broadcasters just sign with the first agent who calls them because they were flattered or because they felt that it was the right time.

You know why bad things happen to good broadcasters? One reason is: They don't do their homework when it comes to themselves and what's best for them.

When someone is beginning a career, many reputable agents can help you find "a job." Fewer representatives, however, understand the concept and practice of *choreographing* an individual's career. It's analogous to the difference between someone bowling and someone playing chess. There are a lot of bowlers out there. You roll the ball, and you (hopefully) hit the pins. Great! Similarly, if you are a bowler-agent, you send tapes out; you see what hits; and your clients take a job. Task done. However, there are few master chess players out there. These are representatives who, in concert with you, devise a step-by-step strategy and a big picture game plan in which career move after career move is well thought out and made with a specific goal and with the big picture of your unique abilities and heartfelt aspirations clearly in mind.

Arguably, early on, bowlers are fine. However, as you begin to grow, a more sophisticated and advanced career manager may be more appropriate.

Additionally, if you aspire to go to the network or to a syndicated show, there are just a few agents who do most of the business with those venues, who know both the ropes and the key players, and who have the access to the critical information which can materially enhance your career.

In essence, at a certain point, you may want to seek the help of a specialist, and not a generalist, to choreograph your broadcasting career. This is analogous to seeking medical help. If you have a cold, the flu, or even something a bit more serious, you may (initially) seek and may well be perfectly fine with the help of a general practitioner. However, if you have something more acute, you may well be best served to enlist the help of a *specialist*, someone who has a proven track record and is an expert in the field. In essence, one agent may not fit all. Do your homework regarding people's track records for accomplishing what it is that you aspire to do. If an individual has been successful at a task many times before, you may well increase your chances of attaining your most cherished goals by seriously considering that person to represent you.

However, all of the most well-respected and successful representatives had to start somewhere. It wasn't until my clients grew, and they stayed with me, that I gained day-to-day access to top network executives, syndicators and top-market news managers. I understood my clients, and they trusted my instincts — even if I did initially lack experience. And, we've all grown.

Martina Hingis, Boris Becker, Steffi Graff, and Chris Evert didn't have a major tournament track record until they had the chance to play on the center court of the U.S. Open or Wimbledon — and when they did, they rose to the occasion and eventually became champions.

If you're talented and you trust your agent and his or her instincts, you can grow together. Your talent, your agent's understanding of you, and your agent's hard work and thoughtfulness regarding you and your career can equal great success. (Nevertheless, experience in the specific field does help.)

In selecting which individual will be the most effective representative for you, carefully weigh all of the pros and cons.

Understanding Revisited

It is key for your representative to truly understand what makes you special and what your strengths and your non-strengths are. This is so for at least three reasons. First, in putting together a demo tape for you that shows the very best of what you can offer to an employer, your representative must know what you do well and must make sure that your very best work is presented on that tape. Many people have said that I have a keen eye for spotting talent. Part and parcel of this perception is my ability to transcribe what makes someone special on tape, so that their demo tape stands out above the rest.

It is also important for your representative to understand what a particular prospective employer looks for in a tape. This can indeed vary from recruiter to recruiter; so, sometimes tapes need to be tailor-made, depending upon the tastes of the specific recipient or the requirements of the position to be filled. In essence, the representative does target marketing. If a representative knows a recruiter's preferences and dislikes, this kind of marketing can, in many instances, materially increase an applicant's chances of securing a desired position. This is an instance in which years of experience and being familiar with the key recruiters can tangibly help a client. However, if someone puts a tape together that most people feel is great, experience with recruiters can mean nothing. I would say that knowing what makes a client special is more important than knowing what a particular recruiter wants. However, having recruiter familiarity is certainly an added advantage.

Finally, it is crucial for a representative to understand what makes you special, when he or she has to counsel you regarding what the most enhancing (next) position is for you to take. Every talent is different. And different positions can impact different individuals in different ways. An effective representative must understand how a particular position can help or hurt a particular client, depending upon a client's strengths and non-strengths, when taken in the context of the person's stage of development and goals.

Contract Sophistication

Once again, having a representative who understands your goals and values should help him or her negotiate the most appropriate and enhancing contract for you. This contract should reflect and effect your short and long-term goals and values. As we discussed above, having a representative with some experience, or at least access to what is attainable in a particular contract and with a particular employer, obviously can be very helpful in this endeavor.

Don't Coast; Make the Most

It is also of great importance that whomever you choose as your representative continues to help you to keep growing, by continuing to critique your work and to search out and create new enhancing opportunities with your current employer, or other employers for whom your employer would allow you to render services.

Here's an example of my being able to enhance and expand my client's present and future career opportunities with his current employer.

Years ago, my company secured the representation of a very talented individual who was between jobs. After a stint as a reporter and then host for a nationally syndicated program, we helped him to secure a host position of a network entertainment program. About two-and-a-half years into his network contract, the O.J. Simpson criminal trial was about to begin. After a couple of conversations with my client, I called my client's employer to suggest that my client anchor the network's live coverage of the O.J. trial from Los Angeles. To the best of my recollection, here's what took place.

I opened my call by saying that it appeared that the trial might well be the entertainment and news story of the decade, and that if the network's main anchor didn't want to anchor all of the trial coverage from LA, that my client would love a chance to fill in.

I went on to say that because the O.J. Simpson case was a huge entertainment story, my client would be the natural person to be involved in the coverage, as he hosted the network's entertainment show of record. I then respectfully explained that there may be some aspects about my client's background that some executives and other individuals at the network might not be aware of.

I began, "For example, did you know that my client was a practicing California attorney before he began his on-air career?"

The executive responded, "I didn't know that."

I continued, "Did you know that my client's first job in TV was as a legal reporter for KABC?"

Once again, the response was, "I didn't know that, either."

Now, on a roll, I inquired, "And did you know that my client anchored the Monday through Friday morning newscasts at KCBS?"

He quickly shot back, "I knew that one! We love his anchoring."

Ready to ask for the order, I said, "So, because this is the entertainment *and* the legal story of the decade, I really believe that my client is uniquely qualified to have the opportunity to anchor some of your O.J. (trial) coverage."

The executive said that my timing could not have been better, and that he had just met with his main anchor, who had chosen not to come to LA — at all — to anchor the O.J. coverage. As a result, my client would be given a two-week tryout. After one week, we were advised that my client would anchor the O.J. coverage indefinitely. As it turned out, he anchored the coverage throughout the trial. He thereafter was asked to fill in on other network news (instead of entertainment) programs. Because of this assignment, my client's persona had been modified and enhanced — big time — for the better.

My client now anchors Monday-Friday evening newscasts for his network as well as his entertainment program. With the national exposure that he has received for his anchoring and live interviewing (at which he is excellent), coupled with the warmth and personality that he displays on his entertainment program, my client is poised to host and to anchor many other national shows in the future.

Knowing your client and seizing and creating appropriate additional opportunities can enhance your client immeasurably, and forever.

The Psychology of Contracts

One of the keys to enjoying a successful career in broadcasting is to secure contracts which reflect and effect your most important values and goals. Therefore, before you enter into any contract, it is of the utmost importance for you to identify and to list your priorities. Then, depending upon what stage you're at in your career, and what you need and want to accomplish, you will want a number of contract clauses to be written into your contracts in very specific ways.

In connection with almost all middle and major market news and reality-based programming positions, a contract will be signed between the talent and the employer. In about 99 percent of these instances, the employer — or an outside law firm — will write that contract. It will contain numerous clauses which will protect the employer's monetary investment in the employee, minimize its downside monetary risk as much as possible, and give the employer maximum flexibility in connection with the employee's duties, days-off, schedule, and job security, while at the same time limiting and circumscribing as tightly as possible the employee's rights and options in all areas.

For example, just the other day, a client was offered an agreement with a station which provided for a firm four-year commitment by the talent; however, the station could terminate the agreement at anytime with sixty days notice. When I asked the news director what his rationale is for such a one-sided contract, he responded that, "The station is taking a big risk in bringing new people to the station, and it (the station) needs to protect itself, if things don't work out." I replied, "What about the person who is uprooting her family to accept your position? Doesn't she deserve at least a couple of years to prove herself? And what if things at the station aren't to her liking? Why should she be stuck there for four years? Also, how can you rationally argue that your station's interests are more important than this person's career and family stability? Shouldn't there be equal rights in this contract?" (I knew what his answer would be.)

"Maybe," he replied, "but it won't happen here [at this station]. And besides, Kenny, I don't even have a contract; at least your client gets some protection. I can be blown out tomorrow."

Another example. An anchor at station "Y" had been successfully anchoring there for over ten years. She recently was offered a new five-year contract which called for her to commit for five years firm to the station, but the station had the right to terminate the agreement — without cause — after eighteen months and thirty-six months, successively. In this case, the station knew exactly who they were hiring and they loved her work; yet, she still didn't merit equal rights under her new contract.

"Why?" she asked management.

Management responded, " 'Cause we don't give no-cut contracts."

"But why not?" she asked.

The reply: " 'Cause we don't."

Throughout my career, I've asked employers how they could justify their unfair contracts, as, in most instances, there is no logical rationale or humane justification for them. These employers often reply, "Hey, that's the way it is;" or "That's the way it's always been." Okay! That makes sense . . . right?!

A more exact answer would be, "It's because we [the employers] can get away with it." However, as we discussed earlier, with leverage, sometimes things can (almost) even out.

One more true story. Years ago, an anchor in a small-to-middle-sized market entered into a five-year agreement with her station. Her salary was approximately $37,000 for the first year, $39,000 for the second, $43,000 for the third, $48,000 for the fourth, and $53,000 for the fifth year. The station could terminate her employment at regular intervals, but she was tied to the station for the full five years. This anchor, whom I did not represent until years later, was a true superstar talent, with a horrible — but all too common — one-sided contract. During the second year of that contract, a major network offered her the position to anchor/host its weekday (Monday-Friday) morning program, for a salary between $400,000 and $500,000 a year. Her station wouldn't let her accept the position, and threatened to sue the network for inducing a breach of contract if the network had any more conversations with her. The network, who didn't want others stealing its people, quickly withdrew its offer to this anchor. The conclusion was: The anchor had to stay at the station for three-and-a-half more years under her original contract. And, with timing as critical as it usually is, she was never again offered a position of that magnitude at the network.

To quote a 1970s hit song:

> "It's sad to belong to someone else when the right one comes along."

The moral of the story: Because this anchor didn't have any termination or out-clause for a network or for a top market position, she couldn't accept this career-making offer. Contrary to what lawyers and others say — "Contracts are not made or written to be broken" — they're made to be enforced. And because employers don't want *their* employees to be hired away by other employers while under *their* contracts, they will almost always back away from offering a position, if a newscaster is under someone else's contract. Not because they feel it is morally or ethically wrong, but because they don't want to be hit with a tampering suit, and because, if they steal from others and get away from it, others can, in turn, do it to them. It's the implied law of the broadcasting jungle.

Therefore, the important point to remember here is: At the end of the day, broadcasters often live or die with their contracts. So it is of profound importance to understand them and the provisions that comprise them.

Term

The *term* is the length of the contract. However, keep in mind that there will be a number of provisions in a contract by which the employer can end the contract before the full term of the contract has expired. For example, an employer can usually terminate the agreement, "for cause." Cause for termination is usually triggered if the employee is insubordinate, refuses an assignment, refuses to show up to work as scheduled, breaches the contract in some way, cannot perform services for a stipulated amount of time ("incapacity"), commits a "morals infraction," etc. In most contracts, the employer can also terminate the agreement without cause — that is, for any reason at all — at certain intervals in the contract (i.e., every thirteen or twenty-six weeks or each year).

The thing to remember is that if you don't plan to stay at a station or in a market for a long time, get as short a contract as possible. If the employer can terminate you without cause on a regular basis, get as short a contract as possible, because, in essence, you have no real security anyway. If you take a position for a comparatively low salary, get a short contract, so in success, you can negotiate a new, more lucrative contract sooner. However, if you plan to stay in the market for a long time, if you are able to secure a lucrative, no-cut deal for yourself, and if long-term security is of great value to you, then, under these circumstances, a long-term deal may well be appropriate. However, I have learned that in success you will make more money by signing a series of shorter agreements, than by signing a long agreement and getting (small) percentage raises each year (which most stations are mandated to give).[1]

It is also important to do your best to secure various termination provisions for yourself, so that you can end the term of a contract when there is a better opportunity for you to take. These

---

1 However, there are many variables that one must take into account before passing up a good long-term, secure deal, which provides for an enhancing position in a desirable market.

provisions will be discussed below.

Regarding the term of a contract, keep in mind that an employer will be reluctant to let an on-air employee end his or her contract during its early stages, as it takes time for an employer to recoup its investment in the talent. Letting someone who the viewers like terminate a contract early can diminish or hurt the on-air product, and result in a loss of ratings and revenues for the employer. So, it is important for talent to understand and to acknowledge that stations and programmers have a real and legitimate interest in keeping continuity of talent on the air.

Cycles

These are intervals during the term of a contract when the employer can terminate the agreement without cause — for any reason — or for no reason — at all.

During the term of a contract, ideally you would like the contract to be firm; that is, without cycles. However, in most cases, there will be cycles. The talent's goal is to have as few of them, and therefore as much security as possible.

As a compromise, you would like to attain maximum security at the beginning of a contract, so that you have enough time to reach a comfort level, and thereby show that you are a valuable member of the broadcast team.

There are many reasons why you want to obtain the most secure contract possible. For example, when a new manager is hired, he or she often makes it a priority to learn who can and can't be terminated in the near future. It is a broadcasting reality that a new manager is more likely to get rid of the person with the cycle coming up, and stick with the person who has a good amount of guaranteed time left on their contract. This is because, as a rule, managers don't like to take people off the air, whom they'll have to pay for an extended period of time. It's cost ineffective. Therefore, those broadcast journalists who have firm (no-cut) contracts, often have a better chance of keeping their positions during news purges, as the news manager either learns to live with them or begins to appreciate them. Additionally, talent with firm contracts can wind up outlasting news managers who were not their biggest supporters.

For many reasons, try to negotiate a contract with as much security as possible.

The Program Cancellation Clause

In many instances, syndicated programs such as *Entertainment Tonight, Access Hollywood, Hard Copy,* etc. — and, to a lesser extent, network and cable programs — provide in their employment contracts that if the specific program that you've been hired to render services for is cancelled, your employment contract can be terminated by your employer, usually with no more than two weeks notice. (Please note that this provision is different than, and in addition to, the employer's right to terminate the contract *without cause* at the end of a cycle.) The thinking behind this clause is that, once a show for which you've been hired to render services no longer exists, the employer wants immediately to eliminate its obligation to continue to pay you.

Be aware that often the existence of this clause in an employment contract is not raised by the prospective employer during the negotiation process, as it frequently appears in the contract as a standard provision of the "boilerplate" terms and conditions. Therefore, it is imperative for you and/or your representative to inquire ahead of time as to whether the contract that you're negotiating contains this clause. It if does, try to delete it. Please note that although in most instances deletion is almost impossible to achieve, with leverage, there may be some negotiation and improvement.

Compensation

This is the money that you earn under a contract. In almost all instances, get as much money up front as possible. I suggest this because contracts usually do have cycles, so there's no guarantee that you'll see the big increases later on in the contract.

I have heard people say that they would rather not be paid too much money, or else stations will be more likely to fire them because of their salary. Be aware, for the most part, stations have money to spend on people who are good. Stations have no money to spend on people who aren't. So get as much as you can within reason, at the beginning of a contract, and be good!

I have been told that with a higher salary comes more and higher profile responsibilities. I believe this. If someone is paying a talent a lot of money — especially if a current manager and regime negotiated the contract in issue — they will be inclined to want to prove to their bosses that the salary is justified. Therefore, they will often put their highest-paid people in high visibility and important situations.

One thing that I have learned over the years is: When a manager says, "I can only pay you 'X' for this contract, but when you become a success, you can 'kill me', 'get me back', or 'get even' in the next contract negotiation (years later)," DO NOT BUY IT!!!! First of all, that manager, in all likelihood, won't be there when your next contract comes up, and the new manager won't care about making up for what his or her predecessor promised. Second, with the passage of time, things can change and memories can become short. My experience is that no one pays you more money in a subsequent contract to makeup for what you didn't get in an earlier one. A good rule is: Get it — or forget it.

Clothing Allowance

Many stations no longer give clothing allowances because of administrative problems, tax issues, and the fact that talent has occasionally abused the privilege by buying clothes more appropriate for personal use (imagine that!).

From my perspective, notwithstanding all of these issues, with some effective station involvement, I would think that it's in the employer's best interests to pay someone a $100,000 salary plus a $5,000 clothing allowance, rather than a salary of $105,000, because the employer gets the value and the guarantee that some amount of money will be allocated to appropriate talent dress. This would enhance the talent as well as the employer's broadcasts.

Be aware that employers who give clothing allowances, for the most part, are afraid that the talent won't pay taxes on this allowance, and that the employer will ultimately be held liable. As a result, employers are now taking taxes out of the clothing allowances up front. So, what may initially seem like a good amount of money for a clothing allowance, may well not be as meaningful after taxes. When negotiating a contract, try to get your clothing allowance "grossed up" or reimbursed to allow for taxation.

Employee's Right-Of-Termination

It is important to try to secure a right-of-termination, with as little notice as possible to your employer, so that you can extricate yourself from your contract when you are no longer being assigned to the duties that you were promised.

A number of stations won't grant this clause; however, if you are demoted, quite often an employer won't want an unhappy employee and/or the employer won't want to pay a salary to the demoted talent which is now inappropriately high for the lesser-newly-assigned position (especially in this present cost-conscious climate). Therefore, you can probably negotiate your way out of your contract (even if you don't have an out-clause) — but it will be on the employer's terms and timetable (which may not necessarily be good for you). Needless to say, if you can negotiate an unconditional termination clause in your contract when a negative change of your duties takes place, you will be in a clearer, cleaner, and better position.

Depending upon your job goals and where you aspire to work next, you may well want to provide for a right-of-termination (an out-clause) for yourself, should you receive a bona-fide offer for a position at a station in a desired larger market, on a syndicated program, or at a network. Generally, it is easier to secure this type of clause if you are working in smaller- and middle-sized markets. You are less and less likely to attain this clause once you're in a Top-10 or even a Top-15 market, or if you're a main weeknight anchor in a Top 20 market.

When negotiating this clause, try to secure a notice-of-termination of thirty or sixty days, but no longer than ninety days. Additionally, the out-clause should be unconditional, in that your current employer should not have the right to monetarily match (that is, match the money of) the offer of a station for which you can contractually leave, and thereby retain your services for the length of the matched deal.

In essence, if you have an out clause, you should be able to use it — with no ifs, ands, or buts.

The Pay-Or-Play Clause

This clause, which is in almost all broadcasting contracts, provides that an employer can fulfill its obligation to you by just paying you your guaranteed minimum salary; but you, in turn, have no right to perform any on-air or other services for the employer. In essence, employers can pay you off, but they don't have to air your work.

Unless you want a long paid vacation, not getting on the air for an extended period of time isn't going to enhance your career. Therefore, once again your best bet is to have a termination clause in your contract which provides that, if your duties negatively change, you can leave.

Moving Expenses

Many employers are now giving lump-sum moving expense checks with taxes taken out. Before agreeing to a moving allowance, make sure that you can move (with airplane fares and temporary housing included) to your new job on the *net* amount of money which you will receive.

Right-Of-First-Refusal

At the conclusion of many broadcasting contracts, there is a right-of-first-refusal or a right-of-last-refusal, which means that for a specified time before and after a contract expires, the employer that you currently work for can monetarily match an offer that you receive from another employer, and keep you there — even if you don't want to stay.

If you have a right-of-first-refusal in your contract, the first question to ask is: Does the employer's right to match an offer extend to all TV employers, or to just the specific market that you're in; or to the specific kind of show that you're doing (talk, magazine, network, syndicated and/or cable)? The employee's aim is to limit an employer's right-of-first-refusal as narrowly as possible. For example, if you work in Phoenix, the employer's right-of-first-refusal should be in connection with that market only. So, if a Phoenix-based employer wanted to hire you away from your station, your station would have the right to match the offer and thereby retain your services. However, if you want to go home to and work in Chicago, the right-of-first-refusal should not be extended to that market, and you should be free to work there after the expiration of your current Phoenix station contract.

Ideally, you would like to include in the right-of-first-refusal provision that the matching (your current) station, must not only match the offering station's monetary terms, but it must also match the position that you're being offered, as well. If you accomplish this, then if the station across the street offers you a weeknight anchor job, your current employer *cannot* match the offer and thereby retain your services (and make the defensive move of precluding you from going across the street to work), by offering to match the other station's monetary offer, along with a lesser or different position, such as weekend or noon anchoring.

Additionally, if a prospective employer offers you a firm agreement (meaning, there are no right-of-termination clauses, or "cycles," for the station), it is to your advantage to have a contract with your *current* employer which obligates them not only to match another station's monetary offer, but also the "no cycle" or "firm" component of that offer. The reason being that if you do not have this obligation in your current contract, your current employer may be obligated to match only the monetary component of the prospective employer's offer. Therefore, your current employer can arbitrarily terminate your new contract — i.e., six months or one year thereafter — depending upon your current employer's "cycle" policy, which could result in a problematic scenario. On the one hand, you've been precluded from accepting a long-term firm deal with a new employer, and on the other hand, six months or one year later, you can be fired by your current employer and there may not be any other attractive positions to go to.

Therefore, a good rule to follow is: The more specific the deal points that your current employer has to match in order to retain your services, the better.

The other component to pay attention to is the length of the first refusal. For talent, the shorter the better; for the employer, the longer the better. For example, if the right-of-first-refusal is sixty days, this means that if the talent wants to accept an offer within sixty days after the expiration of his or her contract, the talent has the obligation to bring that offer to his or her current employer, and that employer has the right to match it and thereby retain the talent's services under the terms of the matched deal.

If you don't want to give your current employer the opportunity to match the deal, and the right-of-first-refusal is sixty days, you can wait sixty-one days to accept another employer's offer — thereby letting the right-of-first-refusal expire. If you do this, you no longer have the obligation to bring the offer to your current employer, and your employer no longer has the right to match the offer.

A problem arises if you agree to an unreasonably long right-of-first-refusal — for example, one year. This period may well be too long for a station to wait for you, and too long for you to sit out with no income. Therefore, you may have no choice but to present the third-party offer to your employer and hope that the employer doesn't match it.

Obviously, an employer will want a long right-of-first-refusal, so as to preclude you from waiting it out, and thereby legally and ethically circumventing it.

One last point. Make sure that you provide that the right-of-first-refusal is only operative at the natural expiration of the contract. If the contract is terminated beforehand, without cause or due to no fault of yours, the right-of-first-refusal should not apply. This way, if your employer terminates the contract because he or she no longer values you enough, that same employer can't preclude you from going to a competitor by matching the competitor's offer. In essence, what you want to protect against is your current employer making the defensive move of keeping you away from someone, rather than making the offensive move of keeping you because he or she truly values you.

The Covenant-Not-To-Compete

> Below is some information that should make us pause,
> About an unfair, anti-competitive clause;
> That's called a covenant-not-to-compete,
> Which precludes one from working across the street,
> For a period of time that's unreasonably long,
> When one's contract is over; and that's patently wrong!
> 'Cause a free market place is supposed to envision,
> An environment based upon free competition.
> So after giving this section your perusal,
> I believe you'll conclude that a right of first-refusal,
> Is the most appropriate remedy
> For both the employer and the employee.
> And from here-on-out, we should strive to delete,
> From all talent contracts, covenants not-to-compete.
>
> — K.L.

The covenant-not-to-compete is a clause found in many broadcasting personal services contracts which provides that for a defined period of time (i.e., six months; one year, etc.), upon the expiration or termination of an employee's contract, he or she cannot appear on-air (and in some cases, work off-air) for a competitor. This competitor can be any station in the employee's local market, if the contract in issue is in local news; or it can be in syndication or cable, if the contract is for a position on a syndicated or cable program, respectively. Essentially, a covenant-not-to-compete clause allows the employer to preclude the employee from rendering on-air services to anyone the employer wants, for any period of time the employer wants, (usually one year or less), depending upon how the employer chooses to write this clause. Some covenant-not-to-compete provisions (hereinafter "covenants") go so far as to preclude employees, for a defined period of time, from rendering *any* services for a competitor (i.e., writing, producing, etc.); they may preclude them from working in other media, such as radio; and/or they may *even preclude them from just seeking future employment.* For example, a person who was let go from a station without "cause," but who would like to stay in his or her current market, would not only be prohibited from working in broadcasting in that market for a one-year period, but he or she couldn't even *seek* employment there until *after* the one-year covenant has elapsed.

Does it seem *fair* and *equitable* for a general assignment reporter who was let go from a station (after one year of employment there), because that station didn't care for his or her work, to be precluded from working and seeking employment in the market of his or her choice for one year? *I don't believe so!*

As far as I'm concerned, depending upon how a covenant-not-to-compete is drafted, it can be one of the most *unfair, inequitable* and *inhumane* clauses found in any broadcasting personal services contract.

The test that courts have used in the past for the legality and enforceability of covenants, is whether they are *fair* or *overbroad* both in their *reach* (whether they are overly restrictive and thereby preclude too much), and in their *duration* (whether they last too long). Recently, an Albany Supreme Court Justice enjoined (stopped) an Albany television station (WTEN-TV) from enforcing a covenant-not-to-compete in its market. In that case, *Nigra v. Young Broadcasting of Albany, Inc.,* Justice Hughes, in his opinion, reasoned that "Once the term of an employment agreement has expired, the general public policy favoring robust and uninhibited competition should not give way merely because an employer wishes to insulate itself from competition from a former employee." Additionally, on August 7, 1998, the Massachusetts Senate and House of Representatives signed into law a bill that will prohibit that state's TV and radio stations from requiring on-air broadcasters to sign non-compete clauses. As a result, Massachusetts is the first state to ban these clauses.

My inclination is that many, many broadcasting *covenants* would be struck down by courts as *overbroad* both in reach and in duration. The problem, however, is that talent almost never want to incur the great expense of bringing a suit against a company with deep pockets. They don't want to spend the time necessary to fight a suit through to its conclusion; and they're *scared to death* to incur the silent wrath of the broadcasting community by suing one of its own.

The last reason is a *big* one. On-air individuals (often rightfully) feel that if they publicly fight a broadcasting employer — even if they are *absolutely correct* in their position — other employers will brand them as a "malcontent" and/or "troublemaker," and be reluctant to hire them for fear that they may one day cause *them* problems, too. Therefore, on-air individuals, out of practicality and fear, bite the bullet and don't challenge clauses, such as covenants-not-to-compete, which preclude them from earning a living in their field for as much as one year, in a city in which they would like to make or keep their home. This is a sad broadcasting reality.

From the employer's perspective, they have made a legitimate and substantial investment monetarily, promotionally and in on-air time in the broadcast journalists that they hire. The employers argue that they will be *materially damaged* if, as soon as their contract with an employee is over, that individual works for a competitor. *Employers* feel that this would be unfair and inequitable to *them*.

I believe that there *is* merit in their argument, up to a point. But just as a punishment is supposed to (ideally) fit a crime, so too, should the breadth and scope of a covenant-not-to-compete be adjustable to *appropriately* fit the situation and the station's *real* investment in the *particular* talent. *One covenant does not fit all.*

For example, should a general assignment *reporter* who earns $45,000 annually, and is let go after one year of service, be subject to *the same* one-year covenant-not-to-compete as a main weeknight anchor who is promoted all over the place, earns $300,000 annually, just completed a five-year contract, and who is offered a new five-year contract by his or her station, beginning at $400,000 annually? Does the station in issue have the *same* monetary investment in the reporter as the anchor? Does the station have the the *same* promotion and on-air investment in both individuals? Is the station *damaged* to the same extent, if the reporter is immediately employed by a competitor, as compared with the anchor?

I would argue that there are *material* differences here, but rarely, if ever, are these differences taken into account and reflected in the way covenants are drafted.

Let's continue. What if the *reporter* mentioned above,

began his career in a market, by working for five years for station "A"? He then leaves station "A," sits out a one-year covenant-not-to-compete to join station "B" (in the same market), which then fires him one year later, because they no longer like his style of reporting. In this case, station "B" (that fired the reporter), didn't pay his moving expenses when he first came to the market; nor did it *introduce him* to the market.

I would argue that station "B" had invested *very little* in the reporter, and that its one-year covenant-not-to-compete is *unfair*, and would be held to be *illegal* by a court.

Let's consider three other scenarios:

1) Susan is a single mom anchoring the weekend newscasts at "Station X." Her station decides not to offer her a new contract at the expiration of her current one. In order to maintain custody of her son, Billy, Susan must continue living in her market and must maintain her current salary level. The general manager at Station X says that he must enforce its covenant-not-to-compete, and not allow her to seek or accept on-air employment in the market for one year. The general manager says that he feels "badly" but he can't set a precedent regarding the elimination or negotiation of the covenant. He explains that Susan has been a wonderful employee, but that her style of delivering news does not have the intensity and immediacy that his new news director wants for his anchors and reporters. As a result, Susan, whose current employer has *no* intention of retaining her services, is *precluded* from earning a living anchoring or reporting for any TV or radio employer for one year in the one place that she needs to live to retain custody of her son. And while she is allowed to secure a position as a writer or producer in her market, neither position will enhance her on-air career nor allow her to earn near the salary that is required for her to keep Billy.

2) Ted is a husband and father of three. He is a noon anchor at "Station Y," earning $75,000 per year. At the end of his contract, "Station Y" demotes Ted to a reporter and occasional fill-in anchor, and stands firm

that his salary needs to be cut to $50,000. Ted also has received serious interest regarding a 5 P.M. weeknight (Monday-Friday) anchor position, starting at $100,000 per year at a station in the same market. Ted has a six month covenant-not-to-compete during which he cannot *accept* employment in his market. The prospective employer, with the 5 P.M. anchor opening, tells Ted that the position may not be available in six months, and that Ted will take a substantial risk if he sits out for six months hoping that the position will still be available for him to accept when his covenant elapses. Ted reluctantly decides that he can't play Russian Roulette with his family's income, so he accepts the position at his current station for $50,000.

3) Ann is a weeknight anchor at "Station A" and earns $500,000 per year. Her station offers her a new three-year contract beginning at $700,000 per year. She is very popular, and both of her newscasts are rated #1 in the market. Ten days before the expiration of her contract, "Station B" offers Ann a five-year, no cut deal, starting at $1 million per year. Ann's current employer, "Station A," says that it will enforce her one-year covenant-not-to-compete. "Station B" can't wait one year for Ann, so they revoke their offer.

For most people, Ted's and Susan's cases would probably be *more compelling* illustrations of why covenants-not-to-compete need to be *more appropriately* limited and written. However, in a capitalist society, should Ann (the $500,000 per-year anchor) be precluded from attaining the true market value of her services during her prime earning years? Does this not smack of restraint of trade?

My perspective is that, in the case where someone is demoted or asked to take a pay cut, *no* covenant or a minimal covenant of no more than 30 days — *for which the employee is paid* — is appropriate. The covenant-not-to-compete should be used as a *shield* by a station to protect its investment and *continued interest* in the fair and gainful employment of an employee — *not* as a *sword*, to preclude a competitor from hiring someone whom the current employer no longer values enough or at all, and thereby, professionally and financially hurt that employee.

In the case of Ann, there is somewhat more of a meritorious argument for a covenant-not-to-compete — *to be paid for by the station* — for a maximum of 90 days. (It is also arguable that, unlike Ted and Susan, Ann has the clout and the *leverage* to negotiate the covenant-not-to-compete down to a reasonable amount of time.) However, my best solution to this problem is to follow the practice of the network-owned stations in markets such as Los Angeles. These stations have rights-of-first-refusal, but no covenants-not-to-compete. Therefore, if Ann's current station wanted to keep Ann, they would have to match "Station B's" offer and pay the market price of one million dollars per year. I would argue that, in the case of Ted, his current employer would have to match the money *and* the position in order to keep Ted.

In a situation such as Susan's, where someone isn't renewed (or is terminated without "cause") by an employer, that employer should *not* be accorded *any* form of covenant-not-to-compete or right-of-first-refusal. Once again, the right-of-first-refusal should be used as an *equitable shield*, not an *onerous sword* — so that a station can make a *defensive* hire. I would also limit the scope of any right-of-first-refusal to the market in issue *only*.

"Negotiate" vs. "Discuss"

It is of the utmost import for you to know what you can and can't do during your contract.

A number of contracts say that during the term of your contract you can't discuss future employment with a prospective employer; some say you can't negotiate with them; and many contracts say that you have to negotiate exclusively with your station until the end of your contract with them.

These provisions reflect employers' feelings that they do not want their employees discussing or negotiating future employment with other employers while their employees are still working for them. Their perspective is understandable. The employers believe that they deserve the best opportunity to try to re-sign their own employees while they are still under contract to them.

The converse of this is: How can talent know what is available to them and on what terms, if they can't discuss employment with prospective employers until their contracts have expired and they're out of work?

My recommendation to talent is to make sure that you're not precluded from discussing future employment with other potential employers during the term. It's okay to grant some period to exclusively negotiate with your employer. But during the last sixty days of your contract, ideally you should be able to seek and negotiate offers with all perspective employers, so that by the expiration of your contract, you can make an informed decision regarding what your options are. Your employer is still protected by his or her right-of-first-refusal at the expiration of your contract. This way, you have the best opportunity for ascertaining and/or receiving the fair market value of your services.

Exclusivity

This clause provides and circumscribes what, if any, services talent can render, *in addition to* the duties to be performed pursuant to their current employment contracts. In news contracts, it is rare that you are allowed to do anything outside of working for your news operation. In reality-based programming, there is generally a bit more potential for leeway.

The concept of exclusivity is that an employer is paying you a certain sum of money for your exclusive services. Therefore, employers don't want you working for competitors, for others who might do what your employer does, or in any situation that could, in any way, present you in a less than flattering light, or could diminish your energy, focus, and enthusiasm for your employer's duties, etc. In connection with news operations, employees must not be involved with anything that could compromise their objectivity to report the news. Therefore, commercials, industrials and infomercials, 99.9 percent of the time, are out.

Additionally, employers do not want talent appearing on any programs where the employers cannot control the quality or the content. For example, what happens if the outside product is shabbily produced, written, researched, shot and/or lit? All of these occurrences could dilute and/or tarnish the value of the employee, if seen by the employer's viewers. Additionally, employers want their employees energized and sharp when they render their services to them . . . not tired, because they were out earning extra money and/or working extra hours at another job.

I believe these are all legitimate concerns and values of the employer, depending upon the situation in issue.

If you appear on a network, there are other problems. The networks now own local stations, cable outlets and syndicated shows. Additionally, they have affiliates that they must please and not anger. So, for the most part, networks don't want their talent competing with them, their other stations, their programs or their affiliates. This doesn't leave much room for working for anyone else but one's own network. If you're on a syndicated show, another issue is that syndicated shows — by definition — are essentially sold station by station in each market, and air at different times of the day in different markets. Therefore, if you were to perform outside work, there is a question as to whether that work could potentially air against your own syndicated show (or vice versa). Additionally, if your proposed outside work is also syndicated, it will be almost impossible to get your management to approve it. The reason is that if your current employer is selling your show each year based upon your unique presence, your employer won't want other producers diluting its presentation and product, as a result of the other producers offering your services too.

However, there have been isolated cases and individuals who have been on network and syndicated shows at the same time, and on network or syndicated shows, along with cable. And because of leverage, the creativity of the individuals involved, and/or the unique nature of the shows in issue, there have been extraordinary instances of someone being on two competitive networks during the same contract. This happens in the rare instances where the two shows are so diverse that 1) the networks do not see it as any conflict; 2) the shows could not possibly conflict with each others' time periods, and therefore would not directly dilute the audiences for either show; and 3) both networks see some benefit from loosening their exclusivity provisions.

Your goal in most instances is to convince your employer, that allowing you to do the outside work will somehow benefit both you and your employer, or, at the very least, you and your employer will not in any way be diminished.

Incapacity

Almost every broadcasting contract contains a clause which gives the employer the right to terminate the contract, if the employee becomes unable to effectively render his or her services. For example, contracts often provide for an employer's right to terminate for incapacity if the employee loses his or her voice, becomes visibly disfigured, contracts a disease or sustains an injury that materially detracts from or limits his or her performance, etc.

The key is to make sure that an employer can't terminate you for incapacity unless you are incapacitated for a minimum amount of time; for example, for at least four or five consecutive weeks in any one contract year. Optimally, this incapacity period can be longer.

I would also argue that a station should not be able to terminate a contract for incapacity if the injury or illness sustained is a result of some work-related event.

Morals Clause

A morals clause provides that if the employee commits an act or does anything which might negatively affect or reflect poorly on the employer, or which tends to or does, in fact, offend a portion of the community, the employer can terminate the agreement.

In real life, whether or not a company will exercise this clause can depend upon the flagrancy of the offense and how important the offender is to the employer's ratings and profitability. The rule of thumb is: If you bring in ratings, employers will do all that they can to rehabilitate and to save you. If you don't, and the offense is serious, you're toast.

Indemnity Clause

In broadcasting, you often rely on writers, producers, and reporters to supply you with information. Hopefully, the material supplied to you is correct. But what if it isn't and you and the station are sued? Or, what if you report or ad-lib something which offends someone, and the next thing you know, someone files a suit against the station and names you as a co-defendant? Your best defense is to provide a clause in your contract which says that if you act in good faith and within the scope of your employment, you will be indemnified and held harmless by your employer (who should be insured) against any and all claims, suits, actions, damages, expenses, and awards — in connection with the alleged wrongdoing. This language isn't always possible to attain — but try to get it, anyway. In any case, take comfort in the fact that I have not seen an instance where an employee acted in good faith, and the employer didn't indemnify the employee for all of the employee's costs in connection with the claim or suit.

Please note that a number of the provisions that I have discussed above may not be attainable from certain employers. However, some can be secured, and you should make efforts to have them incorporated into your employment contract.

News Tip: It is your aim to secure contracts which reflect and effect your most important values and goals. Your best chance to accomplish this is to 1) know what you want in the short- and long-terms; 2) have leverage (or perceived leverage) with which to bargain with your employer; 3) have a reputable and knowledgeable professional assist you.

Remember! Employers negotiate contracts all of the time. You don't.

V. The Psychology of Breaking Into Broadcasting and Developing Your Career

The Psychology of Breaking
Into Broadcasting

Through the years, I have been asked many, many times by aspiring broadcasters, "How do I break into broadcasting? What's the best way?"

In answer to these questions, I suggest four possible routes.

Route 1 "The Initial Large Market Experience"

This route calls for you to secure a position, for instance, as an intern or as an assistant, at a high quality, large market station or news operation. And then, as time goes on, you can hopefully befriend a reporter, producer and/or photographer there from whom you can learn. Optimally, these individuals will take you out in the field so that you can get some off-air reporting experience. Hopefully, you can develop a "demo" tape of your work with which you will be able to market yourself and find your first on-air job.

Route 2 "The Initial Small Market Experience"

In this instance, you begin your development by getting an assisting, writing, producing, or assignment desk position at a (very) small market station, and then graduate into an on-air position there.

In an extraordinary situation, you may be fortunate enough to start on-air immediately — without a demo tape or prior newsroom experience. This can occur if the market in issue is small enough and/or you have good timing, because there's an opening at the station when you apply, and/or a news manager there believes in you enough to give you the opportunity.

Route 3 "The Grad School Experience"

This is where you attend a graduate school of journalism before having any real newsroom experience. From this route you can attain a good deal of theoretical knowledge; and, depending upon whether the school in issue has an affiliation with a nearby local station or whether it has its own news operation, you can also get some real-life experience and a demo tape with which to market yourself.

Route 4 "The Course Or Private Instruction Experience"

In this situation, you take a course or set of courses in broadcast journalism, given at a college or university, from which you can generate a demo tape of your work; or, you work with a private instructor or coach who will help you to develop your performance or voice skills and who has access to individuals who will help you to produce, shoot and edit a demo tape. With this tape, you can go shopping for your first job.

* * * * * * * * * *

As different individuals have different aspirations and financial and geographic constraints, etc., one particular route may not be the most appropriate or effective for everyone. Here are some perspectives.

For on-air individuals, I believe that Route 1 is an excellent means by which you can begin to lay a strong journalistic foundation. The reason: If you can spend about a year in a high quality, sophisticated news operation, you will be exposed to *how* things are done by seasoned, highly skilled broadcasters; and learn *why* they are done that way. Thereafter, when you work in smaller markets, alongside beginning broadcast journalists and inexperienced or less-experienced management, you will have in your mind's eye how things are done by the "pros." This big market experience and big picture perspective can be invaluable in helping you to more quickly develop your good news instincts, your news sensibility, and your off-air and on-air skills.

Quite often, top graduate business schools require applicants to have a minimum of two years of practical business experience before matriculation. Their perspective is that with real-life business exposure and experience under your belt, you will understand more and contribute more to classroom discussions. In essence, you'll have had enough exposure to real-world business issues to see and to appreciate the big picture of business once you're in school. I believe the same thing is true of broadcasting. By initially spending time in a high level news operation, when you thereafter go to work in smaller markets, you will have a greater understanding and a big picture perspective of what's going on there.

Additionally, having an initial large market experience will give you exposure and access to individuals from whom you can learn a great deal. Hopefully, you can cultivate a mentor or two, who will answer your questions, critique your work, and will take the time to explain things to you. Many individuals who took this route as their first real-life broadcasting experience say that it is amazing how much they learned through osmosis — that is, from just being around top professionals in a good news gathering organization. It set high standards for them to live up to throughout their careers. These individuals also believe that beginning their careers in a top market station gave them the taste and hunger to strive to make it "back there" (to the large market station) full-time, in the on-air or off-air position of their dreams. It gave them a realistic picture and a goal to shoot for.[A]

In contrast, if you start out in a small market, with no sophisticated news operation experience, you will be surrounded and taught by, and exposed to, individuals who, for the most part, are as inexperienced as you are. There will be few, if any, great off-air and on-air talents to learn from and to emulate.

When I asked top news managers for their perspectives regarding the large market route, the great majority thought it was the optimal way to begin a career. However, one news manager voiced the concern that if you start out as an intern or an assistant in a large market and you get promoted there, because of union requirements and the generally high standard of pay, you quickly earn big market wages. The problem, she says, is that, "These young kids begin to make good money, and because they (often) live at home and have few expenses, they feel flush. So they don't want to go to some small market for a third of their wages and pay their on-air dues. Seduced by the big market money, they wind up staying in the large markets, in off-air jobs, and they never go to the smaller markets to pursue their dream of being on-air."[B]

To these individuals I say, "Your career is a marathon, not a sprint. Don't sacrifice your dreams for a quick buck or a fast break."

Additionally, you should also be aware that the routes that I've outlined are not exclusive. When beginning your career, there are no hard and fast rules — just some tried and true courses. For example, you can have a Route 1 along with a Route 4 experience. That is, you can intern or work in a large market news operation along with taking broadcasting courses or private instruction. You can also intern at both a small and a large market station before seeking your first on-air position. This, in many instances, is an excellent game plan.

Route 2 for many broadcast journalists is also an effective means by which to begin your career. You lay a solid foundation by going up the ladder, learning as much as you can as a writer, assignment desk person, and/or producer, etc., before going on-air. You can make rookie mistakes and grow from them in small market news operations, where errors and inexperience are more readily accepted.

Two issues are:

1) As I discussed earlier, a number of my clients started their on-air careers in relatively large markets, because they lived or went to college there and worked themselves up to on-air positions at their large market stations. The inherent problem with this apparent success is that you don't have the chance to make your many novice mistakes in the smaller markets, where they are

more forgiveable. In larger markets, you are competing with more experienced individuals. You can't afford to make mistakes; and as a result, you are inhibited from stretching and taking risks — because with risk-taking come mistakes. Therefore, you have a much harder time finding your comfort level and your true voice. As we all know, it's hard to find the groove and your "zone" when you're always uptight. It can be done, but it's a much tougher process.

The key is: In small markets, you can experiment with your writing, packaging, delivery, etc., try things, grow, make mistakes, and re-group. This is why the small market experience is so valuable to your development. Remember: It's not how fast you initially go, but how much in the long run you ultimately grow.

2) A second concern about starting your career in too large a market or ascending market sizes too quickly is that you may not give yourself the opportunity to try your hand at and develop varied skills, such as reporting *and* anchoring. For example, if you start in a large market as a reporter, and, in time, you decide that you want to anchor there, you will have had no prior anchor experience and you will be competing with others who may have already developed their anchoring skills in two or three smaller market positions. As a result, you're completely overmatched, and you may never get to (learn to) anchor (in a safe and nurturing environment).

Earlier, I told a story about a client who was a noon anchor in a small market and was offered a five-year reporter position in Philadelphia. Had she taken the Philadelphia job, she almost certainly would have left the development of her anchoring skills behind, with the result that, in all likelihood, she would have to go down significantly in market size in order to begin anchoring again (after having lost five precious years of anchor seasoning).

The key is to move up in market size with a purpose; not as a way to make you (momentarily) feel good about your career, or as an (often false) litmus test for you to determine how well you're currently doing. Choreograph your career for the long run with intelligence and discipline.

The question of whether or not attending journalism graduate school is the optimal way to begin an *on-air* career elicits varied responses. Some news managers say that this move isn't necessary, as, "News is more of a trade than a profession. There are no tests to become a good reporter or an anchor. You get ahead if you're good and experienced at your craft."[C] Another observed, "There's no way to (learn to) be a reporter, other than to be a reporter. You must do it."[D]

On the other hand, my on-air clients who attended graduate school all felt that the education they received was well worth the time and money spent. One individual said that the ethical and professional responsibilities of being a journalist that were instilled in her during grad school have been invaluable. She believes that laying a solid intellectual and psychological foundation when one is beginning any endeavor of importance increases your chances of success and fulfillment. This woman continues to receive kudos for her reporting at a network-owned station. Two others felt the same way about the ethical and other practical information that they received in grad school. One of these individuals is now a network anchor; the other is reporting in Los Angeles for a network-owned station.

All of the individuals whom I spoke with felt that having a graduate journalism degree on their resumé had helped them at one time or another in the job search process, because they were accorded more respect — if for nothing else than that they had made an effort to lay a solid foundation.

I have found that attending a reputable graduate school of journalism is an asset that draws positive attention from news managers. It won't get you a job — your demo tape, your interview, and your personal qualities will do that — but it can help, depending upon the position sought (i.e., at a network) and the particular employer's value system. And, who knows? If more individuals attended journalism graduate schools, maybe there wouldn't be as many ethical and quality-control problems as there are in broadcast journalism today.

If you aspire to be an executive producer or to be in news management, journalism graduate school, and the business and economic information that you can learn there, can be of tremendous value. A number of news directors, who aspire to become network executives or local station general managers, said that if they had it to do over again, they would have attended graduate school, or at least taken specific courses there.

In connection with Route 4, I would definitely recommend that you have a large market (or at least some market) newsroom intern or assistant experience along with this route.

Finding Your First Job

In connection with Routes 1,3, and 4, one of the main fruits of your time and labors is getting a demo tape with which you can market yourself and get your first job.

I recommend at least three ways to find your first on-air position — any and all of which can be used together:

1) Send your tape and résumé to each station in every small market that is geographically desirable to you. Then follow up with phone calls. If success doesn't come within a reasonable period of time, try to get some feedback on your tape and/or résumé. If you can make beneficial adjustments make them, and then widen the scope of your geographic search.

2) Call news directors ahead of time, to set up appointments, and then take a road trip to meet some of these managers in person. Personal interaction can make all the difference in the world in positively separating you from a crowd of impersonal tapes and résumés. A meeting can get you the job, if there's one immediately available, or it can keep you in the news manager's thoughts when an appropriate position opens.

When interviewing, it is important for the interviewer(s) to get a strong sense of your passion for journalism, your work ethic, and your character. It is also important for news managers to know that you aspire to be the best writer and storyteller possible, that you're constructively competitive, and that you're a team player and not going to be a newsroom problem. And even if you aspire to be the world's best anchor, it's important to impart to the news manager in issue, that you are aware that the best anchors understand the context of the stories that they're telling. Therefore, your *first* goal is to be the best reporter possible. Anchoring can come in time.

3) Send your tape and résumé to consultants[1] who may show or forward your tape to prospective employers who are their clients. Generally, consultants can be more and more helpful as you move up in market size.

The Question Of When To Hire An Agent

This is a question with no simple answer. It really depends upon the talent and the agent.

First off, as we discussed earlier, if you are considering hiring an agent very early in the process, do your homework. It is important for you to find a representative who has a track record for helping people develop careers, which, in part, requires that the agent have an ability and an enthusiasm for effectively critiquing your work as you grow. As discussed earlier, broadcast journalists rarely receive critiques to begin with, and when they do receive critiques in small markets the critiquing can lack big market and big picture sophistication. (No offense meant to small market managers.) Additionally, even if your small market station hires a consultant to coach you, that consultant is coaching you to be successful in Eureka, Paducah, or Redding — the specific market that you're currently working in. A sophisticated and effective representative can give you critiques that may well help you to be more attractive to larger and a greater variety of markets.

Additionally, a good agent can help give you big picture advice regarding your career. This, too, can be quite beneficial. However, in all likelihood, an agent will not be effective in securing your first or even second job, as many small market stations

---

1 Unlike agents who work for on-air or off-air individuals, consultants are hired by stations to bring talented broadcast journalists to their attention. Consultants often perform additional functions for their clients, such as conducting research as to how to "fix" newscasts, newscasters, promotions, graphics, etc., in order to secure higher ratings. Please keep in mind that although consultants can be of great help to broadcast journalists by exposing their work and résumés to potential employers, consultants' salaries are paid by and their primary allegiance is to stations and production companies — not to talent.

won't deal with agents. And agents often aren't anymore aware than you are[2] about what small market positions are available. In fact, arguably, small market employers can be scared off by agent involvement, because they feel that as soon as you show any sign of growth your agent will pluck you out of their station and take you to a larger market and to a more lucrative position. The station may also be reticent about someone who hires an agent in connection with a first or a second job, as there's very little money paid for those positions and there's usually no negotiation involved.

I have found that unless an individual has an extraordinary demo tape and/or background, it is usually beneficial to take someone on as a client during their second or third job. However, I can definitely point to a few cases in which I've represented individuals right from the beginning, and we've done wonderful things together. In these unusual cases, I was able to secure career-enhancing first and second positions for them.

So, as I said, the point at which you should retain some sort of representation, and what that representation's function should be, depends upon the particular parties and the circumstances involved.

---

2 That is if you do your homework, by checking such magazines as *Broadcasting & Cable* and *Electronic Media*, as well as Internet services such as *Don Fitzpatrick & Associates' Shoptalk, MediaLine, Talent Dynamics,* and *TV Jobs* for open positions.

Building A Foundation
Step-By-Step

A poignant line from the film *Field of Dreams* is "Build it and they will come."[A] My take on this thought is "Build a rock-solid foundation of journalistic skills and the most attractive broadcasting positions and other sweet fruits of your labors will come."

For example, tennis star Pete Sampras developed the forehand, the backhand, the serve, and the volley, as well as the quickness and the agility he needed to win in almost all situations. By building an all-around foundation, he is able to adapt to difficult, new, and unusual circumstances, and thrive. By mastering all of the requisite skills, he's laid the foundation for all-time greatness.

The key to successfully mastering skills is to break things down into accomplish-able and master-able steps. Then accomplish and master them.

For example, in my athletic endeavors, one small victory often led and encouraged other small victories. These, in turn, led to the confidence and the ability to extend myself and my talents, so that ultimately I was able to attain larger and more gratifying victories. Success bred success, emotionally and technically.

The first time that I played against Arthur Ashe my goal was to concentrate as intently as possible and thereby hit (master) each and every one of my strokes, to the very best of my ability. I believed that if I could indeed do this, the points, the games, and the match would take care of themselves. They in fact did.

On that occasion, I was victorious.

When I began my business, I transferred my Arthur Ashe-match philosophy to that undertaking, by believing that: If I could serve each client to the best of my ability, each client's success and fulfillment would come; then, other clients would come; and, ultimately, the success of my company and my personal fulfillment would come. Step-by-mastered step, they all came.

If I were to teach someone a skill, such as tennis, I would teach that person one master-able component of a stroke at a time. I would have that individual stand just a few feet away, and I'd toss ball after ball to student, until he or she got it right, by taking mental and physical ownership of the step involved. We would then proceed to more difficult and advanced tasks.

When beginning broadcasters ask me what the best advice that I can give them is as they embark on their on-air careers, I say, "If you understand — truly understand — and, where appropriate, personally master the easiest to the most complex behind-the-scenes and on-air duties, then there's nothing that can throw you later on. By understanding and mastering the 'where,' the 'how,' and the 'why,' and the Big Picture of how everything fits together, you'll have the internal foundation to conquer the broadcasting world."

As we discussed earlier, I am a big proponent of starting in a small market or in some other low-pressure, beginner operation, where you can be exposed to and have a hands-on education regarding every step of the news-gathering process. I would:

> 1) Continually work on and develop your writing skills and style. This is of great importance. Listen to and study how more seasoned and accomplished individuals tell a story, craft their language, etc. Learn as much as you can about writing from those who deserve your respect.
>
> News luminary Burton Benjamin said the following regarding the fact that, no matter what form news transmission and news programs take in the future, those individuals who can write will always be valued:
>
> "The good journalist is a treasure, and they won't be able to develop or clone him in a laboratory. The problem that television faces, in my opinion, is for the creativity to keep up

with the racing technology. I don't care whether or not a story is coming to you via satellite, has been written by computer and transmitted by a correspondent with an antenna implanted in his head. If he can't write, he can't write — by satellite or by quill pen. If he can't report, he can't report. And all of the technology in the world can't save him. There is so much at stake today, that if we simply go with the technology, we are going to be in trouble. There was never a time when a reporter who can write, report, analyze, ask the right questions was needed more."[B]

2) Develop proficiency in as many areas as possible. Ask for opportunities to report both hard news and softer news stories. Work on developing your live reporting skills as well as your packaging. The ability to write and craft a compelling and/or moving piece is an art. Become a Picasso. Try your hand at anchoring; see how it goes and if you like it.

3) Read books on the history of broadcasting, and learn how the most accomplished individuals in the field think and how they act in various situations. Understand your profession's roots and ideals, and how broadcasting has evolved.

4) Objectively review tapes of your on-air work as frequently as possible. Identify the areas that need improving, and figure out how to improve upon your product and performance. Also, take note of the things that you do well, and consciously integrate them into your on-air repertoire. Be your own coach.

5) Try to enlist the critiquing of well-respected consultants, news managers, producers, and on- and off-air individuals in larger markets. But remember, everyone has his or her own subjective point of view, and the things that they suggest may not be right for you personally, for what you aspire to be, or for where you aspire to go. One rule of thumb to follow regarding critiques is: If a comment about your work comes up often, it should probably be given due consideration.

6) Study what the most effective communicators do. See why they and their pieces and styles work. There are good things about most individuals in top markets that you can emulate in your own personal way. Try to identify what those valuable qualities are and integrate them into your repertoire.

7) As you grow, try to push the envelope, bit by bit. Try new (appropriate) things in writing and delivery. See if they work and enhance the effectiveness of the manner in which

you deliver your message. Continue to keep growing, improving, and polishing.

8) Study and immerse yourself in the news. Read well respected newspapers on a daily basis, as well as periodicals such as *Time, Newsweek, U.S. News And World Report*, etc. Watch programs such as *60 Minutes, Nightline, Dateline NBC, 20/20*, etc.

News Tip: The above eight suggestions are just a few that will help you to develop into a compelling storyteller and communicator. And remember, if you can master the basics and develop a strong and diverse foundation, the (valid) feeling of empowerment will be huge, and this mastery will serve you well throughout the rest of your broadcasting career — whatever you do.

Knowledge and mastery can equal power — the power to communicate effectively and compellingly.

Attaining "Understanding" and "Ownership" of Your Work

Years ago, a story was told to me, about a reporter who was assigned by his TV station to cover a serious accident. The story allegedly unfolded this way:

Upon arriving at the scene of the accident, the reporter quickly, and without great care, scanned the area. He then went on to do some other things — such as watch a baseball playoff game on TV — until it was time to deliver his report. As the reporter began his presentation, he did his trademark walk-and-talk routine, by walking around the accident scene and directing the camera to various points of interest, while he flawlessly delivered the facts that he had memorized earlier.

When the reporter finished, the studio anchor advised both the reporter and the viewers that an unexpected development had just occurred. The anchor shared the development with the reporter and the viewers, and then asked the reporter to "analyze how the new information might affect the situation." Upon hearing the question, the reporter immediately panicked. His brain apparently locked, and he couldn't speak — for what seemed like an excruciatingly endless amount of time. As the reporter had only surveyed the surface facts of the story, he didn't understand its essentials, and therefore, he had no clue as to how to intelligently respond to the ever-changing situation. A moment or so later, the anchor nervously asked the question again. The reporter continued to stand there, speechless, staring blankly into the camera. Finally, the reporter began to speak. However, to everyone's embarrassment, he began to regurgitate the memorized facts, word for word, that he had given moments earlier — while never attempting to answer the anchor's question.

As he did this, a near-hysterical producer implored the anchor to segue as soon as possible out of the report and back to the studio.

The reporter was fired soon thereafter.

On the other end of the spectrum, there are reporters who pride themselves on attaining a thorough understanding of their material. They can deliver their stories during torrential downpours, amidst gunfire, in the face of gale force winds, and with curve after unexpected curve being thrown at them. And through it all, they don't lose their presence of mind or their ability to creatively and effectively deal with and thrive when major changes or delicate nuances are presented. By familiarizing themselves with and understanding the elements of their story, they can see everything in the insightful context of the big picture. These individuals are said to have ownership of their work. They've mastered the material and made it their own.

Having been in the news business for fifteen years, I see examples of both ends of the spectrum every day. Some individuals take responsibility for, and master their actions and decisions in a healthy and wise manner. Others, passively and/or destructively, do not.

We are all performers in life, as day in an day out, we perform hundreds of functions. The reporter who froze was a performer who didn't understand the why and the how of the story that he was reporting on. He only knew the superficial facts. He didn't care enough to have a deeper understanding of the situation. Therefore, during a crisis period, when others with a more thorough knowledge and understanding might well have insightfully and adeptly reasoned through the anchor's question, this reporter was unprepared. He froze; he didn't know what to do or say; and eventually he ran for cover to his old script — literally!!!

Through the years, I have noted that a disproportionately large number of individuals who are great live reporters, anchors and hosts, received their initial broadcasting training in radio. When I asked two or three of these individuals why they are so comfortable in the face of the most frantic live situations, they essentially said the same things: In radio, since you have no TelePrompTer or script to rely on (or to constrict you), you just absorb the essential facts and then talk with the listener. You get the big picture, take ownership of the material, and then off you go. Because you're not relying on anything or anyone — if you're good — you develop the wonderful abilities to ad-lib and to speak off the cuff.

I often see beginning and seasoned reporters try to memorize and to cram in every fact they've learned into their stories. The problem is that the communication of this memorization seems unnatural and non-conversational. Similar to the radio philosophy discussed above, the key to natural and effective communication in live TV, is to absorb the essentials and then talk to us, share with us, and thereby engage us. Having a basic understanding of your material, and then taking ownership of it, is the way to do this.

News Tip: Broadcasters who inspire respect, confidence, and trust have understanding and take ownership of their work.

VI. The Ideal Fate of Broadcast Journalism

The Ideal: To Secure Higher Ratings And Also Produce A High-Quality Newscast or Reality-Based Program

The content of your character
is reflected in the character of your content.

—K.L.

The Ideal — The Content Component

Earlier we discussed the dilemma that many executives and news managers face, as they perceive that gratuitously reporting on crime, murder, scandal, and negativity results in viewers watching their newscasts and in a more profitable business. On the other hand, these managers also have a duty and a responsibility to supply *necessary* information to the public.[1] So the issue

---

1 I assume that most station owners and executives do feel a sense of pride when in fact they provide a valuable public service (along with owning and/or running a profitable business.) Therefore, I also assume that most owners and executives would enthusiastically embrace any formulas or ideas enabling them to provide a quality news product, along with garnering high ratings.

becomes: How do you ideally air news that people need, and still get ratings?

Recently, a longtime #3 station in Los Angeles aired a compelling series of investigative pieces on health code violations the station had uncovered in that city's restaurants. The ratings for the newscasts on which these reports appeared *increased dramatically*. What makes this occurrence even more interesting is that these pieces aired during sweeps. Therefore, viewing habits were significantly changed because of the interest generated in and the effectiveness of these reports, during a time when the other higher-rated stations in the market were airing *their* most viewer-attractive and commercial material.

What these and other instances of exceptional reporting that resulted in substantial ratings increases signals to me is that reports and newscasts that truly supply viewers with information that they can use, and that are reported and produced with flair, can very definitively compel viewers to switch stations in order to watch them.

Recently, a large number of my clients confirmed that ratings on their newscasts increased substantially when these newscasts aired information segments in which they supplied the viewers with news that they could use day-to-day, or from which they could benefit. These clients also noted that the many viewer letters and phone calls that their stations received in response to these information segments expressed sincere viewer interest in and appreciation of the station presenting information that helped them (the viewers).

From this kind of consistent feedback, I conclude that:

   1) By supplying quality information that viewers want and need, in order to live and to enhance their daily lives; and,
   2) by presenting this information in an attractive and compelling manner;
   3) the supplier-stations will get individuals to watch and to feel good about their newscasts and their stations.

It has been said and written that most stations that attempt to take the high road, by choosing not to gratuitously air tabloid news, do not fare well in the ratings. In response to this assertion,

I argue that there are a number (albeit a relatively small group)[2] of very strong stations that have for years been — and continue to be — highly respected ratings giants, as a direct result of serving their communities with *quality* news. KCRA in Sacramento, WFAA in Dallas, and WCVB in Boston are three such stations. All of these stations effectively cover news that viewers need and want to know, with high quality, in-depth reporting. As a result, these stations have developed, a very high level of viewer good will and trust, which have endured over time.

So let's say that you, as a station owner or executive, want to emulate the standard of quality and long-term success of the aforementioned three stellar stations, and you plan to accomplish this by winning your viewers over by doing high quality and relevant news. One question for you to consider is: To what extent will viewers, who specifically tune into your newscasts for compelling and pertinent reports, stay around for the long term, if you don't want to resort to manipulating or titillating them into regularly watching your newscasts by airing a large ration of crime, violence, sleaze, and gossip?

To effectively answer this question and re-position your news product, you may want to consider the following other questions and thoughts:

1) How do viewers perceive your station? Do they trust you? Do you have equity with them?

If you haven't built a good deal of viewer trust and equity, you can earn them by consistently doing high quality and relevant stories for each and every newscast. This growth process requires a long-term investment and mind-set by you and your company.

---

2 I believe that the number of highly-rated, truly non-tabloid news stations is relatively small, *not* because they have adopted a philosophy of doing high quality news; but rather, I believe that these (non-tabloid) stations have failed to attain high ratings, because: 1) they have not given their non-tabloid approach enough time to make an impact; and 2) these stations do not have the appropriate constructive internal news philosophy (which I discuss in the next section) that enables stations and broadcasts to develop true viewer loyalty.

2) What news content and philosophy do viewers expect from you?

If they don't expect high quality content and information that they can use, you may need to re-position your news product, as well as viewer expectations through appropriate promotion. Then be sure to deliver what you advertise.

3) Does your station currently have the requisite reporting, producing, and writing staff members to produce quality news, in an interesting manner, on a full-time basis?

Quality, in-depth reporting and producing do require more and better staffing. Therefore, you must be willing to make the requisite monetary investment in order to deliver a high-quality news product on a daily basis.

4) What kinds of news (i.e., the degree of tabloid content) are the top stations in your market airing?

The answer to this question should give you a good idea as to what has been successful in your market and what many viewers there have come to expect.

5) Taking all of the answers to these questions into account, what is the best formula for your particular station to adopt in order to entice viewers to sample your newscasts, to like them, and to eventually watch them on a regular basis.

In figuring out the right formula for your particular station, here are a couple of thoughts. If your station is in a market where the (other) top-rated stations are relatively non-tabloid, it should be easier for you to be non-tabloid right from the start. (Because this has proven to be successful in your market already.) The key, then, is for your station, story by story and promotion by promotion, to be better than the competition.[3]

However, if you are in a tabloid news market, and this philosophy is working for the highly-rated stations there, depending upon what you, your management and your consultants feel is the most appropriate course to take, you can:

1) Produce a counter-programming news product by doing great non-tabloid news; or,

---

3 Also, be better and different by effectively implementing the internal pact/proposal outlined in the next section.

2) Produce a news product that contains a combination of quality news and some sexy and provocative stories — but no gratuitous sleaze, degradation, or (potentially) harmful gossip.

For example, a few weeks ago, I asked a successful and very well-respected news director what his formula was for building the #1-rated newscast in his large market. He replied: "I consider myself half-Edward R. Murrow and half-P.T. Barnum. On the one hand, we do news that we feel is important, and we mix it with some sexy and fun stuff that entertains the viewer. This way, we give viewers the news, and they stay interested — and entertained — at the same time. It's a combination that's really worked for us."

I am not by any means a news production expert in connection with advising stations as to what the right combination of necessary information and entertainment news should be in a newscast. This is best left in the capable hands of talented news managers, producers, and consultants. However, I am immersed in the news business; and day after day, I hear people say that they can't watch (local) news because it's too negative and too depressing. I, for the most part, concur. I also believe that many would agree that we live in a society whose morals and ethics sink lower and lower each day. Broadcasters can choose to encourage this, or they can choose to inform us and truly help lift the state of our society, depending upon the news philosophies that they embrace.

I don't have the specific sure-fire answers as to how to alter the content of your newscasts, so as to secure higher ratings while at the same time delivering quality news. However, I firmly believe that:

1) There is clear evidence that when stations air reports and information that viewers can use and are interested in; and these reports are communicated, packaged and promoted in an interesting and compelling manner, the viewers will switch stations in order to watch them.

2) Generally, people do what's advantageous for them, and they often react to events and stimuli by asking the question, "How will this affect me?" Therefore, it makes sense, that if a station's newscast supplies (the self-focused) viewers with

information that is *relevant* to them, of benefit to them, and interesting to them, these viewers, out of self-interest, will watch that station's newscasts; and,

    3) If a station supplies relevant and beneficial information on a consistent basis to viewers, these viewers will viscerally (and hopefully, consciously) realize that this station legitimately cares about their interests and their well-being, as opposed to other stations that air trash, in order to hook them. By supplying relevant and beneficial information, over time, a station can develop a trust and an equity level with viewers that can lead to long-term viewer-loyalty. The kind of loyalty that stations such as KCRA and WFAA — for years and years — have enjoyed.

The choice is yours.

Creating A Climate Of Character

Another content issue involves the current controversy as to whether news organizations may be implicitly placing a higher value on securing the get than they are on truthful, balanced, accurate, and compassionate reporting. As a result, broadcast journalists have taken their cue from their employers, and in turn have adopted this same flawed value system.

Ron Alridge, publisher and editorial director of *Electronic Media*, wrote an excellent article discussing the instances of "malpractice" in broadcast journalism that have recently come to light and those that have presumably taken place but have not been discovered and/or exposed.

Alridge says that efforts of such organizations as CNN and NBC to create ombudsmen to enforce professional standards and practices, to dismiss and to discipline guilty parties, and to issue candid confessions and sincere apologies — although admirable and well-intentioned — aren't nearly enough to remedy the problem. As he warns, "You can't treat cancer with Band-Aids."[A]

Alridge believes that, "You can't force people to be honest. They must *want* to be honest."[B] Therefore, if news gathering organizations — owners, general managers, news directors, executive producers, and other newsroom leaders, as well as talent recruiters — consistently stress and positively recognize and reward such values as honesty, accuracy, balance, and compassion, talent, in many instances, will take that cue and also follow along. Mr. Alridge continues:

> "At the same time, this climate of character will probably mean de-emphasizing, at least a bit, the values of beating the competition or boosting the ratings. Call it a healthy re-balancing."[C]

In the above quotation, Alridge suggests de-emphasizing the value of boosting ratings — "at least a bit" — in order to begin to achieve a climate of character. I am sure that some — or many — executives and managers fear that with this de-emphasis will come a decline in ratings. I believe that in this current climate, in which broadcast journalism is suffering from major esteem, credibility and relevancy problems, taking a bit more time to report a story truthfully, accurately, and in a balanced, and humane manner, will not, in fact, result in a long-term ratings decline. I would suggest that laying a foundation of truthful, accurate, balanced, and humane reporting that is produced in a manner so as to connect with and engage your viewer in a positive fashion, may well result in long-term viewer loyalty and ratings success.

I agree with Alridge that TV station, network, and program owners and managers will achieve character in their content by positively reinforcing character in the way that their staff members gather, write, and report the news.

Broadcast journalism, step by step, can indeed make a content comeback — but appropriate first steps must, in large part, be taken by owners and management.

The Ideal — The "Pact/Proposal" Program

Stephen Covey, in his highly acclaimed book, *The Seven Habits of Highly Effective People*, writes that shortly after World War I many individuals and companies adopted a manner of acting, which he terms *The Personality Ethic*.[D] In discussing the post-World War I years, he writes that personal and professional "success became more of a function of personality, of public image, and of attitudes, behaviors, skills and techniques that lubricate [and manipulate] the process of human interaction." When discussing how *Personality Ethic* individuals (consciously or subconsciously) want their problems solved, Covey writes that they want some quick fix advice or solution that will relieve their pain and make things better.[E] *Personality Ethic* individuals will find people[4] who will fulfill their wants and teach and/or implement quick-fix solutions; and for a short time, these recruits' skills and techniques may appear to work. In fact, they may eliminate some — or many — of the cosmetic or outer problems through (often manipulative) social aspirins or band-aids. But the underlying chronic condition often remains, and eventually, new acute symptoms will appear. Covey warns that,

> The more people are into and rely upon the *quick fix*, and focus upon the *outer problems*, the more this very approach contributes to and exacerbates the underlying chronic condition.[F]

The Personality Ethic individual also frequently perceives that he or she needs to take some kind of dramatic action, by making heads roll and by shaking things up.[G] *Personality Ethic* people feel that there's always something or someone "out there" . . . some quick fix — that will provide the golden answer or solution.

As the news director (mentioned earlier) allegedly said, "The worst anchor in the country is the one that I hired three months ago; the best anchor in the country is the one that I'll hire next."

When I read Covey's thoughts regarding the *outer-directed/Personality Ethic* individual, I felt that he described the management philosophy of many news and program executives and their advisors to a "T."

Throughout the fifteen years that I have been working in

---

4 Such as, new general managers, news directors, executive producers, consultants, etc.

local news, I have seen a plethora of management changes, and, in a great majority of these cases, material changes of on-air talent quickly followed. However, I cannot recall many instances of significant rating increases by stations and/or programs that have had revolving door management and/or on-air staffs. I would think that there have been some anomalous situations, in which ratings success occurred in spite of constant change, not as a result of it — however, I can think of only one.

WSVN, the Fox affiliate in Miami, presents an interesting case study. Before becoming WSVN, this station was WCKT, an NBC affiliate. When this station lost its NBC affiliation and its value was about to plummet, Joel Cheatwood was hired and he created a counter-programming news product which has been called (and criticized as) tabloid. What Cheatwood envisioned and created was an energized, attention-getting, fast-paced format and style for presenting the news, which visually, viscerally, and emotionally reaches out, touches, and involves the viewers. And, however one feels about the tabloid nature of WSVN's content, style, and delivery, Cheatwood found a formula that caught and kept the attention of a significant portion of the Miami audience. As a result, he increased WSVN's ratings. Additionally, many stations across the country, as well as various syndicated programs have adopted many elements of Cheatwood's and WSVN's style of delivery, music, graphics, and sets, etc.

As I discussed earlier, WSVN's newscasts are format-driven; and notwithstanding the fact that for budgetary reasons WSVN has chosen to let a number of its newscasters come and go, it has maintained its ratings over time (while earning large profits). So it would appear that this station is an exception to my belief that in order to significantly increase ratings and win in your market, you must have continuity of on-air talent. However, upon close examination, WSVN has maintained continuity in other key areas, which has helped it, *to some degree*, to overcome having revolving door anchors and reporters.

First of all, WSVN has adhered to the format and style that Cheatwood first brought to WSVN. The Miami viewers have grown to expect a certain kind of content, pacing, energy, music, graphics, etc., from WSVN, and day after day, year after year, they get it. And it is these qualities, as well as WSVN's innovative "news-plex" set that the station promotes — not its on-air talent (so viewers are less disappointed when there are talent changes). Additionally, this station has had the same owner and general manager since it became WSVN, and the news directors who have succeeded Cheatwood have all worked at WSVN prior to becoming news directors, so they all have understood and appreciated WSVN's product and appeal and have stayed the course by making few, if any, material changes.

Although Cheatwood was successful at envisioning and building the financially successful WSVN, and later doing the same thing (with less of a tabloid feel) at WHDH in Boston, I have always believed and have told Cheatwood that his stations would be *even more* successful, if — along with having continuity of format, style, ownership, and management — the station had *continuity of talent.* I am sure of this.

So, while the *Personality Ethic* philosophy of, "Shake it up baby, now!" sounded good to the Isley Brothers, the Beatles, and their fans, I believe that it doesn't play well — and never has — with the viewing public. As a means for stations to attract and/or to maintain viewership — constant change has not met with any consistent success.

Covey believes that the way in which the *Personality Ethic* individual sees the problem, *is* (the crux) of the problem.[H] Albert Einstein wrote that, "The significant problems we face cannot be solved at the same level of thinking that we were at when we created them."[I]

I would argue that during the past twenty years, many station owners, general managers, advisers, etc., have adopted the *Personality Ethic,* "Outside-In" approach, as a means of increasing the success of low-rated newscasts. This is in direct contrast to Covey's inside-out approach. Combining Covey's and Einstein's theories, with my belief that the formula of constant change by stations (and programmers) until they "get it right" rarely works, I offer the following "Internal Pact/Proposal."

The Win/Win/Win/Win Pact/Proposal

Geoffrey Chaucer wrote, "If the gold rusts, what shall iron

do?"ᴶ Leadership *must* start at the top. If a general manager, station group owner, or the head of a production company doesn't endorse the implementation of this Pact/Proposal, news managers, executives, consultants, etc., cannot be expected to follow through with it; especially when the fix may not be quick, and substance, in many instances, will be at least as important as form.

As owners and those in true decision-making power positions must be the first individuals to accept my long-term approach, I address you, as well as news managers, producers, consultants, etc. Covey writes, "*If there is little or no trust, there is no foundation for permanent success.*ᴷ It is character that communicates most eloquently." As Ralph Waldo Emerson put it, "What you are shouts so loudly in my ears, I cannot hear what you say . . ." ᴸ In the last analysis, what you are and how you conduct your business communicate to your viewers and to your employees far more eloquently than anything that you say or advertise. There are people whom we trust because we know and have witnessed their good character and their consistency; and there are those individuals and institutions whom we don't trust, because of their lack of character and/or their lack of consistency.

I believe viewers viscerally know that when a station continually changes, fires, or demotes its newscasters (individuals whom they watch and with whom they have established some relationship), that station is truly not committed to anyone or to anything — except itself; not to the on-air staff, not to the employees, and not to the viewer.ˢ As Covey explains, "It's how you treat the 'one,' that reveals how you regard [others], because everyone is ultimately a 'one.' " A number of women have said to me, "I watch how a guy treats his mother, because that's how he'll treat me." If a station treats its on-air staff with no respect, viewers will know it and will act (and have acted) accordingly. Viewers won't invest in you, because they know that if a station cannot commit to its employees, there is no reason to believe that the station is truly committed to them (the viewers) either.

Recently, there has been a good deal written about how sports fans — especially baseball fans — no longer feel the same allegiance and identification with their once-favorite sports teams. This is so because the advent of free agency has resulted in players switching teams with great frequency. Therefore, player loyalty — and team loyalty — have eroded. I believe that sports fans viscerally feel that sports has become too much of a cold, bottom-line business. And, although news, like sports, is a business, it too, in the past has been held to a higher intellectual, visceral, and emotional standard.

Therefore, no matter how a station advertises and promotes its product, the true litmus test is how a station conducts its business — not what it promises. Besides, in all likelihood, the (unsuccessful) station has made advertising promises before, and has not delivered. For example, when a station advertises its anchor team, it is, in essence, saying to the viewer, "We are behind these anchors — they are our link and connection to you. These anchors will be there for you, in your home, night after night." Then, all of a sudden, they're gone and replaced — thereby disappointing the viewer. Once again, the station fails to deliver what it implicitly promised. Not keeping a commitment or a promise, or failing to fulfill a valid expectation, Covey teaches, is a major source of lack of trust. Continually letting individuals down results in very little or no trust between the parties. I submit that this kind of station behavior is one of the major causes of poor viewership. (Besides, all low-rated stations in the U.S. can't be built on ancient Indian burial grounds — there must be some other common reason for their non-success.) I would certainly argue that low-rated stations have very low viewer-trust quotients.

To drive the point home, Covey writes, "People *will* forgive mistakes, because mistakes are usually *of the mind,* mistakes of judgment. But people *will not* easily forgive *mistakes of the heart,* the ill intention, the bad mistakes, the *prideful justifying cover-up of the first mistake.*"[M] Once again, if a station continually treats its on-air staff with no conscience, no respect, and no commitment, and consistently seeks to manipulate the viewer, the viewer might well not forgive the station and, for a long time thereafter, withhold its viewership. (I believe that this is how ancient Indian burial grounds get started.)

So, if one accepts any of the points that I've made above (that a station cannot continually [only] change its facade), I ask that the reader consider a different strategy — one based upon

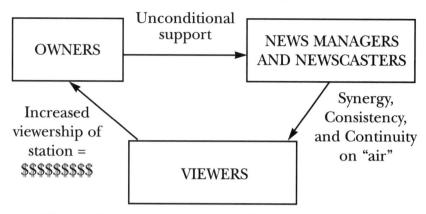

Viewers begin to grow attached to the newscasters
and the news product of the station.

station change from within. As Covey says, "Change — real
change — comes from the inside-out."[N]

I am proposing a "win/win/win/win" scenario. Owners
would commit long-term to their news managers, program executives, and to the on- and off-air news staff members. Managers,
consultants, etc., would work together to maximize the talents of
the newscasters by putting them in positions that showcase all of
their strengths. All employees would receive unconditional
owner and manager support. Individuals would begin to feel
secure and positive about what they do and how they do it.
Continuity and consistency would reign. Internal relationships
based upon trust could begin to develop. The viewer will viscerally and visibly identify a difference, and begin to develop a relationship with the station, its on-air talent and its philosophy,
which can result in increased viewership and ratings.

In order for my pact proposal to flourish, it is of the
essence for all levels of management to allow time for strong
internal and external relationships to develop, and for a positive
and strong talent/viewer rapport to evolve. As discussed above,
owners need to commit *long-term* to the on-air news staff and to
the news managers in order to implement this plan. Covey writes,
"We need to approach [a] win/win [concept] from a genuine
desire to invest in the relationships that make it possible."[O] In my

scenario, the station's internal relationships with its newscasters and management, and its external relationship with the viewers, must be nurtured over time.

As Goethe wrote, "Treat a man as he is and he will remain as he is. Treat a man as he can and should be and he will become as he can and should be."[P] Covey adds, "You have to water the flowers you want to grow[Q] . . . inspire them [your employees] toward a higher path." Covey writes, "Trust is the highest form of motivation. It brings out the best in people."[R] But [the development of trust] takes time and patience. Covey also discusses the story of the goose who laid the golden eggs (Aesop's fable), and how important it is to nurture, preserve, and enhance the goose, so that it will continue to lay the golden eggs. He says that true success "is a function of two things — what is produced (the golden eggs) and the producing asset (the goose)."[S] Covey continues, "Always treat your employees exactly as you want them to treat your best customers. You can buy a person's hand, but you can't buy his heart. His heart is where his enthusiasm, his loyalty is. You can buy his back, but you can't buy his brain. That's where his creativity is, his ingenuity, his resourcefulness [lies]."[T]

I believe Covey would conclude that if a station owner implements an unconditional support system and a long-term positive relationship with his/her on- and off-air employees, many of those employees would rise to the occasion, and, as they say in the army ads — be all that [they] can be. Interestingly, I recently watched a network special about the National Basketball Association and its all-time great playoff performers and coaches. During the program, former star Bill Walton discussed the career of Red Auerbach of the Boston Celtics, who was probably the most successful general manager/coach in NBA history. When former Celtics players were asked why the Celtics were so extraordinarily successful under Auerbach and why there was such cohesion in their organization — to the point where players willingly trained their successors — the players, in essence, responded that Auerbach above all valued loyalty, longevity, and continuity among his players. In addition, he was totally supportive of his staff.[U]

Individuals generally perform better when they are confident and feel good about themselves. Being in a supportive and nurturing environment can help build confidence. A broadcast journalist will perform better — on air, as a writer, or in any other capacity — in a positive, nurturing environment. Stations hire potential — the potential of a new on-air individual to make a positive impact on both the news product and the viewers. By providing a positive environment, by giving constructive, thoughtful feedback, etc., to the newscaster, that individual is more likely to grow to achieve the potential that ownership and management envisioned. On the other hand, if the performer is not supported, becomes defensive, or is afraid to take risks, the opposite may occur. No growth. No connection. No impact. Nada.

Assuming station owners agree that nurturing and enhancing one's prime producers is in their own best interests, under my proposal, news managers would then receive the unconditional, long-term backing of the owners. Managers will begin to feel more secure about themselves and their positions. A news manager would perceive, "I am in an environment where I can choose; I am responsible for the product. I can be independent, and make independent decisions, because I will be at the station long enough to see my decisions implemented and supported. In turn, as news management gives its long-term, unconditional support to their on-air staff, newscasters can feel less vulnerable to the subjective whims of owners and management, and can begin to feel independent, empowered, and confident. An on-air individual in effect would say that, "I am valued, I am an integral part of the 'program' and its future. I have a home. I can now buy into a 'program' and work for the greater good of the news product, instead of always worrying about my job security."

In essence, if station owners begin to take a more "inside-out" approach to their relationship with their management and their news staff, a stronger, healthier station environment, and a more compelling and engaging news product, can begin — over time — to evolve.

"Interdependence" and "Synergy"

In Covey's "Maturity Continuum," a person can grow from "dependent;" to independent;" to "interdependent;" to a truly synergistic person. "Dependent" people are "outer-directed."[5] Independent people perceive that "I can do it; I am responsible; I am self-reliant; I can choose." Covey says that the "interdependent" person has the perspective of "we"; "we can do," "we can cooperate," "we" can combine our talents and abilities and create something greater together.[v] It is interdependency that owners and managers must strive to create at their stations.

In implementing an environment of "we are in this together for the long haul," owners can make management feel more secure; managers and owners can make newscasters and producers feel more secure. Both groups would feel more comfortable with their long-term roles at the station; would learn to trust; would not be afraid to give up their defenses ("old scripts"); would take risks; and would begin to work towards the betterment of the product as a whole.

One result of the adoption of the interdependent behavioral pattern is the concept of "synergy." Covey writes that the phenomenon of synergy occurs when the whole is greater than the sum of its parts.[w] Individually, John Lennon, Paul McCartney, George Harrison, and Ringo Starr attained varying degrees of success — but together as The Beatles their success was unparalleled. Synergy can produce that indefinable, but so identifiable chemistry that great sitcoms, movies, and newscasts, etc., have. It can occur when two or more individuals let themselves go and flow; being in many ways selfless, yet strong — so that the end product is a "hit." (These are qualities seen in the characters of such all-time hits as *M*A*S*H*, *The Cosby Show*, and *Seinfeld*.)

I remember watching an anchor years ago, who impressed me so very much because, unlike most anchors who only focused on their own performances, he thoughtfully and sensitively made sure that every person on the set was as comfortable and effective as possible. He knew the substance of the reports which would be in his newscast ahead of time, and asked relevant questions of the reporters, which enhanced both the report and the reporter. He

---

5 Outer-directed individuals are those who look for solutions and validation, etc., in and from others, in order to solve problems and to evaluate their self-worth, respectively.

also took pains to establish a genuine rapport with his co-anchor, the sportscaster, and the weathercaster. Like a great point guard in basketball, he controlled the ball, and at the right time knew when and how to give it up, so that all of his teammates flourished. He indeed "made the sum bigger than the parts." That anchor (and his on-air teammates) worked interdependently to create synergy that resulted in 1+1+1+1+1 equaling 25. The extraordinary ratings reflected the wonderful chemistry of the overall product.

If the on-air individual is secure within himself or herself, because he or she is given support by management, it is certainly easier to give up some of his or her defenses and prior (self-focused) ways of doing things in order to achieve a greater result. If one is always worried about, and in jeopardy of losing one's position, and every on-air appearance is a potential demo-tape performance, one is much less likely to care about enhancing others and ultimately the product as a whole.

Covey writes that the phenomenon of synergy occurs when "a group collectively agrees to subordinate 'old scripts' [old defense mechanisms and old ways of protecting oneself] to write a new one"[X] (in which the end product — the broadscast — is more important than the individual performances).

Identifying Differences and Strengths in Broadcast Journalists and Using Them to Their and To Your Advantage

Just as no two snowflakes are exactly alike, all individuals are different as well. Every newscaster brings something different and unique to a news product. Covey says that, "The essence of synergy is to value differences."[Y] ". . . to respect them, to build on strengths and to compensate for weaknesses."[Z] When new management inherits a newsroom and its news product, instead immediately instituting change, I suggest that they think about, "How do I take advantage of the investment that my station has made in the individuals that are currently on our air?" Richard Bach, in *One*, says that, "Hatred is love without facts."[Aa] My take on Bach's quote is: Dislike of a newscaster's performance, oftentimes can be the result of an initial assessment, reached without appropriate time taken and homework done in order to learn about each on-air individual and what makes him or her special and (positively) different." Before reaching any conclusions about a talent, management should learn all that he or she can about each on-air person, and what he or she can positively contribute to the overall news product. A newscaster's strengths and non-strengths should be identified. The manager should also take time to learn the specific tastes and preferences of the unique market that his or her station is serving. It should then be decided how best to take advantage of the time that the individual has spent in the market and the relationships that the newscaster has formed. (For example, relationships with sources in the area and with other station newscasters — which could result in an engaging on-air chemistry between them.) In addition, the manager should value the equity that a talent has built in connection with a (franchise) reporting position and with the viewers, etc. After taking all of this data into account, the management team, along with its consultants, should develop a format or "program" that allows for all of the on-air individuals to contribute positively. This is what some of the most successful professional sports teams, such as the San Francisco 49ers, have done. They have developed a program that specifically fits the team's unique personnel, strength, and character. These programs allow the sum to be greater than its parts. Covey writes, "Once people [news staff and station's viewers] have experienced real synergy, they are never quite the same."[B] Hopefully, the right program will be the vehicle and the catalyst for real synergy to develop. This also means that general managers, news directors, and consultants must be willing to put their usual quick-fix scripts in abeyance, until they have openly and honestly explored whether those scripts are still appropriate, or in fact need to be modified or replaced, due to management's long-term commitment to them, to the station, and to the viewers.

Once a well-designed program and the appropriate on- and off-air individuals are put into place, owners and managers must stick with them . . . for the long-term. Richard Bach, in *One*, says that achieving excellence is not easy, and the greatest of rewards can take time before they are ready to be reaped — but the rewards that are reaped can truly be great.[C] The formula of "Build it, and they will come,"[D] once again is applicable here. My thesis is: If station ownership commits long-term to building the right internal environment, along with constructing the right program or format that, over time, enhances all its contributors, the viewers, the ratings, and the profits will come.

Two Caveats

1) It is not expected that everyone can be integrated into every program, no matter how "inner-directed" and "interdependent" owners and managers attempt to be. And if, after owners and managers do their best to take advantage of a newscaster's strengths and contributions, that newscaster just doesn't fit in, owners and news managers should be humane in how they part ways with the individual. After all, the newscaster has invested an important portion of his or her life and career in the station. This investment should be treated with the highest regard. For example, should the station decide to terminate or demote the individual, the station should waive its covenant-not-to-compete and right of first refusal. If the newscaster is no longer employed in the position for which that he or she was hired, don't force that individual (once again) to uproot and to leave a market, in order to earn a living. Let him or her attempt to work in the market of his or her choice. Additionally, ownership and management should make the parting as amicable as possible, both emotionally and financially for the individual. In the long run, aren't people more important than things (i.e., a few extra dollars to a station)?!

2) When a general manager or a news director leaves a station, the owner or head of the station group should be proactive in ensuring that the replacement-individual brought in stays the course already set by the prior inside-out management. Preserve the on-air individuals; preserve the off-air individuals; preserve the tailor-made program; and keep intact the relationships already established with the staff and the viewers. (Remember, if you cut off the roots, you won't reap the fruits.)

A Final Note

For the most part, constant change of on-air individuals, format, and management at local stations has not resulted in any appreciable ratings gains. Maybe a different approach is needed.

I believe that many of the ideas set forth above can be implemented, to varying degrees, by station owners and news managers. To summarize: Station ownership would create an enhancing work environment based upon stability, confidence, and trust. Newcasters and news managers would then work to become more and more interdependent. The development of a tailor-made program that would make the most of the abilities of the on-air staff members, who already have time invested on the station's air, is the third step. With time, the evolution of a news product with synergy and chemistry, that is viewer-engaging, would take place. Attracting a substantial number of new viewers, while keeping a station's current ones, is the hoped-for result.

I termed the above proposal as "win/win/win/win." Newscasters and management staff members win, as they are given unconditional support emotionally, contractually, and in connection with their on-air and off-air contributions, respectively. Viewers win, because:

> 1) they can watch newscasters with whom they can develop or have developed a relationship;
> 2) stations will keep their explicit and implicit advertising promises, so viewer expectations will be fulfilled; and
> 3) in the end, viewers can watch an engaging, compelling, consistent news product.

Station owners win, because as viewer satisfaction grows, ratings will increase, thereby increasing news profitability.

However, there is one more "win" in the scenario. While how profitably you run your business may be important, isn't the manner in which you live your life and treat others ultimately more important? Isn't it more satisfying to nurture, to support and to develop individuals, than to treat them as dispensable cogs?

If you are a station owner or station executive, when you look back on your life, will treating individuals with respect, thoughtfulness, and humaneness give you greater joy and peace than the (extra) profits that you earned for, or derived from your company, as a result of treating people insensitively or poorly? I do not believe that the one who dies with the most toys — and the best profit-and-loss statement — wins.

Ideally, there's a better way.

VII. Closing Thoughts

The State of Broadcast Journalism

Day-to-day, I clearly detect
That network news has lost the respect
Of viewers who have had their fill
Of Clinton/Lewinsky overkill.

And although maximization of profits is a corporate must,
Polls say that news is now *less* worthy of trust
Than the scandal-ridden President of the United States,
And Kenneth Starr, whom almost everyone hates.

To me, these startling developments
Reflect news' lack of revelance;
And that news divisions would be wise to concede
That they must spend more time airing news that viewers need;
And produce it in such a compelling way
That airing news of importance will *also* pay.

But until news divisions change, I suspect
They will continue to lose credibility and respect;
They will make big bucks, but seal the fate
Of broadcast journalism's sorry state.

— K.L.

P.S.

As we milk tawdry stories to their extreme,
Broadcast journalists lose self-esteem,
As being well-paid can only go so far,
When you feel bad about what you do and are.

The State of Broadcast Journalism

"Sensational, superficial, pandering to the lowest common denominator — Why, the critics ask, is (local) TV news the way it is?"

The answer is simple . . . It [local TV news] is, in fact, a finely tuned, highly calculated, money-making machine.

It is all driven by money . . .

The Los Angeles Business Journal,
August 24, 1998[A]

Three years ago, I took a series of trips to various cities to visit my clients and to get a general grass roots education as to how people were feeling and what they were thinking about regarding their jobs. What I came up with, much of the time, were individuals expressing their feelings of unhappiness, frustration, resentment, and resignation as to where broadcast journalism was going and how this direction was negatively affecting them professionally and emotionally.

In many instances, these disillusioned individuals worked at low-rated stations, which they perceived lacked ideals, had no continuity, and would do anything, cover anything, and would hire anyone in order to get a boost in their ratings. In essence, they believed these stations would sell out at the drop of a hat, and this perception caused many of these on-air individuals to feel badly about their employers, their work, their profession, and themselves. For the most part, those individuals who felt more positive, worked at stations which they perceived cared about the content and the quality of the material that they aired. These stations also highly valued the persons who worked for them and those that the station served — their viewers. Interestingly, but not surprisingly, all of these latter stations did well in the ratings.

By and large, however, the feedback about the state of broadcast journalism that I received from my trips and from many, many subsequent conversations, has been disturbing.

As we have discussed, most local news-gathering and talent decisions today are driven largely or solely by the goal of increasing ratings and revenues while reducing expenditures. The problem is that these values are often in stark contrast to and in profound conflict with the ones that initially led many broadcast journalists into the profession. The result is that with quality diminished and compromise pervasive, talent often feel dissatisfied with, compromised, and resentful about their daily assignments. And, as I have discussed, the effects of severe financial pressures on station management have also led broadcast journalists to feel undervalued, frustrated, and disillusioned.

A most poignant example of a prominent broadcast journalist's disillusionment with broadcast journalism's apparent loss of its "moral compass," came when NBC's Keith Olbermann delivered the senior convocation speech for Cornell University on May 23, 1998. When discussing the endless hours upon hours of programs on MSNBC devoted to the Clinton/Lewinsky affair that he has hosted, Olbermann said:

> *There are days now when my line of work makes me ashamed, make me depressed, makes me cry . . .*
> Forty years ago, Edward R. Murrow got up in front of the convention of radio and television news directors and announced that without *moral direction*, all this great medium would become was "wires and lights in a box," and there are

days when I wish that it would still be even that idealistic.

About three weeks ago, I awakened from my stupor on this subject and told my employers (at NBC) that I simply could not continue doing this show about the endless investigation, and the investigation of the investigation. I had to choose what I felt in my heart was right over what I felt in my wallet was smart. I did not threaten them. I let them balance for themselves their professional and moral forces. I await their answer.[D]   (emphasis added)

To make matters worse, *the profession* of broadcast journalism itself recently has been subject to a tremendous amount of criticism for lowering its standards, for its commercialism, and for its pandering. In essence, for being just like every other business today.

For example, Ron Alridge writes the following about TV news' coverage of the relationship between President Clinton and Monica Lewinsky, and how poorly the public now views the news media:

> By all reasonable standards, the coverage was wildly excessive and, at times, almost as reckless and inappropriate as Mr. Clinton's conduct.
>
> Too many leaks were chased and reprinted blindly by a braying and salivating pack . . .
>
> The public got a lot more noise than light from news organizations entrusted with the sacred responsibility of informing them.
>
> As the Clinton/Lewinsky scandal and its scandalous coverage raged on, one of the polls that caught my eye showed *the public to be substantially more disapproving of the news media than it was of the disgraced President Clinton or the despised Ken Starr. To me, that's a mind-boggling indictment of how we in journalism have conducted ourselves of late.*[B]   (emphasis added)

Today, we read more and more about how we, as a society have lost our *moral direction*. If nothing else, our values and ideals in many areas have been severely compromised and lowered. Intellectually and viscerally we all know this to be true. The reality is that broadcast journalism — which was once supposed to check the ills and the shortcomings of our society — now, in many instances, reflects and embodies them. As a result, broadcast journalism is experiencing a period of deserved low self-esteem.

We all agree that television news is a high-stakes and an extraordinarily lucrative business. However, the pressing problem is: We need broadcast journalism to be more and to give us more.

Years ago, John Chancellor warned that television news was in serious danger of being corrupted by commercialism. Today, we move ever closer to that point with each instance of compromise.

This is a sad — but a very necessary reality — to acknowledge. Necessary, because it is only with the recognition and acknowledgement that we, in broadcast journalism, have some serious problems to address and to remedy, will we be more inclined to explore and to seriously consider appropriate solutions.

Don't Lose Sight of "The Gift"

Throughout this book, I have presented a number of the pressing issues, tough conflicts, and harsh realities of broadcast journalism. However, talent and broadcasters must never lose sight of the access, the platform, and the power that you have to truly help your fellow man and woman, by supplying them with the essential information which they need in order to intelligently and effectively live — and lift — their lives. This opportunity is a gift. It is the gift of being able to truly serve others.

As your salary escalates, as the competition for the most coveted positions intensifies, as the stakes regarding your career appear to get higher and higher, and as your life becomes more and more complex, remember the responsibilities of your position.

For all of our sakes, don't lose sight of the wonderful reality, that being a broadcast journalist or a broadcaster can be a noble profession. It is a position of trust, and a gift to be made the very most of . . . and cherished.

Carpé Diem.

A Broadcaster's Mission Statement: To Aim Toward Attaining 'The Ideal'

For a moment, picture the "ideal,"
And think about how great it would feel
If we *really* focused upon achieving the mission
Of making *viewer-enhancing* decisions.

Through all of the stories we'd discerningly sift,
And then air the ones that would unquestionably *lift*
Our quality of life, and those of others,
Thus enhancing ourselves *and* our sisters and brothers.

If we try to make fewer content slips
And proactively undertake ownership
Of our standards, our product and of our choices,
Acting congruently with our Inner Voices,
Which tell us while we're here and alive
That we should make *every* effort to strive
To not be solely driven by ratings and greed,
But instead impart information that we truly need,
And thereby make choices, fueled by the zeal
Of making broadcasts *extraordinary,* and close to "ideal."

And if I try with all of my might,
To be a constant source of light,
And do all I can in hopes that I might,
Lift all those I touch to greater heights,
Then when I face my final day,
I'll be better able to say
That I've reviewed my broadcasting history,
And for raising the bar, *I'm proud of me.*

— K.L.

Bibliography

Advancing The Story
A.   *Dead Poets Society,* (Peter Weir, Director),
     Touchstone Pictures.

Thoughts For The Journey
A.   *Dead Poets Society.*

The Conflict of: It Smells But It Sells
A.   Schlosser, Joe, "Jerry Springer: Scraps or Scripts?," *Broadcasting & Cable,*
     27 April 1998, 50;
     Extra, Telepictures Productions.
B.   Ideas for these four points came from Meidel, Greg,
     "Jerry Springer Serves Its Purpose,"
     Electronic Media, 16 March 1998, 44.
C.   Borden, Jeff, "Regular Laugh Riot: Springer Takes The Low Road To
     Success," *Electronic Media,* 16 March 1998, 4, 44.
D.   Rosenberg, Howard, "Russian Roulette Of Live News,"
     Los Angeles Times, 2 May 1998, F1, F18.
E.   Information for this story was based upon the following articles:
     Abrahamson, Alan and Corwin, Miles, "Man Kills Self As City Watches,"
     Los Angeles Times, 1 May 1998, A1, A37.
     Lowry, Brian, "Grisly Death Is Broadcast Live On Local Stations, Cable

Network," *Los Angeles Times*, 1 May 1998, A36.
Braxton, Greg and Lowry, Brian, "TV Stations Reconsider Live Coverage Policies," *Los Angeles Times*, 2 May 1998, A19.

The Conflicts Between Our Needs And Our Wants
A. Bliss, Jr. Edward, *The Story of Broadcast Journalism*, (New York: Columbia University Press, 1991), 10.
B. Ibid, 11.
C. Ibid, 11.
D. Ibid, 11-12.
E. Ibid, 47.
F. Ibid, 47.
G. Ibid, 459.
H. Gartner, Michael, "O.J. Circus? Blame TV," *USA Today*, 3 October 1995, 11A.
I. Bliss, Jr., 460.
J. Cohen, Richard M., "The Corporate Takeover of News," *Conglomerates and The Media*, Barnouw, Erik, et. al., (The New Press, 1997), 32.
K. Rosenberg, F18.
L. Bliss, Jr., 306.
M. Ibid, 460.
N. Mason, Dave, "We Just Disagree"

Change
A. Liss, Walter, President, Buena Vista Television.
B. Cheatwood, Joel, NBC Television Stations Division.

Affirmative Action Versus Racial Discrimination
A. Bliss, Jr., 327.
B. McConnell, Chris, "Court KO's EEO," *Broadcasting & Cable*, 20 April 1998, 6, 10.
C. Papper, Bob and Michael Gerhard, "About Face," *Communicator*, August, 1998, 29. (This quotation is from Jim LeMay, Vice President, News, WJLA-TV, Washington, D.C.)
D. Ho, Man Keung, *Minority Children & Adolescent In Theory* (New York: Sage Publications), 8.
E. Ibid, Part II.
F. Ibid, 12 and Part II.
G. King, Jr., Dr. Martin Luther, *Why We Can't Wait*, (New York: Signet Books,

1964), 134, 135.
H.   McConnell, 16.
I.   McConnell, Bill and Paige, Albiniak, "Court Denies Recruitment
     Rehearing," *Broadcasting and Cable*, 21 September 1998, 26.
J.   McConnell, op. cit., 10.
K.   Papper, 30.
L.   Ibid, 31-32.
M.   Ibid, 31.
N.   Ibid, 32.

The Realities Of Being An On-Air Female
A.   Marin, Rick and Yahlin Chang, "The Katie Factor," *Newsweek*,
     6 July 1998, 53.
B.   Adalian, Josef, "Pauley Keeps 5 Mil 'Date'," *Daily Variety*, 30 June 1998, 1,
     17.

On-Air Males
A.   Sadker, Myra and David, *Failing At Fairness*, (New York: Touchstone,
     1994), 198.
B.   Ibid, 204-206.
C.   Gray, John, *Men Are From Mars, Women Are From Venus*, (New York:
     HarperCollins 1992), 17, 29-36.

Lack Of Feedback
A.   Peck, M. Scott, "The Road Less Travelled," (New York: Touchstone,
     1978), 15.

The Pay Disparity In Broadcasting Journalism
A.   Browne, Donald V., President/General Manager, WTVJ-TV,
     Miami, Florida

The Pressure To Secure "The Get"
A.   Chung, Connie, "The Business of Getting 'The Get': Nailing An Exclusive
     Interview in Prime Time," *The Joan Shrenstein Center On The Press, Politics,*

and Public Policy, Harvard University, John F. Kennedy School of Government, 8.

B.   Brill, Stephen, *Brill's Content*, August 1998, 124-132.
C.   Ibid, 123-151.
D.   Ibid, 123-124.
E.   Starr, Kenneth, in a letter to Stephen Brill, 16 June 1998.
F.   Brill, 123-151.
G.   Ibid, 130-131, 133, 140-141.
H.   Ibid, 134.
I.   Ibid, 136.
J.   Ibid, 134.
K.   Abrams, Floyd, guest on *The Charlie Rose Show*, Public Broadcast System, 6 July 1998; written excerpt from *Electronic Media*, 13 July 1998, 46.
L.   Statement of Fred Brown, President, Society Of Professional Journalists in the San Francisco Chronicle.
M.   Kalb, Marvin, *Perspective On Journalism*.
N.   Ashe, Arthur, with Arnold Rampasand, *Days Of Grace*, (New York: Knopf, 1993), 19.
O.   Ibid, 8-10, 17, 19-20.
P.   Ibid, 20.
Q.   *Jerry Maguire*, (Cameron Crowe, Director), TriStar Pictures, 1996.

The Three "D's" Of Constructive Decision-Making
A.   Peck, 15.
B.   Robbins, Anthony, *Unlimited Power*, (New York: Fawcett Columbine, 1986), 73.

The Enhancing Niche
A.   Goethe, Johann Wolfgang von, in Stephen Covey, *The 7 Habits Of Highly Successful People*, (New York: Fireside Books, 1989), 301.

At The Beginning — Less Is Often More
A.   Berger, Alan, Executive Vice President, International Creative Management.
B.   Ibid.

The Compromise In Broadcast Journalism and The Value Of Emotional Intelligence
A. Goleman, Daniel, *Emotional Intelligence*, (New York: Bantam Books, 1995), xii.
B. Brill, 123-151.
C. Carman, John, "CNN Retracts Story On Nerve Gas — Report Said It Used On Defectors," *The San Francisco Chronicle.*
D. McClellan, Steve, "CNN Takes A Fall," *Broadcasting & Cable*, 6 July 1998, 10.
E. Alridge, Ron, "Amid Scandals, Journalism Looks Suddenly Very Common," *Electronic Media*, 13 July 1998, 22.
F. Tharp, Paul and Dan Kaplan, "Down the Tubes For The Nets," *New York Post*, 18 September 1998, 35.
G. *Dead Poets Society.*
H. Karras, Chester L., *The Negotiating Game*, revised ed. (New York: Harper Business), 3.

The Psychology Of Breaking Into Broadcasting
A. Feder, Bart, News Director, WABC-TV, New York, New York.
B. Fair, Cheryl, News Director, KABC-TV, Los Angeles, California.
C. Fair, Cheryl.
D. Browne, Donald V.

Building A Foundation Step-By-Step
A. *Field Of Dreams*, (Phil Alden Robinson, Director) MCA/Universal Pictures, 1989.
B. Bliss, Jr., 469.

The Ideal: How To Secure Higher Ratings And Also Provide A High Quality Newscast Or Reality-Based Program
A. Alridge, Ron, 22.
B. Ibid, 22.
C. Ibid, 22.
D. Covey, 19.
E. Ibid, 40.
F. Ibid, 40.
G. Ibid, 41.
H. Ibid, 40.
I. Ibid, 42.
J. *Barlett's Familiar Quotations*, 16th ed., (Boston: Little, Brown & Co., 1992),

30.

K. Covey, 21.
L. Ibid, 22.
M. Ibid, 199.
N. Ibid, 317.
O. Ibid, 222.
P. Ibid, 301.
Q. Ibid, 232.
R. Ibid, 178.
S. Ibid, 54.
T. Ibid, 58.
U. The NBA's Champion; Greatest Teams, NBA Entertainment, CBS/FOX Video, date unavailable.
V. Covey, 49.
W. Ibid, 263.
X. Ibid, 265.
Y. Ibid, 274.
Z. Ibid, 263.
Aa. Bach, Richard, *One,* (New York: Dell Books, 1998) 269.
Bb. Covey, 269.
Cc. Bach, 68, 114.
Dd. *Field Of Dreams,* MCA/Universal Pictures.

Index

A

A Current Affair 20, 80
ABC xxi, 98, 99, 157, 192-193
Abrams vs. United States 13
Access Hollywood 79, 224
ad-libbing 154, 238, 256-257
African-American Coalition 43
allowances 225-226, 227
Alridge, Ron 266-267, 287
Alvidrez, Phil 46-47
appearance 177-178, 225-226
Applegate, Jodi 155, 157
Arnett, Peter 189, 190, 191
Ashe, Arthur 102-105, 251-252

B

Bach, Richard 277, 278
Benjamin, Burton 252-253
Bliss, Jr., Edward 12, 14, 16, 19-20, 37
Branzburg vs. Hayes 13
Brill, Steven 96-99, 189
Brill's Content 96
Broadcasting & Cable 53, 234, 249
Brokaw, Tom 62, 97-98, 191

C

cable television 25, 31, 53, 67, 96, 116,
    153, 162, 224, 227, 230, 236
CBS xxi, 16, 27, 99, 150, 157, 192
Cheatwood, Joel 269-270
Chung, Connie 50, 95

Clinton, President Bill 79, 286-287
CNN 79, 99, 104, 161, 189, 191-192,
    266
Cohen, Richard M. 16-17
competition 228-231, 280
content 7-10, 79-81, 105-106, 162, 120,
    255, 261
contracts 29-30, 32, 44, 51-52, 65-69,
    71, 115-116, 123, 169, 179, 197-198,
    203, 206, 213, 216, 217, 219-238
consultants 247-248
Couric, Katie 34, 35, 49, 50, 89, 90,
    155, 161, 164, 191
Covey, Stephen 267-268, 270, 271, 272,
    273, 274, 275-276, 277, 278
Curry, Ann 157, 191

D

Dateline NBC 30, 68, 80, 95, 254
David Letterman Show 123-124
Days of Grace 102-104
Dead Poets Society xviii, xx, 193
demo tapes 177-178, 216, 241-242, 246-
    249
demographics 31
Desert Storm 79
discipline 127-132, 134, 171

E

education 242-243
Electronic Media 6, 249, 266, 287

entertainment reporting   162-163, 264-265

Entertainment Tonight   xxi, 17, 79, 210, 224

Equal Employment Opportunity (EEO)   38, 44-46

ethics   189

exclusivity   235-237

Extra   xxi, 17

F

Failing at Fairness   61

Federal Communications Commission (FCC)   12-13, 38, 45-46

Federal Radio Act of 1927   12

Federal Radio Commission (FCC)   12, 14

Fernandez, Giselle   157, 191

Format-driven newscasts   161

Fox   xxi, 27, 79, 160, 269

G

Gartner, Michael   15-16

H

Hamn, Barbara   46, 47

Hard Copy   80, 163, 224

Hingis, Martina   150, 215

Hispanic Coalition   42-43

Ho, Man Keung   38-39

The Hollywood Reporter   52, 234

Houchins vs. KQED   13

I

Inside Edition   xxi, 80, 163

internships   241, 242-247

J

Jennings, Peter   62, 191

K

Keating, John   xviii, xx, 193

King, Jr., Dr. Martin Luther   39-40, 41, 44

L

Lauer, Matt   35, 51, 89, 155, 157, 161

leverage   197-201, 210

Lewinsky, Monica   79, 97-99, 189, 286-287

Lifestyles of the Rich & Famous   17

long-form reporting   160

Los Angeles Times   18

M

McRee, Lisa   115, 155

morale   76, 77, 79, 81, 83, 162, 226, 275, 285-286

motivations   168-172, 191, 219

MSNBC   99, 161, 191-192

Murrow, Edward R.   19-20, 265, 286

N

NBC   15, 49, 80, 89, 97-99, 157, 184, 266, 268, 286

Newsweek   98, 254

Nightline   99, 254

Nigra vs. Young of Albany, Inc.   234

O

Oklahoma City bombing   105, 106

Olbermann, Keith   99, 286-287

One   277, 278

"Operation Tailwind"   189, 190

overcompensation   140-143

P

Pauley, Jane   49, 161

Peck, M. Scott   85, 129

Pell vs. Procunier   11, 13

personality-driven newscasts   161

Policinski, Gene   102-104

print journalism   98, 254

Q

"Q"   SEE recognizability quotient

R

Radio & Television News Directors Association (RTNDA) 14
   Code of Ethics   14

Rather, Dan   50, 62, 191

ratings   1-2, 6-10, 15, 25, 31, 68, 79-80, 91, 95, 106, 154, 162-165, 180, 187, 262, 267, 269, 279, 286

reality-based programming   xxi, 5-6, 11, 15, 18, 67, 87, 95, 150, 163, 177, 277

recognizability quotient   28

relationships   186-187

representation   204-218, 248-249

reputation   191

right of assignability   67, 73

rights-of-first-refusal   227-229, 233-235

right-of-termination   44, 226, 228

risks   177

Rivera, Geraldo   80

Roberts, Deborah 157, 191
Rosenberg, Howard 18
RTNDA Communicator 46

S

salaries 49, 52-53, 89, 90, 115-116, 130, 192, 198-201, 221-222, 224-225, 231-233, 244
Sampras, Pete 122, 251
Sawyer, Diane 33, 49
scheduling 159-160
scripts xxii, 131, 139-142, 180-181
Shapiro, Neal 95-96
Shipman, Claire 97-98
Simpson, O.J. (trial) 16, 79, 142, 217
60 Minutes 67, 254
sports broadcasting 157, 210-211
Starr, Kenneth 96-98
strengths 153, 154, 155, 215-216
sweeps xxii, 19, 160, 179-180, 262
syndicated programming xxi, 25, 29, 162, 209, 224, 227, 230, 236
synergy 276-278

T

tabloid-based programming xxi, 18, 79-81, 262-265
termination 179, 220, 222-223, 229, 237-238, 256, 279
termination clause 227-228

The Jerry Springer Show xxi, 1, 2, 6, 20
The Oprah Winfrey Show xxi, 28, 67
The Road Less Traveled 85, 129
The Seven Habits of Highly Effective People 267-268
Today 35, 49, 52, 90, 155, 184

U

unions 179, 185, 244
USA Today 102-105

V

vacations 143-147
Vargas, Elizabeth 157, 191

W

Walters, Barbara 49 ,52
Watergate 97
weaknesses 153-154, 215
Westin, David 192-193
William Morris Agency 123-124, 132
Williams, Brian 157, 161, 191
Winfrey, Oprah 6, 49, 50, 52, 89, 155, 156, 177
(The) Women in Cable and Telecommunications (WICT) Foundation 53
Wright, Will 46, 47
writing 186, 238, 241, 245